make your own music video

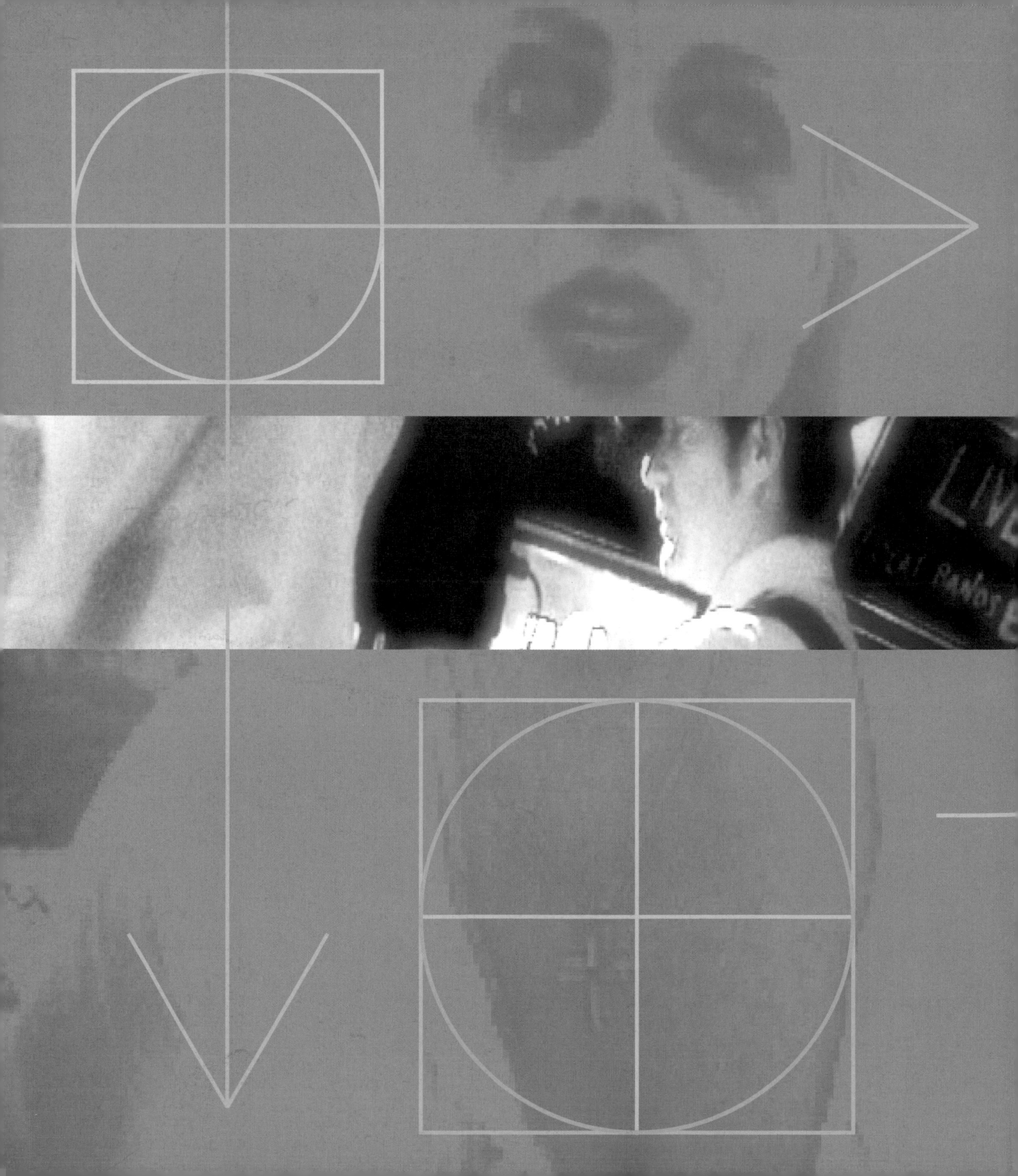

make your own
music video

Ed Gaskell

ILEX

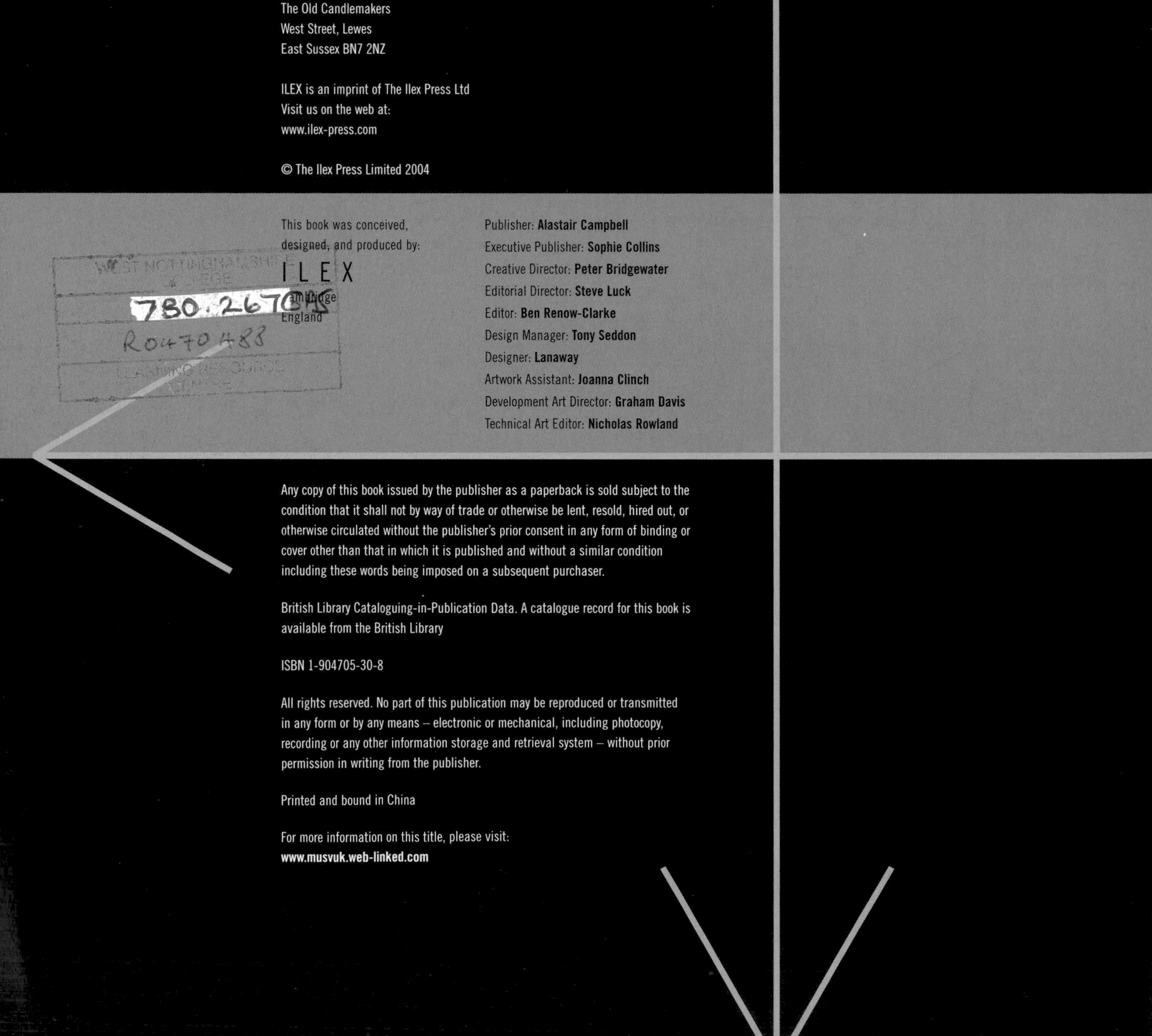

First published in the United Kingdom in 2004 by
ILEX
The Old Candlemakers
West Street, Lewes
East Sussex BN7 2NZ

ILEX is an imprint of The Ilex Press Ltd
Visit us on the web at:
www.ilex-press.com

This book was conceived, designed, and produced by:
ILEX
Cambridge
England

Publisher: **Alastair Campbell**
Executive Publisher: **Sophie Collins**
Creative Director: **Peter Bridgewater**
Editorial Director: **Steve Luck**
Editor: **Ben Renow-Clarke**
Design Manager: **Tony Seddon**
Designer: **Lanaway**
Artwork Assistant: **Joanna Clinch**
Development Art Director: **Graham Davis**
Technical Art Editor: **Nicholas Rowland**

British Library Cataloguing-in-Publication Data. A catalogue record for this book is available from the British Library

ISBN 1-904705-30-8

Printed and bound in China

For more information on this title, please visit:
www.musvuk.web-linked.com

CONTENTS

1 **INTRODUCTION:**
BUSINESS AS USUAL 6>17

2 **CLASSIC CONCEPTS**
& DJ CLICHÉS 18>43

3 **PRE-PRODUCTION:**
SINGING TO THE SAME TUNE 44>63

4 **PRE-PRODUCTION:**
FUNKIN' TECHNO
& ALL THAT JAZZ 64>85

5 **PRODUCTION:**
BETWEEN ROCK & A HARD PLACE 86>123

6 **POST-PRODUCTION:**
RAPPIN' IT UP 124>169

7 **MARKETING & DISTRIBUTION:**
BURN BABY BURN 170>183

GLOSSARY 184>187
INDEX 188>191
ACKNOWLEDGMENTS 191

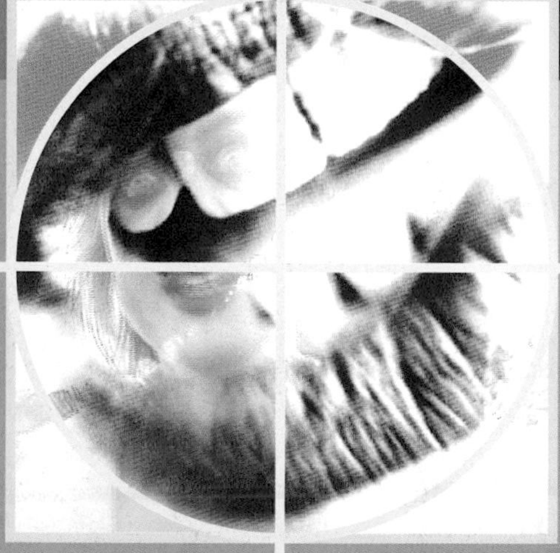

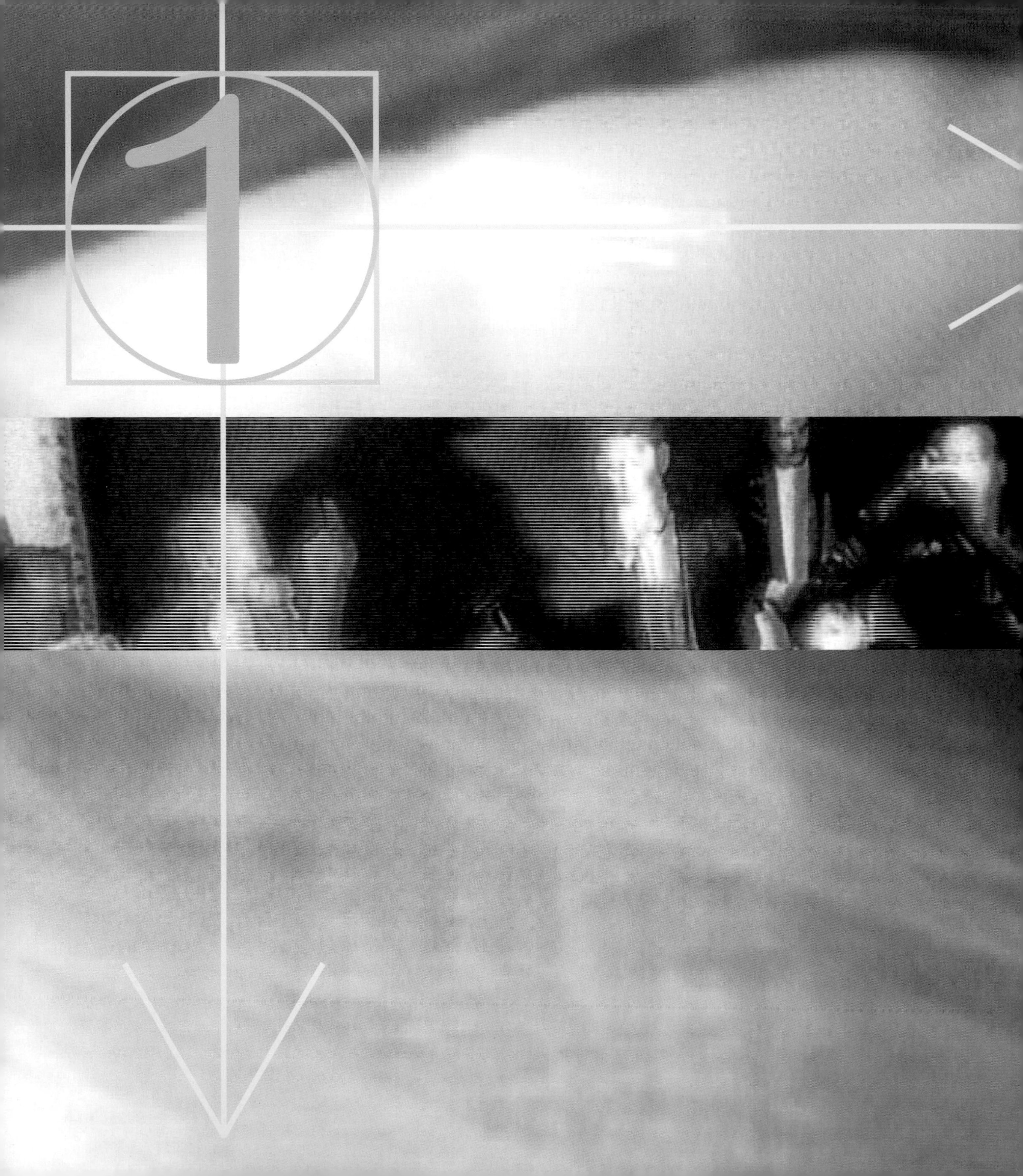
1

INTRODUCTION: BUSINESS AS USUAL

There's more to the history of the music video than those old clichés that *Bohemian Rhapsody* was the first, and *Video Killed The Radio Star* was the most influential. The fact is that music has always been used to sell visuals, and now the visuals sell the music.

Why do art galleries play classical music at viewings? Why do clubs cut random movie clips together for video walls? In each case, the visuals and the music are disassociated, yet there is an implication that they work together. But how do they 'work?' What do they do? Does music make us buy more paintings? Do video clips make us want to go to a club? Absolutely not. What they do is make a more stimulating environment. More stimulating environments appeal; they make us stay a while longer, make us more willing to buy into it, or to buy.

The bottom line is that music videos sell music in exactly the same way that PR stunts of sex, drugs, and cock-and-bull sell music. They create word of mouth and tabloid headlines, they give a band personality, they make them sexier or scarier, they create a mystique, and they open up marketable sexualities. Most of all, they get musicians and bands remembered.

BELOW LEFT: Everyone knows a band or a musician or somebody that can sing or dance – or at least somebody that thinks that they can do any of these things. Music videos make great showreels for yourself and for the talent you're filming. It's backscratching, but if you've got a DV camera, all that scratching may well be making you itch.

BOTTOM LEFT: It starts with a track, an introduction, an agreement…

RIGHT: …runs through production, concepts, and treatments…

UP TO YOU: **SEX AND DRUGS IN ROCK AND ROLL**

First there was music – let's get that straight. After music came the motion picture. Then came the musical motion picture, and then the music video.

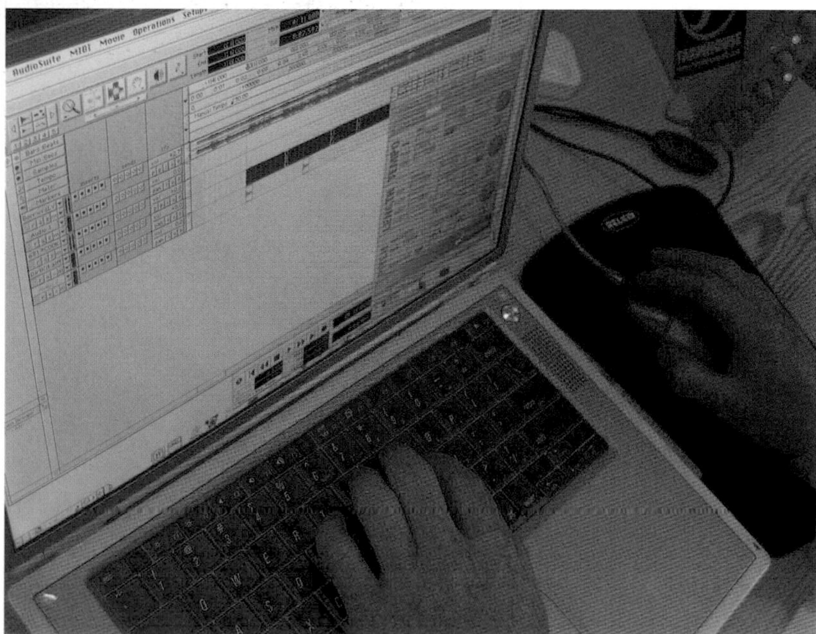

Commercials rarely rely on 'buy this: it works' tactics any more. Those days are numbered, if not history. *These* days, it's all to do with branding—wanting and buying. If it's not that, it's *needing*. CDs are tagged 'essential' or 'indispensable'. It is the music video that helps create this whole package of personality and image – the things that the music itself cannot do. They make a band remembered whatever the music, and this widens market appeal.

Only a small slice of everyone's expenditure is dedicated to leisure and entertainment as a whole, and only part of that slice will go on music. It is that small part of the slice that all musicians are fighting for. The way to engineer this is not making better tracks especially, it is to be noticed and remembered by the broadest demographic. And while music is suitable for the radio, more people watch television. Visuals can quadruple exposure. A band needs a video, and they need it *now*.

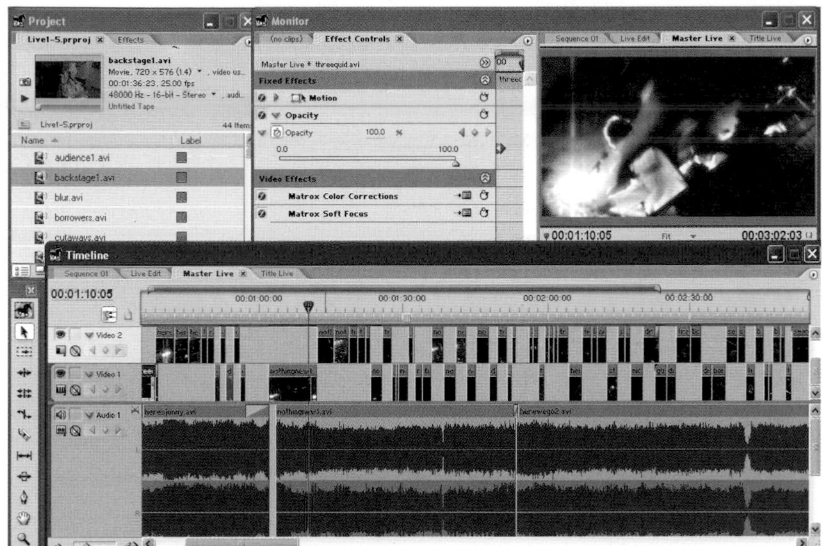

THE TIME IS NOW

>It used to be that music sold itself. It doesn't any more.

>Music is like comedy: taste is impossible to explain.

>In early videos, musicians were always put in glamorous locations, such as Duran Duran in Rio. Nowadays it pays to be more down to earth.

>Before video, nightclubs were the only place to go to see the music, now music is everywhere thanks to the video.

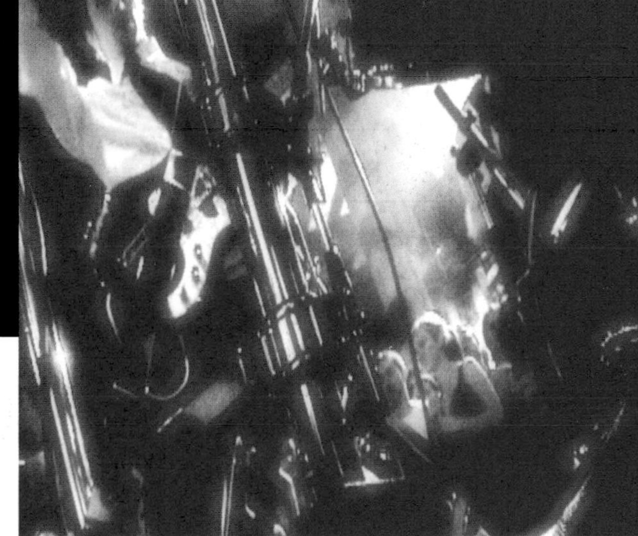

ABOVE LEFT: ...the performers perform, and after the wrap comes the construction of your dream...

ABOVE RIGHT: ...and after all that, they're on set for three minutes.

Music is a sign of the times. Don't give any musician an ounce of credit if they tell you that their music is written to last. Nothing lasts, least of all music. Music 'reminds us of a time when...'. Video for music has this privilege. It can be as dated as it wants in twenty years time as long as it's cutting edge and memorable *at* the time. This is why music videos are such a creative video-making experience.

Back to the paintings. Would we really expect classical music at the opening of the latest Jeff Koons exhibition? Would it work as irony? This is the nature of the music video: working *with* (usually), or *against* (often) the music. The reason for utilizing irony is not that it's particularly clever, it's just not subscribing to our very first instinct. The human mind works logically and Koon's quirky *Balloon Dog* – if you were pushed to find compatible music – might inspire thoughts of Beefheart more than Mozart. Irony is lateral thinking. It's out with Captain Beefheart and in with Captain & Tennille.

Logical and lateral thinking (primary and secondary) are important in the music video for the one reason that whatever environment the video puts us in, the goal is to make us remember it. Why? Because the gallery and the club are retail outlets and the music video markets the music.

The music video *is* a commercial. And while a Hollywood movie has 90 to 120 minutes to tell its story, a music video and a commericial are bound by permissible time parameters – in fact, this is one of the only boundaries that they do have.

Because tracks are much shorter than Hollywood movies it can be a race to put across ideas. A music video can virtually mimic a Hollywood plot, only without the complications that take the conflict to a two-hour running time.

POPPING UP: THE LANGUAGE OF THE MUSIC VIDEO

The music video has progressed through many different styles. At first it merely showed us the musicians playing their track, which then evolved into showing us the musicians miming to their track, then to showing the musicians doing something completely different, and finally to not showing the musicians at all. With this progression has come major advances in the associated technology. The music video breaks the boundaries of space, time, technology, and imagination.

But what *is* the language of the music video?

Cutting

Hollywood movies usually cut to another shot somewhere between every 3 and 7 seconds. The average cut in the music video is much shorter, about once every 1 or 2 seconds. This is exactly the same as for a television commercial.

ABOVE TOP: Confounding time and space is the kind of thing that dreams are made of. This is why music videos often have that same quality to them. Defying the rational allows you to use effects in a music video that would not ordinarily be seen in any other visual genre.

OPPOSITE TOP: Digital technology makes the illogical and irrational a reality. Compositing images and making them work with each other is just one of the tools readily available. Truly terrific images come from directors directing a shoot and knowing exactly how each part of the composite will interact in the edit.

Space and Time

To understand the way music videos break the rules of space and time, think of any conventional music video. Why are Oasis waiting in London's Docklands for a helicopter? Why is Bono riding through the streets of Dublin in the back of a truck? Taking a band or musician out of their habitual surroundings (recording studio, concert hall) and inserting them somewhere else breaks their space.

The rules of time are broken by visual shifts between locations, or showing the band doing different things as the track progresses. A listener understands that a track is like an isolated conversation – no matter how the music was recorded, it is delivered to the ears in real time. Imagine a Hollywood movie where the dialog continues over a reverse shot that suddenly cuts the speaker from being in a warehouse to being on the moon. There *are* no continuity errors in the music video. Space and time can be crossed, compressed, or protracted, as the viewer is not looking for logic or believability.

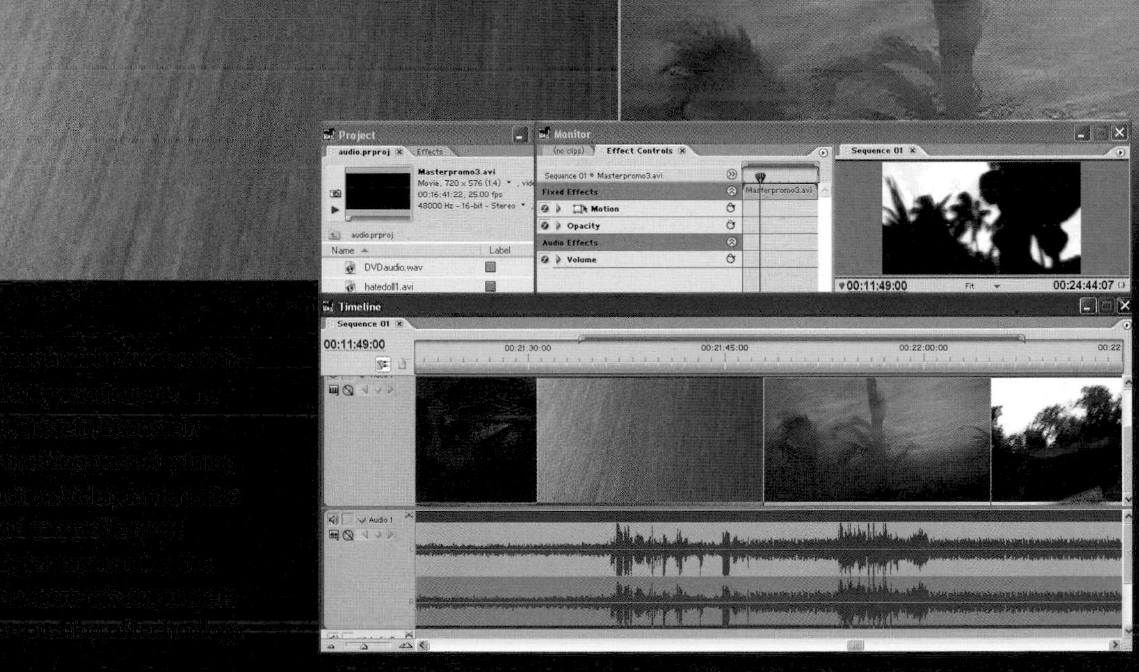

Project
audio.prproj
Effects
Masterpromo3.avi
Movie, 720 x 576 (1.4)
00:16:41:22, 25.00 fps
48000 Hz - 16-bit - Stereo
audio.prproj
Name
Label
DVDaudio.wav
hatedoll1.avi
Monitor
(no clips)
Effect Controls
Sequence 01 * Masterpromo3.avi
Fixed Effects
Motion
Opacity
Audio Effects
Volume
Masterpromo3.avi
Sequence 01
00:11:49:00
Fit
00:24:44:07
Timeline
Sequence 01
00:11:49:00
00:21:30:00
00:21:45:00
00:22:00:00
Audio 1

Technology

Sync, therefore, becomes the most crucial part of a lot of music videos. It ensures that an audience *believes* that the lead is really singing and that the rest of the musicians are really playing. Viewers are required to believe in this if they are to understand that the band that they buy is the same as the band that they see.

Of course, that is not to say that the effect isn't all just an illusion. Computer and camera tricks can now promise anything, visually; promising anything sonically has been going on for quite some time. Boney M, Black Box, and Milli Vanilli have all been held up to the light and exposed for various lipsync-related infractions. This says a lot more about their good performances on- and off-camera.

THE LIPSYNC

The lipsync is the classic music video. Most tracks with music videos have vocals, and the vocal lead is usually the face of the band. The lead gives the band a personality.

In order to create that personality in the music video the lead singer usually dominates the visuals – and a lead singer who isn't singing is a peculiarity, although that's not always a bad thing.

A track is recorded for release in a studio. It is in the interest of marketing that the product displayed in the music video is the same as can be bought in the shops or online. There are very few exceptions to this with the music video. This, coupled with the nature of music video production (consistency, not continuity, take after take) requires the artist and musicians to mime to their track.

Sync is the synchronization between the played track and the performance of the band: it is the effect of performing to the track without actually performing it. Miming is action without words, and as such, what you are asking of your musicians is a true physical performance.

ABOVE TOP: The control given to the degree of the lipsync depends upon your track, and your framing. Your vocalist has to be directed to show the right amount of exaggeration or temper of mimed pronunciation. Different effects and rhythm are negotiated between the size of the frame and the emphasis of the mouth in action. Using an intimate frame and letting the talent go hell for leather is confrontational...

ABOVE LEFT: Challenging an audience, alternatively, is shooting the lipsync close-up – and upside down but a close-up the right way around can prove to be a dead giveaway with the slightest of mistakes...

Notice that there is no history of a musician being asked to qualify themselves as the individual who played on a track. This is largely due to the fact that playing an instrument is an open and honest display; vocal acrobatics, on the other hand, take place somewhere between the diaphragm and the throat. It is, in effect, a hidden talent that only a few have chosen to project. Judge for yourself whether a Céline, Mariah, or Barbra performance makes you want to believe or hurl.

A lead will have adopted a style of singing and emoting long before you get to hear them. As with any performance in the theatre versus one in a movie, there is a difference between a concert or gig and the music video.

Film and video are largely utilized as intimate media – a way of getting closer to the stars. Over-exaggeration with sync jeopardizes this believability. If the band haven't been directed for a music video before, then it may come as something of a shock.

***RIGHT:** Quieter mime can work with wider shots and longer clips to create a slightly unnerving quality. Whispering vocalization at a distance – specifically with louder tracks – can be wonderfully odd to watch.*

No matter how gregarious or vivacious they might be, a slightly tempered performance always works better with sync on video. The track itself is likely to be mixed to a degree that won't sound like a big-bass, low-vocal gig anyway, so the talent won't be SHOUTING *that* LOUDLY on it.

This combination of believability in an entirely unbelievable world is the crux of a music video. In the Hollywood movie, the job is always to convince the viewer that whatever the horror or the science fiction or the incredibly serendipitous romance, it is a real and believable two hours; it is the music video's job to provide a credible sync as the thread to keep the audience watching. If it isn't credible, it is instantly dismissed as a sham and a fraud.

The job of synching isn't easy for a performer, no matter if they've written the song and sung it a million times. Because the nature of production is so artificial, you may require a performance that is alien to the talent – miming at half speed or miming at twice speed are widely-used techniques. Miming to a track in reverse is a skill all of its own. Musicians can find it extremely difficult to mime while being asked to perform with their instrument in a way that is at odds with their instinct. It's a rubbing head/patting stomach scenario – some have got it and some haven't.

Sync in the edit has to be frame accurate, or you'll be razoring, speeding, slowing, using cutaways, and generally doing whatever you need to do to get a mouth to appear to move in time with the track. This is the horrible truth with sync. There is no room for even half a frame of mismatch during the shoot because three minutes into the track it will be obvious. The ins and outs for success will be discussed, but don't even think about going in for sync unless you have the equipment to do it properly.

THE AS-LIVE

The 'as-live' is a variation on the synched music video. While the sync video takes the musicians through an artificial landscape, miming to their track and creating the believable untruth, the as-live recreates the believable truth: the gig, concert, or live performance.

Musicians play live music: it's the one outlet that they have for displaying their skills (marketing themselves) to an audience. Whether or not they are faithful to their recorded tracks is neither here nor there for the as-live music video. This is because they are still miming to that track.

Recording a live gig for digital use can be an absolute nightmare. Recording off a camera mic is hopeless, and likely to result in a bassy and indistinct sound – probably an accurate recreation of the gig. Amps and mixers for gigs are often analogue-output. This doesn't help a digital input that distorts anything over 0 decibels. If you're shooting a gig and recording the live sound into the camera to sync to the pictures, you're on dangerous ground. It's physically restrictive, it requires a separate mixer to control levels, and you'll be at an utter loss for pick-ups.

***ABOVE LEFT:** As-lives create the utmost in believability. Good vocal sync is the linchpin on which it all hangs, though, and if this is questionable, it throws the entire video into doubt.*

***TOP LEFT:** It's a lot easier to shoot musicians in an as-live. Because instruments are large, often away from the face, and require a fundamental understanding of how they work, it is often possible to use clips that aren't necessarily from that specific moment – let alone from that track at all. This is the versatility that you need in the edit.*

***TOP RIGHT:** Any audience that you can drum up for an as-live are the ones that give it credibility. Don't forget that they can just walk out at any time if they don't feel appreciated....*

As-live is a broadcast term for programmes that are perceived live but aren't – even if that is a 10-second delay for mixing video and audio. An as-live will be perceived as a live performance, but it is edited in the same way as any other music video that's set to a recorded track. This is one of the reasons that musicians record as-live music videos.

This recorded track can be one of two things. It can be the track recorded by the musicians at the time of the live performance, or it can be a track that the musicians mimed to as part of the 'live' performance. The first of these is a level-controlled mix of the audio output. If this is what you are using, it will be recorded to a DAT before a CD and may well not be accurately matched to your visuals. Why? Because DAT is tape and DV is tape, and both are prone to slight stretching and wear. The combination of both add up to a possible problem – and if there is a problem, it will be a very difficult edit, or you'll have to shoot again.

WHY SHOOT AN AS-LIVE?

Choose to shoot an as-live for all the right reasons:

- **The marketing strategy is to sell the musicians as a live band**
- **The musicians have dynamic stage personalities**
- **There is an opportunity to shoot them as-live**
- **They are performing in an irresistible location**

Getting musicians to mime to their pre-recorded CD is by far the less troublesome method. Aside from achieving sync confidence, you will also be able to replay the exact same track to get the shots that you missed.

The other reason for miming is exactly the opposite of the first two mentioned. If a band or artist *hasn't* established themselves as a live act as yet, turn the whole strategy around. Studio bands can get a whole new audience and lease of life if they break out of their mould and dust themselves down. It's one of many methods of visual reinvention.

To create the believable truth, as-lives work a lot better with audiences. It is quite extraordinary how patient an invited audience can be, but if you choose to shoot this way, your job – and the performers' – will be to keep their enthusiasm going. Not only does audience excitement put a positive vibe in the music video, it can also help with the sync and useless shots make great cutaways.

As-lives are often cut into conventional sync music videos – and more often than not, it's to promote a tour or celebrate the passing of one. Cutting live footage into videos gives an opportunity to do away with sync altogether. The way this works is that the recorded track becomes a theme to the wallpaper of performance montage, and audiences will buy into this without the need of a sync. This kind of promo can get a little grating because it is transparently a marketing strategy.

As-lives are technically hard work, but the pay-off is that the shoot will then be over relatively quickly. Audiences forgive all sorts of visual errors (but never audio problems), and often any wobbly shots will lend the footage a sense of the hand-held, 'being there', experience. Edits can also be quicker, provided that there are no sync issues. Viewers of as-lives tolerate longer shots because they suggest a reality of sorts. In the language of the documentary or fictional docu-drama, longer shots equate to 'home video' reality.

Better still with as-lives, and unlike a studio shoot, *you* can be a part of the fun. There's also something challenging and hopefully rewarding about making a silk purse out of a sow's ear.

ABOVE LEFT & RIGHT: What's the difference between an as-live and a live? Usually it's the difference between the quality of shots, audio, and camera angles in a controlled environment, versus those in an all-out live scramble that ends in a bitter edit of forced decision-making.

ABOVE TOP: Let the audience react how they would normally react. Cheering and taking photos should be actively encouraged.

This may sound unlikely, but in fact there are quite a few reasons why you might end up without anyone to sync the music to.

> You haven't been commissioned to make a music video for the artist (but you're going to anyway)

Welcome to the free world. This is the school of ripping, of experimentation, of simply trying your hand at something. There is absolutely nothing stopping you from creating a music video to a track by your favourite artist – nothing except the entire legal department behind that artist. If you just want to have a go with your kit, and learn to work with existing audio, there is no better way to do it.

Some benefits of this method are: you will have no-one to answer to, and the track will usually be as clear as a bell and will have all the whistles intact. The downside is that it can only be used personally, and even online someone else might just blow that whistle.

> It's practically impossible (and I mean practically)

Sometimes, a logistical issue will stop you shooting with a band. They may be on tour, unable to congregate on a day that you can rent gear, or they might just be hopelessly disorganized.

THE ABSENT

The last form of video is where there are no musicians and there is no gig. Where have they gone? Well, maybe they were never there in the first place.

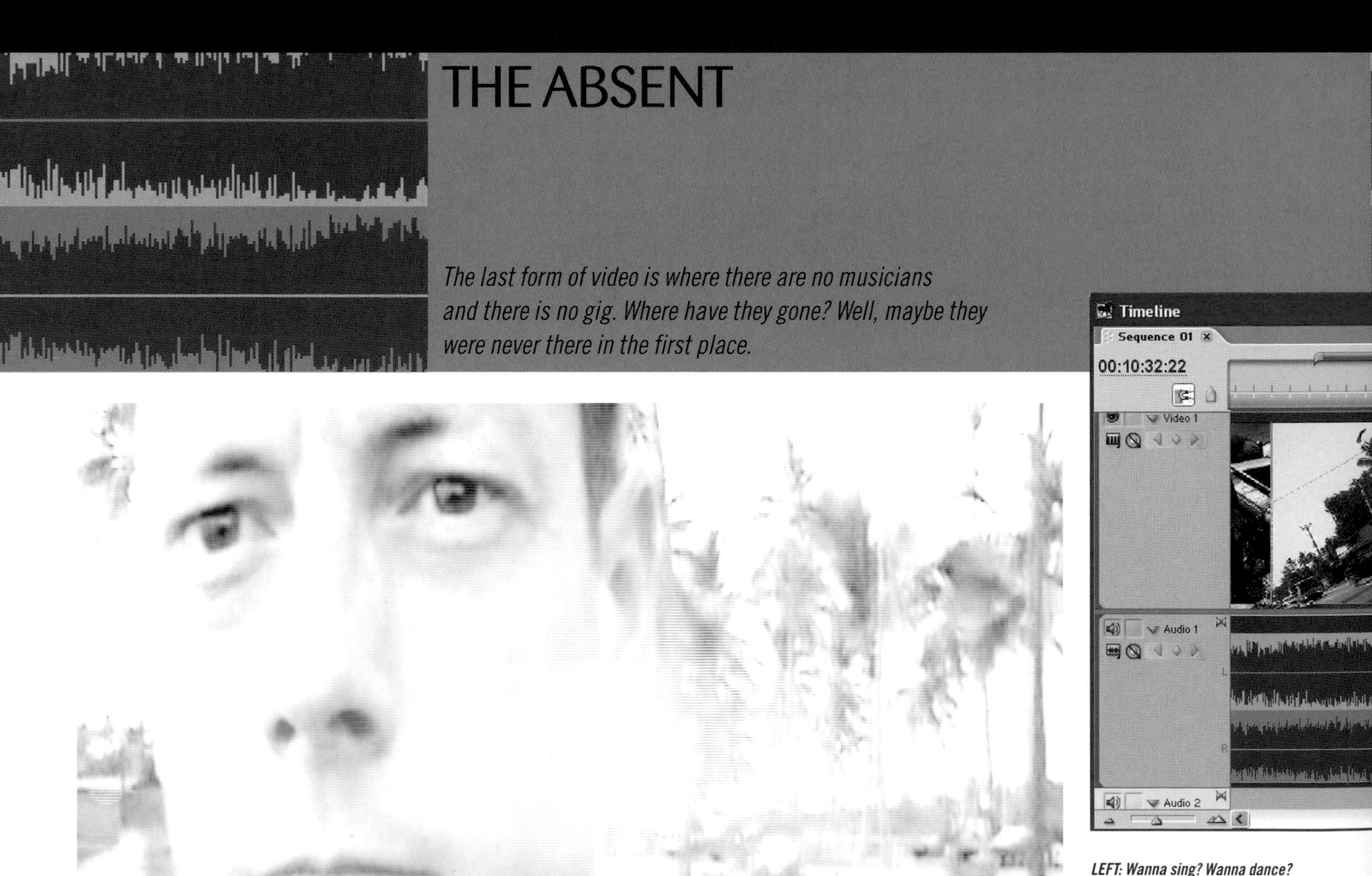

LEFT: Wanna sing? Wanna dance? Nobody to help out? Turn the camera around, flip the screen, and direct yourself. Shoot as you move and you've got yourself a bargain basement body rig.

In the left-hand corner…iiiiiit's SONY! And in the right, George MICHAEL! (Boos, applause, as appropriate.) Working for a band in a legal dispute may seem unlikely, but contract wars can blow up at any time – yes, even in the middle of production.

How this relates to you is based on your own contracts (if you have any). Deadlocks and stalemates, though, can mean that your video for the band cannot be shown, or that you cannot represent them visually. There are always ways around this – and one of them is not showing the musicians at all.

You might have other ideas than the obvious. This can mean that you're working with a DJ (Fatboy Slim's *Praise You*), you want to represent them in another way (Fatboy again, *Weapon of Choice*), you want to use animation (George again, *Shoot the Dog*), or the entire marketing strategy requires that they are absent (The Gorillaz).

> They don't want to be in a video (well, why bother hiring you?)

If your musicians are shy, anarchic, or disagree between themselves or with what you are doing, they may not want to be in the video. The first task as director and producer is to talk them out of it. If that fails, you need to agree on a video blueprint that they will be happy with. This may well be to avoid using them at all – especially if you sense that it will be a waste of time.

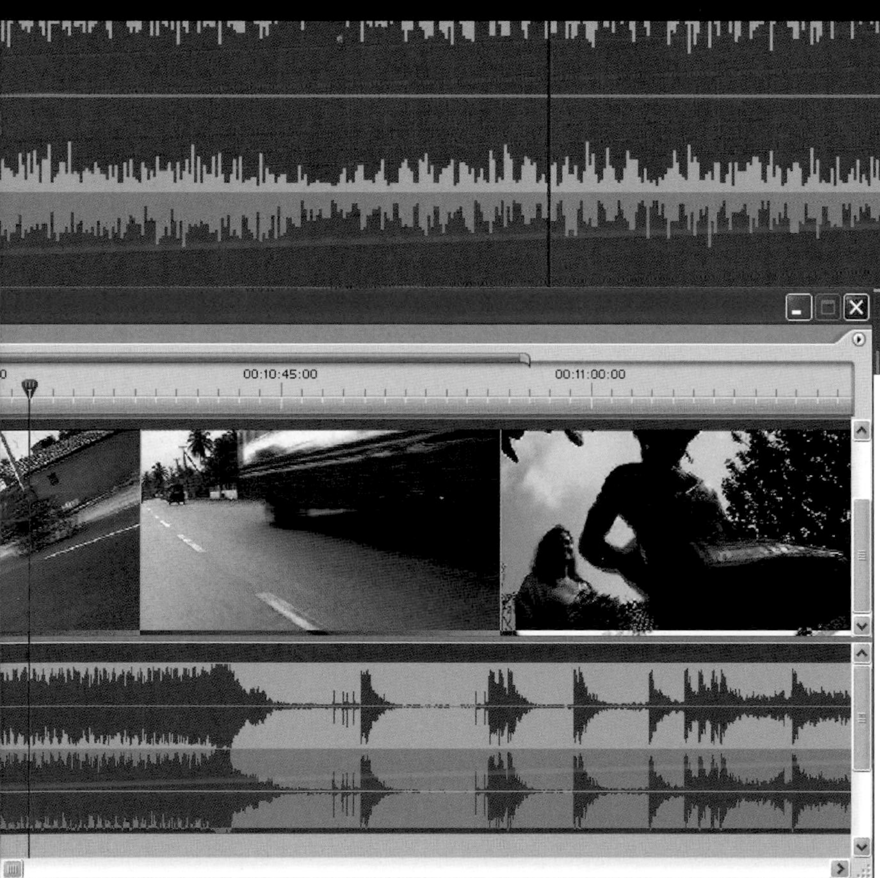

ABOVE: When there are no parameters, look for rhythm in life that fits the track. Think about ways in which attributing speed in the edit will marry with the music.

If it is simply a question of just one musician in a band who refuses to appear, decide whether or not this compromises everybody else on-screen. Embarking on projects like this can be quite deflating. You will be working in a vacuum with little or no energy and influence from the musicians themselves. You'll be in a parameter-free wilderness, and somewhat in the dark.

The upside is that you can do what you want, however you want to do it. You might choose to shoot specifically, or use stock, or a combination of both. Whatever you do decide, treat it exactly like any other music video. Work out what you are going to do with it and where you might show it before you start planning. Move on to finding that one idea, giving it parameters and nailing the themes. Experiment and determine cuts, transitions, edits, and grading that will consolidate all the disparate parts of your venture.

Cutting your teeth on a video in which the musicians are absent is a good start when it comes to editing. Making something out of nothing is a healthy challenge. What it can never prepare you for, unfortunately, is the heaven and hell of working with and synching a band or artist and their music.

CLASSIC
CONCEPTS
& DJ CLICHÉS

LEFT: Pop is instantly attractive. It doesn't have time to waste because it isn't going to hang around. Remember this if you are visualizing a very 'pop' track. The viewer wants something that appeals as soon as the track begins. If it doesn't, you'll lose them just as quickly.

POP UP

[illegible] semantics: pop has taken on a new life and meaning of its own.

Popular music is music which sells. The charts are full of music that sells because that is what a chart charts: sales. The charts, though, are also full of rock, hip-hop, rap, dance, and R&B, as well as the occasional country and classical tracks. Indeed, it is these latter two that hold the explanation. Country and western and classical orchestral tracks have their own charts. This gives them commercial viability and secures them in a world where popular charts dominate sales.

The percentage of the world's population aged between 14 and 25 apportions more money to entertainment than any other age group. It follows that to hold maximum appeal to this demographic, you get a music business that is stuffed full of commercials, endorsements, advertising, sponsorship, and – most of all – sex appeal and aspiration. For example, US pop queen Madonna is widely considered to be a master of self-promotion and reinvention; an overall theme of sexuality is always present in her music, however, and nowhere is that more evident than in her videos. Even her increasingly more meaningful personal and socio-political lyrical dabblings are most often represented visually with sexual metaphors or allusions to fetishism. The result? Her tours continue to sell out and fill auditoriums all over the world – after 20 years of provocative videos, people still can't get enough.

Britney Spears is another very good example of successful visual marketing. Although her songs are very well-produced pop tunes and certainly merit attention on their own, it is obvious that much of the attention Britney gets is due to her visual image. Her videos are laden with sexuality and fantasy, which translates into popularity and strong CD sales.

This is no small feat: the market is bloated with music. Just like the MTV video, we want quick cuts, changes, transitions to monotony. The buying public want their music and they want it now. And because of

In the case of a Hollywood film soundtrack, the video for the hit single is usually just a trailer for the film, but the film is being exploited to sell the track. The trick is to use the video to bridge the gap and link the song to the feelings people have about the film, whether they've seen it or not.

Marketing tries to control what people want and when they want it. The buying audiences, though, are getting wise to this – and cynical. It is a fragile and strained relationship. Trying to stay one step ahead of the game is a marketing challenge, and it is often undertaken by promoters and producers with little respect for musicians. This is why a lot of musicians don't want to be part of it.

ABOVE TOP: Pop always has a good time. It has to, otherwise it'll realize it's a business. A pop music video is a shiny gloss that reflects the surface back to the viewer. If it's polished enough, there won't be a glimmer of anything sordid underneath.

ABOVE: Pop singer status turns an average Joe or Josephine into somebody that turns heads. While this may be flattering, confusing, and rewarding for the lead, it is very useful for your music video. Sex sells, so don't be afraid to use it.

the market saturation, they'll just go somewhere else if they're not given what they want. Those artists that do want to compete, then, must have more than just good pop tracks. A pop star needs engaging, slick visuals that enhance his or her image – so don't be afraid to shoot and edit the video like a TV commercial. In other words, cut frequently.

The fickle buying audience can move from one genre to another, depending on what they want, and depending on what is currently in the spotlight. It is the inventive marketeers who move that spotlight. The marketing pop feeders jostle to get someone in that light quickly for the time that the light remains there. While the music comes about through a collaboration between the artist and a producer, the pop video is often a strict marketing exercise. The artist's image for that particular single is the main concern. The artist might be portrayed as sexy, dangerous, or mysterious – whatever helps to build intrigue or stir interest will help to sell the track.

Intelligent and creative video-making is becoming more popular with discerning pop fans. These days there are many bands and musicians that have die-hard audiences and buyers – Radiohead, Coldplay, or Missy Elliott, to name a few – who chart occasionally while still maintaining credibility with their original fan bases. This status is earned through respect by those in the industry and those who buy into it. As such, video accompaniment to songs from these groups will often eschew image in favour of overt artistic or technical innovation, sometimes including social or political statements. In the cases of now-famous video makers Spike Jonze and Michel Gondry, such pop video innovation ironically led each to careers in Hollywood.

ROCK UP

Rock is the primary alternative to pop. The fundamental difference is that rock uses the electric guitar to drive the music. There are many types and hybrids of rock that serve specific audiences – thrash, metal, indie, goth, rockabilly – and even within these, there are more labels that a band or musician might identify themselves with.

A standard rock video loves movement. Those driving guitars propel the music as much as the video. K-Tel and Time Music know this and pump out CDs full of drivetime tunes that are chock-full of rock.

For a rock video to hold any credibility, it has got to live on the edge. It's not cool to be shiny, smiley, and poppy, but it *is* cool (credible) to be sweaty, grungy, snarling, and unkempt. Credible rock is not safe, nor sober. To be believed as a rock band or rock star, there has to be no indication of any kind of PR machine behind the musicians.

PR is primarily dedicated to pop. It works hard to create a sheen of musicians untouchable by sin, evil, or leaving a sock in the dryer. Sin and evil are the feeding ground for rock. This is why so many in the bible belt get so wound up about it. PR in the rock arena works in the opposite way to pop, and deregulates and exaggerates activity. Normal everyday social drinking becomes a 48-hour binge; rock stars are seen as drug fiends because they're actually allowed to *admit* that they take drugs once in a while – it's carte blanche and expected.

If your musicians need this credibility, it's easy to convey. Get out there with a camera and shoot the band in a bar. Swearing is not only allowed – it's recommended; giving the bird to the camera works, as does a complete disregard for public property. It's fun being a rock star – you're permitted to do anything that you wouldn't normally do....

This is why rock musicians are often considered 'a type'. The fact that they are seen as credible while getting away with all those things that PR machines normally conceal means this is a job for the gregarious, the outspoken, the funsters. As such, capturing all kinds of exciting, wild, or candid clips should not be a problem – if you accompany almost

ABOVE LEFT: Rough-and-ready rock is more about the angry things in life. While goth rock looks forward to the return of the living dead, thrash metal and hard rock often complement an action movie. Explosions, guns and fast women contribute to the sense of a life on the edge.

ABOVE RIGHT: A low shot for a rock star doesn't just help to incorporate their guitar. It works with a hard rock video to display the talent on a podium. For the humble viewer, this gives them the impression of authority and empowerment. It elevates the musician's status.

any young band on the road for a week you'll probably end up with more video footage than you can handle.

Editing this footage then becomes a matter of using the clips that express that particular side of the band's personality that you are trying to emphasize: wild, morose, skilled, tormented, stylish, sexy, or any combination of these.

Rock musicians live for the day. The reason that many rock stars have long hair is that they gain credibility by looking as though they don't care about themselves. The reality is that they do: everyone has in-built self-preservation as a standard feature. Indeed most rock stars want to look good and this – like the whole PR machine – is in the presentation of chaos within the parameters of control.

The extreme of rock existing as if it doesn't care about itself or about the world is not anarchy because it is not political. It is all about decadence, free-spiritedness, and having fun. It is living fast and dying young. Elvis Presley, Kurt Cobain, Janis Joplin – all the most credible artists had tabloid-friendly lives and rocked themselves into an early grave. Even if your rock band or musician is a little too academic for their own good (and your video), look for an edge. This might mean shooting them in an opium den, getting them to grow stubble, or smashing up the set with their own guitars.

While this sounds like punk, it is reined in with a controlled abandon and hedonism. This creates the sexiness of rock. Musicians look as though they are making love or just having sex: their music, clothes, expressions, and body language – even the way they operate the guitar – all infers the sexy side of the free spirit. Rock stars didn't create groupies without good reason. They are wild, untamed, carefree sex machines who need servicing and are up for anything.

Sex up your rock star and you're halfway to a decent rock video; alternatively, over-sex them and hit the heady heights of *glam* rock. . .

ABOVE: Glam rock didn't die in the seventies: it got modernized. It avoids being dismissed as pastiche or sheer camp by still maintaining its rock roots. Add some acidic lyrics, guitar genius, and some hard rockin', and you've got something as suspiciously credible as the Scissor Sisters. . .

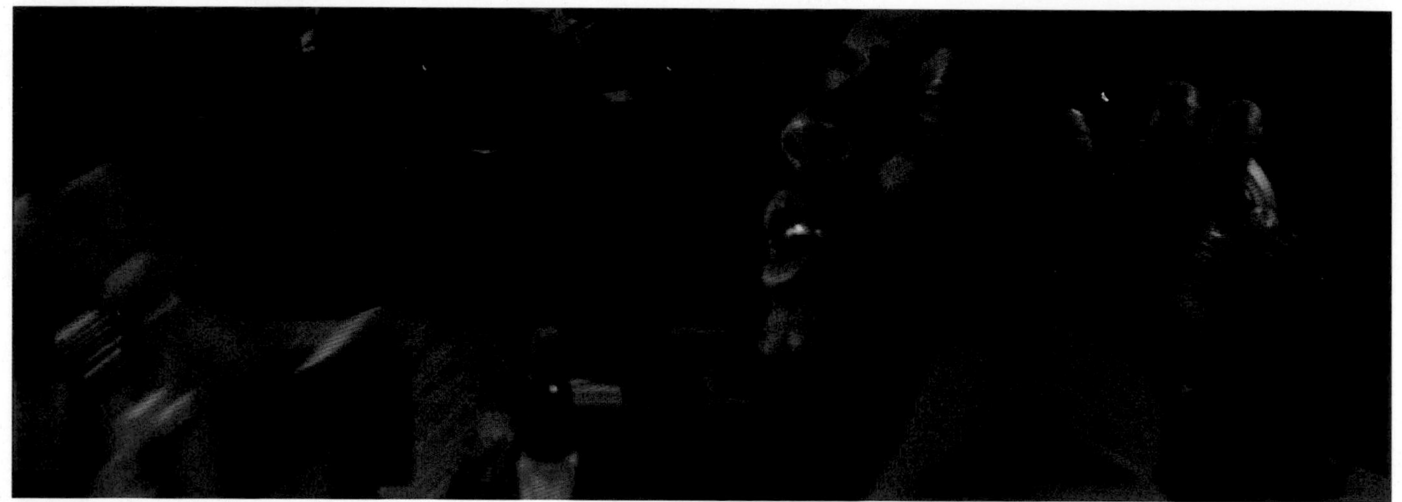

GET DOWN: **R&B**

Rhythm and blues is an ever-changing mood, and has moved from blue hues (Miles Davis, Louis Armstrong, Billie Holiday) to heavy soul (Marvin Gaye, Stevie Wonder, The Drifters) to contemporary R&B (Destiny's Child, Usher, Jay-Z).

In the early twentieth century, R&B was conceived as a way of getting across meaning using musical metaphors and double entendres. The music promised love, sweet love. Nothing has changed – it's still mid-tempo groove. It's the musical equivalent of bedroom eyes.

The huge variety of R&B tracks underlies its consistent popularity. It may have come out of the ghetto, but it did so a long time ago and was embraced by pop. The mid-tempo beat has often been used to hang a more romantic lyric on. In its original manifestation, rooted in the black culture of the time, the R&B lyric presented a predominantly male point of view. This, though, was arguably the nature of the business and not understood as sexism.

With changing political and social climates, the R&B scene has changed dramatically, with a huge succession of female artists entering the equation. Released from ideas of male dominance and incredibility, there is a wealth of emotions born from relationships and socio-politics to plunder. To some people, this may seem about as fresh as burning bras, but there are still plenty of interesting situations to be found in R&B.

R&B uses what it has to the max. If it isn't highlighting the masculinity (or lack thereof) of an ex-boyfriend, it's making suggestive remarks. It's chatting you up and, in turn, will help you to chat someone else up. It's a self-help guide to modern life based on loose and often naïve experience. But you don't want to show this in the music video.

By and large, R&B focuses on the vocals. R&B bands tend to be vocalists with an anonymous backing track or pared band. The genre is very production-based and the vocals are left clean and clear above the rhythm. For this reason, sync from the lead is the most important feature of an R&B music video. Presenting them to work with the music is a regular makeover.

***ABOVE:** The honesty of R&B or Soul can be represented with subtlety within realistic and candid environments (however contrived) in the studio itself – and often is.*

***LEFT:** R&B inherits Soul music's emotion and truth. This has a devout and unfailing belief, and wears its heart on its sleeve.*

ABOVE: R&B's roots are those of singing from the soul. Reflecting this with seemingly very pure visuals can bring that soul and emotion right back.

Attitude is one thing that you *do* want to show. Arrogance in R&B is based on the firm understanding that the vocalists (and sometimes musicians) are in control. The talent is likely to have acquired this attitude naturally later on in their successful lives. At the start, though, you might have to create this personality.

Attitude is created by confidence. The audience reciprocates by giving the artist credibility. Therefore it is this confidence that the talent has to find or the director has to portray.

If it is you that has to construct the artifice, the confidence trick is created on set. Whether the attitude you need is arrogance or sex appeal, it is constructed by allowing the talent to appear superior. A typical R&B video features a large amount of low camera angles, which look up to the artist. These often make up the master shot, and serve to demonstrate superiority in terms of both the performer's importance and sexual prowess. The subject is elevated, the legs lengthened, and the hips centre-frame. Sex, superiority – and if there's a monitor on set, a huge boost of confidence for the talent.

The outcome of R&B and rap's progression in recent times is two-fold: the first is that rap has to distance itself visually from R&B, and the second is that rap has a harder time establishing credibility within the pop market.

Credibility is the lip-service that is paid to rap's original ghetto roots. It has to establish that this is not simply a case of fraudulent desperation, or an artist that's just trying too hard. The roots of contemporary rap lie within the parameters of Jamaican patois and the New York underground scene. Thereafter, it is popular culture that has to assert its potency as pure rap.

through. The syllables and emphasis of patois can be very different from those of conventional English, and allow the same words to have different rhythm. Rap is all about strong percussive rhythm.

What this means in technical terms is that the sync in your edits must be extremely accurate and must push the song forward with a solid, bouncy pace. Everything and everyone in your video must move to the beat.

Back to the bling. Gold may go in and out of fashion, but it never loses its worth. This leads to the question: why would you want your rap lead to be adorned in gold? You may not, but the reasoning behind it is that it *proves worth*. It is asserting their credibility as successful artists.

HOP UP: **RAP**

As R&B has progressed and rap has become more pop, only a fine line remains between the two. As vocals for R&B have become less soulful, rap vocals have become more so. While hardcore rap stays in the ghetto, the popular buying vote goes to rap that adopts a pop sensibility and subscribes to pop standards.

Pure rap…nothing is that easy. Hip-hop is the sub-culture that was built around rap music as it developed in inner-city New York. Hip-hop took the language and made it graffiti – it was music video on a wall with a beatbox blowing its subwoofers next to it. For all intents and purposes, and for the sake of your music video, they are arguably married to rap. They are the wild-card of rap, and if you are making a music video for hip-hop, find the *other* side of it. It will have one, whether C&W, R&B, rockabilly, or pop. In a way, it's the slightly more straightforward version of rap in that the picture (your concept or video) is a little more shaded in.

The interesting thing about rap is that it shows its colors almost as easily. As a pared-down artform, it has no Mariah Carey-style 'eight-octave clause' to hide behind. Instead, it relies on rhythm, delivery, attitude, and lyric. To the rapper, rhythm is absolutely essential, but rhythm is delivered by the lyric. This is where the roots of patois can shine

Of course, this is a double-edged sword. Rap bases itself on the genuine to gain credibility. Musicians don't have that until they prove themselves, unless they want to risk exposure and skip a step. Attributing accoutrements to new rap artists or groups in your music video is a dangerous game: you may win, or you may lose everything.

The 'look' of rap in the music video and the fact that it is now an incredibly popular music genre means that it is very easy to get right, to get wrong, and to pastiche. Most current visual representations of the music simply regurgitate the same old images,

***ABOVE LEFT:** Rap is the one genre that has progressed dramatically in recent years. Eminem led the way for credible white rap artists. The genre's pop acceptance has come with recognition as a credible art form in terms of audio and video.*

LEFT: Rap often focuses on political issues. If you find yourself working on such a music video, understand who or what part of the culture is politically important and why. Above all, understand it to a point where you are using icons for a reason as well as aestheticism: respect the culture.

BELOW: Rap directs itself towards the camera and offers confrontation to beliefs. In this respect, it is visually active and not passive.

because this is is seen as the safest method of attaining instant 'street cred' and attracting the attention of what is seen as the 'typical' hip hop fan. Getting it right doesn't necessarily have to mean that you are subscribing to portraying the talent being fawned over by models, making booty calls, riding in fur-lined limousines, or adopting a po-faced, low-slung, fast-monied attitude. It means that whatever it *is*, you are being true to the lyric and talent of the band. N.E.R.D. can resist…can you?

Dance is still a factor in all forms of pop music, in terms of the more specific (The Macarena, C&W line dancing, Steps) to the more generic (formulation dancing). Formulation dancing is the staple diet of many genres of music and their videos. It feeds the visuals.

The birth of the music video as we know it coincided with the phenomenon of *Saturday Night Fever*. This era insisted that delivering visuals of dancers would instill in the audience a sense of the same excitement. It was fun by proxy. Unfortunately, it was a misguided concept – but it's still used extensively in all genres of music video.

A lot of this has come out of drug culture. Pure dance music allows for the body to find its own rhythm, rhyme, time, and space. It has gone beyond the realms of chatting up (this is left to every other form of music), and now has the effect of an ants' nest: individuals working together for a common cause. This common denominator is to be lost in music.

As a sexual expression, dance is concerned with building oneself up into a sweaty frenzy. All the traits of this are described in the music: the slow intro, the rhythm, the teasing harmony break, the rapid build of the snare crashing into the crescendo of the hook. It's both predictable and repetitious – but a foolproof formula that provides a framework for musical experimentation. It's described as anthemic.

***LEFT:** Dancing in studios – especially rigged studios – can be awkward for the talent if they're not trained. Any sign of awkwardness shows, and the only way of getting rid of it on playback is by making some edit decisions that you might not want to make.*

DUB DOWN: **DANCE**

Everyone likes a good dance: the foxtrot, the jitterbug, the Madison.

Dancing used in the music video is used to inform an audience that this is what you do when you hear the track at home or in a club. Of course, it's just not that *blatantly* portrayed, and dance is used in the music video to work with rhythm and set a scene. Indeed, *not* seeing a lead or musicians move to the music in their own dance video can often seem staged. Dance in the *pop* music video today is more *Haven't Stopped Dancing Yet* or *Don't Stop Moving*: impulsive dancing has become compulsive dance.

Pop dance, though, is very different from pure dance. Pure dance is born out of club and DJ culture. The rise and rise of the superclub has turned dance music around, and given it new life.

In the eyes of the pure dance faithful, pop dance has been getting it wrong for many, many years. Today's club music has nothing to do with ghettoism. It may be an all-embracing, all-forgiving community, but once you are there it is all-concerned with *personal* expression.

Experimentation is a musical journey to find *that* harmony, *that* beat and rhythm that is the perfect representation of ecstasy and release. This is made possible because club dance is very much an electronic artform. Mixing, compression, dubbing, sampling – playing with music in exactly the same way that pop art or cut-ups did before – encourages digital wizardry. DJs and engineers are mad scientists trying to create the perfect club single.

The same engineering is available to the music video director, and is a virtual home away from home. This partly explains why some pure dance music videos feature computer-generated graphics. The other reason is purely practical: there is no band or purist musician to shoot. If you're lucky, there's a vocalist...

The vocalist for club dance may be either a sample from another track or a featured artist. Either of these are enough of an excuse not to use that particular artist in the video for the music. Because the music is digitally engineered, the artist can be created.

***RIGHT TOP:** If you're trying to infuse your music video with the spirit with which the track was intended, play the track on set as sync for the dancers. This might sound obvious, but even though you may be considering speed for slowmo, using the dance track's particular and consistent beat makes it easy to multiply. This is effective in ensuring that your dancers are never out of time in the edit.*

***RIGHT:** Don't be afraid to try something different. If you can't afford a choreographer – or even dancers – there are plenty of other things in life that can be choreographed by instinct and edit.*

They can be a more glamorous representation or even a digital one (Digital Diva). Creating a music video for a dance record, therefore, is a mission to create entertaining visuals to accompany a track that would ordinarily be uncomfortable in a broadcast world. This is why music videos for pure dance often tend to lack budget. Stripped bare in the outside world, these tunes lose their impact, and it may well be that your only viable presentation of the video is in a club environment. Often, they are designed for such a short life that they don't warrant any financial support – videos for DJ Sammy's clubby reworkings of 1980s hits 'Heaven' and 'Boys of Summer' are good examples of economical, yet appropriately flashy, video-making.

Dance tracks can offer a fantastic soundscape to work with. Huge, dynamic ranges and full harmonies, hard beats, and audio stings inform different concepts, cuts, transitions, and effects – and playing up to them makes the visuals shine and the track even better. They can be a real joy to work with.

STRING UP: **CLASSICAL**

Music videos aren't always aimed at the mass market. There are plenty of musical genres that make even more sales, but are simply less suited to visual interpretation. This is not to say that the music is less image-inspiring, but more that they don't have to rely on marketing to sell them.

This is a contradiction of the entire music video industry, and serves to highlight the cynicism that drives the machine. With a classical or ambient track, there is often no vocalist. Without a subject to focus on, there is no-one who can sexually express or appeal to the music video demographic: those who buy music. This makes the video redundant for any show or channel tailored to the buying audience.

Classics are used as soundtracks. Where there is no vocalist, there is no-one to interfere with dialogue. Instrumentals are there to create mood for visuals. This is the direct opposite of the pop music video where the visuals are there to create a mood for the singer, band or musicians. Eliminating the visuals for an instrumental track to create a solely aural experience is like reading a book: the mind creates the visuals. Your video should perform a similar task.

TOP: Can classical string harmonies or soaring minor to major ambient anthems become more beautiful? Sure – by adding beautiful pictures. Tempering this, though, is always wise to avoid overdoing it.

ABOVE LEFT: Visuals to instrumentals often seem to examine human life. When everyday activities are shown in slow motion, the effect can be almost fetishistic. Everyday activities are, ironically, precisely what a viewer might be doing at the time of listening to that track.

Just as the instrumental may be used to be played against dialogue in the media, so the everyday purchaser of instrumentals often uses them as a soundtrack to play as a background to something else that they are doing. They might be having a dinner party, doing the housework, sunbathing, working, driving, or commuting – it's everything *but* watching television, in fact.

London's Classic FM radio station, however, has a dedicated television channel in the UK, that is available via satellite and cable TV. It features visual interpretations of classical and contemporary instrumental music. This includes such things as sweeping deserts, blue skies, star-filtered streams, native cultures in foreign lands exhibiting colourful traditions. You don't have to be this predictable, however. The idea is to go with the music and predict the images it might evoke in the viewer, and then play with these expectations to create something the viewer will notice and remember.

The viewing (and buying) public respond to rhythm in audio and video. Thus, your video events and edits must be closely timed with peaks, rhythms, and other significant events in the audio track. For example, a segment can be slowed down not only to match the beat of a song, but to enhance a mood of reflection or fantasy.

video, only the best visuals will do. It's an edit job based on the existing trailer.

Without any vocals, the same successful enterprise can be achieved by targeting the club audience. Adding modern instruments and a beat to Barber's *Adaggio For Strings* helped William Orbit achieve recognition as an artist and engineer. Club

ABOVE: *Instrumentals are a time for contemplation and the exotic. The sex factor is sensuous rather than sexually charged.*

The instrumental is especially effective when it is the soundtrack to a fictitious life (a movie); James Horner's theme from *Titanic* is an easy example. Without a vocal, it is a classically-themed orchestral instrumental. With the right lyric and the right vocal on board, it becomes a golden ticket. The combination of visuals (Kate and Leonardo hooked the teens) and audio (classical grabbed your granny; Céline snared the 20/30/40-somethings) and lyric (undying love made it a compulsory purchase for wedding soundtracks), took it on a long voyage at full sale, crossing demographic oceans until it hit the iceberg of contemptuous overplay and self-destruction. Okay, that's over egging the pudding a little, but after all is sung and done, it was a classic track.

This proves without a doubt that movie soundtracks containing instrumentals can be incredibly successful. While *My Heart Will Go On* sold (and made) records, it existed to sell the movie. A commercial for the movie is then based on the track. In the music

dance – and more specifically, trance – relies on harmonies with a building beat. Again, if you're working with one of these tracks, they're a joy to edit against, but you mustn't lose sight of the concept behind the original song.

Instrumentals are entirely open-ended in their conceptual possibilities and treatment. An instrumental's purpose is to create mood. There are no vocalists and no lyrics, so always work within the parameters of the mood to give yourself *something* to work with – even if you choose to contradict the mood entirely and create irony.

Think about adding dialogue to the video, or making it highly theatrical. Working with the instrumental onomatopoeia can give great results. Otto Fischinger visually described classical works by scratching film and animating in time, and Michel Gondry composited a view from a train window to emphasize beat and sound. Instrumentals are solid practice for the creative video-maker.

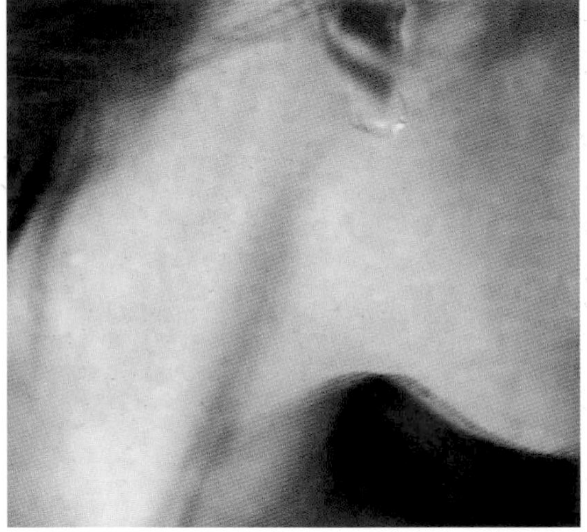

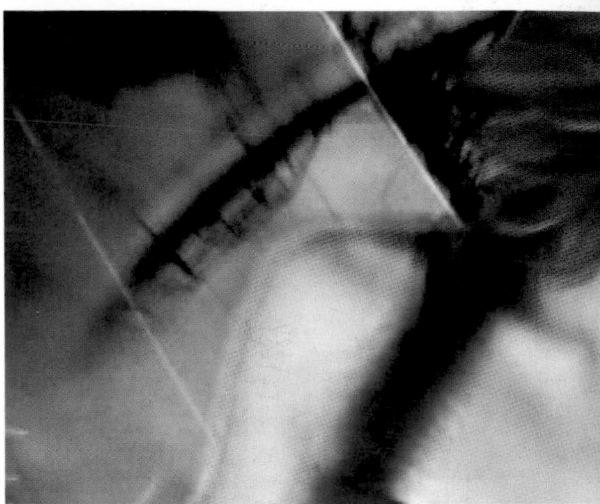

BELOW: Creating fun on set often brings out the flirtatious in your talent. Use this to your advantage. Wardrobe or props (such as furry deelyboppers) can encourage a frivolity that is always appealing in a tough world.

SEXING UP: **SEX IN THE MUSIC VIDEO**

Sex sex sex sex sex. Now that's over with, let's get on with what sells music. Oh...sex.... And co-incidentally, they're probably singing about it, too.

Making a music video sexy isn't just a question of technique; it's very much to do with what your talent is bringing to the screen. Consider from the start that until they become a star who has the benefit of having an established personality (of sorts), then intelligence, articulation, and any sign of personal appeal is out of the window. It doesn't matter a jot anyway: celebrity makes musicians sexy.

You – and they – are entirely in charge of creating sex appeal at a purely visual level. *You* includes yourself and your entire crew. *They* includes the talent, their inherent presentation, and their performance skills.

Sexiness has to be pitched right, depending on the audience and the track. Kids want non-threatening dates, the wistful want romance, and the settled want danger. All of these can be created.

Sexiness can come out of anything, but is considered tasteless if you remain visually faithful to pompous, political, charitable, or worthy lyrics. Fortunately, most lyrics or music have a sexual element. This is because sex sells.

Don't worry about tailoring to sexuality. Sexiness is perceived as sexiness by one and all. Whether or not it appeals to individual taste is out of your control. Indeed, the most unsexy portrayals tend to be those that insist that the talent is sexy. Anything that smacks of desperation is not sexy.

Within all of these categories lies that of a basic instinct: if the talent is the product of a sexy gene pool, it is often quite impossible for them to be anything but a sex object. But while there are plenty of models and actors out there who are aggrieved that they can't be taken seriously because of their looks, it doesn't hinder a musical talent's career whatsoever. Sexiness doesn't necessarily happen on-set, but it can do later – once you get cutting.

ABOVE LEFT > RIGHT & OPPOSITE LEFT > RIGHT: Out of a simple set-up, necks, hair-tossing, the demure eye contact, open mouths, the sleazy and blatant exposure, can all be captured to spell just one thing: SEX.

SO WHAT IS SEXY?

The following are the traits that define sexy:

- **> Humour: A twinkle in the eye, or the cheeky confidence of the class clown**
- **> Accessibility: Not ridiculously gorgeous or unapproachably famous**
- **> Energy: Naturally dextrous moves, or just straight hot, sweaty dynamism**
- **> Confidence level: Vulnerable, blushing virgin, or verging on vain**
- **> Danger: Blatant uninhibited sexuality suggesting irresistible submission**
- **> Safety: Someone your mum would like or who is sexually non-threatening**

Slowmo

Tried and tested, slowmo emphasizes movement to the extent of lingering fetishism. Fetishism is an interest in something that is normally perceived as ordinary. Slowmo takes frenetic dance moves down to gyrations. It examines hair-tossing in the greatest of detail. It fragments conventional movement into sexual allusion.

Shots

Again, the camera works to fetishize, separating body parts to examine them more closely. There is a lot of this in music video – cutaways that aren't quite as innocent as an edit-saving or tedium-quashing cutaway. Too many of these and the exercise becomes a little cynical. Sex sells, but it can quickly become a turn-off.

Moves

Camera moves often work with slowmo to create sexiness. Gentle glides across a face or body, or a gentle zoom in, invite personal intimacy: a one to one with the viewer. Moving into the artist's space is an approach – and this makes them approachable.

Make-up

People can look better with make-up, and the sense of being shot as a screen star can encourage the musical talent. At their most primal, a viewer will respond more favourably to faces and bodies that are healthy, strong, and physically attractive.

Physical perfection is a mix of good genetics, a gym routine, and garb. Facial perfection is a flawless foundation. Alluring eyes, flushed cheeks, and untamed hair are the different guises that can help create sexiness.

Wardrobe

Clothes are the one thing that will always date a video. Out-dated clothes, however, don't affect the sexiness of your talent. It is always how they wear them, and whether they can carry them off. Fashion phases dictate whether revealing is appealing and classy is brassy, or vice versa. There is a fine line between sexy and trashy.

***BELOW LEFT:** The shirtless and sweaty in reality usually just need a good bath; in the music video it's a contrived and contained visual experience that smacks of sex.*

***BELOW:** The directed camera informs the viewer what is sexy. The price that is paid is that a viewer will make their decisions based on what they are given, and reject what is not personally sexy to them.*

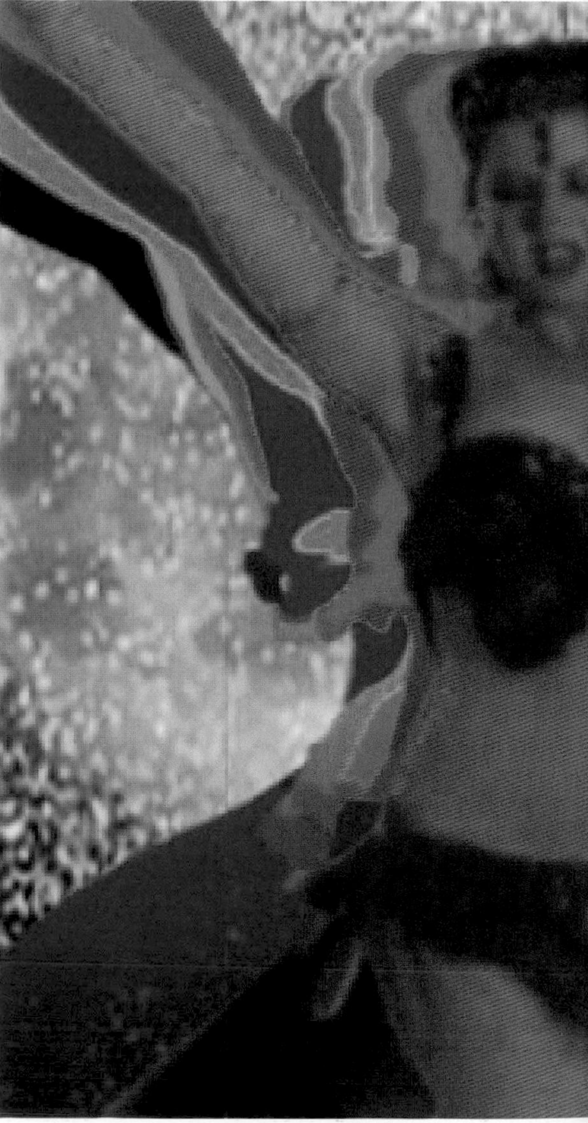

A sexy wardrobe always emphasizes the most impressive parts of the talent's body, no matter the fashion. Most importantly, the talent has to be happy wearing it to evoke sexiness – or indeed, feel sexy.

Whatever it takes, if it works with the song and you can sell the sexiness of the musicians, do it. It sells. And sometimes, if you strike gold, your performers can just *shine* in front a lens. Get a Beyoncé or a Justin Timberlake and you won't have to try too hard at all...

LEFT: Conversely, risking rejection from a viewer raises the chances of success with the strength of the image itself. Making bold decisions with confrontational sexual imagery can challenge the viewer.

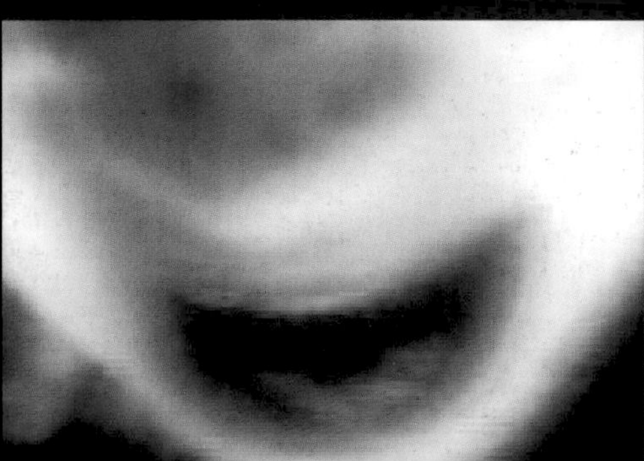

STRIKING DOWN: **DEATH IN THE MUSIC VIDEO**

There is sex, and there is death. Between the two there is a huge grey area that a lot of music videos choose to explore – and it's not so grey after all: it's the dark side.

Goth, trash-metal, and the 'alternative' embrace the dark side. To an outsider, it may appear to be sexually bereft. This isn't true. This genre of music understands the connection between sex and death.

There is a little death in a lot of these generic videos in order to appeal to that specific audience. This dark side is represented in the performer as a malcontent. Malcontents have been around a long time in some form or another – even Hamlet was one. With music, the malcontent is characteristically displayed as a siren to a ghettoized audience. This is why its depiction both musically and visually has to be so specific.

Around this malcontent is a world that empathizes. It is dark and fetishitic in detail; it represents their ghetto and their world and makes them feel at home. Malcontents – both performers and audience – aren't necessarily suicidal. Instead, they do not expect anything of the world – and don't want anything anyway. It is borderline anarchy without the political proactivity. With this comes lack of care for the self. This does *not* represent itself with make-up and wardrobe, but with attitude.

Attitude is superficial. Anyone can have one, borrow one, or steal one – which is why they tend to be temporary and used at a certain age in life. The kind of age, in fact, that buys a lot of music…

The music is bought, or bought into, because is provides an ear and a mouth to the ghetto audience at their time in their place in the world. The music video, therefore, has to represent this visually.

The requisite of the music video when portraying death is the suspension of belief. Dead people aren't very interesting, either. Therefore, the true nature of death in the music video is not the reality, but the sexy allure (the siren), the submission to the inevitable (the harbinger), or the life everafter (the demon).

ABOVE LEFT: ***Fear makes eyes wide, mouths open (or gagged) – it creates sexiness through peril.***

ABOVE RIGHT: ***Death in the music video is not like death in the motion picture. Because the video is selling the music, not the story, the audience knows that whatever happens to your lead singer is not going to affect their future release output.***

ABOVE: Death comes in many guises, and it's comin' right at ya – to the viewer, that is. Most music videos hurl sync and images towards the screen. Doing this with a harbinger of death not only implicates the viewer, but threatens them.

LEFT: Indeed, the threat of death keeps those alive living on the edge. This is precisely where a lot of music feels happiest, and subscribing visually to that theme tailors the package to a death-defying, and defiant, youth audience.

Images of this dark side can both be shown by the performers and any ghetto audience, or by the talent. Wide eyes, screaming mouths, black body and face make-up, masks and armour or fetish wear, convulsive or thrashing physical performance, weapons as props, visions, and metaphoric harbingers of mortality, bullet-shots or crumbling backgrounds, performers threatening suicide, drowning, falling from heights – there are so many ways to convey the submission, confrontation, or the embrace of death.

All of these individual images complete the theme – or at least a videoscape that lies somewhere just *before* death where life is never so vivid or dangerous, teetering on the edge. Completing the distress of the theme is the destruction of the video itself. The techniques of grading or dirtying pictures are often used in this genre to seal the deal with death.

Alternatively, death can be portrayed as beautiful. Beautiful shots, sets, make-up, editing, and grading, work against obvious themes of grim reaping. Choosing irony or finding the flip-side of the darkside (release, relief, explanation of life) can offer just as many visually interesting opportunities.

Sophie Muller's *Stay* and Rocky Schenck's *Where The Wild Roses Grow* are both showcases of beauty, yet both remain uncompromising in their portrayal of showdowns. The question is always whether you choose heaven or hell as your ultimate goal after death in the video.

Just like any comedy, inappropriate, forced humour – or just plain unfunniness – merely serves as a turn-off. A stand-up act can be brutal with a heckler, but for a music video at the mercy of a remote control, it's cut-throat.

The Fun

At the lowest level, this is the promo that is comfortable with being cheerful. Most music videos only allow performances by the talent that are natural – and musicians are naturally serious about what they do. On a practical level, a long shoot can be quite tedious for them. The experience can agitate natural seriousness and turn it sober or exasperated – neither of which are conducive to comedy.

STANDING UP: COMEDY IN THE MUSIC VIDEO

Because the music video doesn't allow for much (or any) dialogue, it doesn't have the benefit of being able to create verbal humour. Spoken language offers so many ways to convey comedy, such as the double-entendre, irony, sarcasm, puns, riddles, and jokes. When verbal comedy is perceived as clever, it is sophisticated and it is cool.

So where does that leave the music video? It leaves it with visual comedy: parody, pastiche, sight gags. These can easily be interpreted as non-sophisticated comedy – and, as such, can be desperately uncool. The marketing machine is fighting too hard for your money to risk being uncool, which is why there are so few laughs in the music video. Marketing is a serious business.

Those that can afford to risk being amusing are those that have established credentials. People are born to comedy, and those that are usually become comedians and not musicians. There are performers, though, who are naturally amusing and both marketing and directors have developed the drive and the video on this part of their personality. The Beastie Boys, Steve Tyler, Anthony Kiedis, and Dave Grohl are all allowed to keep their sense of humour not only intact, but in-frame for appropriate videos.

ABOVE LEFT: Often, the fine line between comedy and death – black comedy – can be a useful tool to help describe a band. It gives them gravity (credibility) with a less throwaway and more conceivably sophisticated sense of humour.

Creating a sense of fun, then, can be quite difficult, take after take. It actually requires acting skills. Deciding on the level of fun for your music video depends on the theme. If everybody is smiling and dancing, this is the momentum and expression that you have to maintain throughout the whole of the video and of the shoot.

Fun is to be witnessed in most up-beat tracks and all dance tracks. If there is an audience representative (a crowd dancing), then it is appropriate that they are having fun.

The Funny

Mid-level comedy is the hardest to judge. Perhaps the best measure is to look at the performers and at the lyric to find some compatibility for humour. D12's *My Band* has a lyric that doesn't allow for much else *but* to be created visually as a joke. The performers are personable and willing, and for this reason, the idea could be taken forward and developed in the video.

How visual jokes actually translate beyond pre-production, the shoot and then an edit can be dangerously hit or miss. Add the fact that humour is so subjective and there's a real danger of isolating part of the target audience.

A visual joke is best utilized as a lever for a performance. OutKast, P Diddy, Eminem, Britney – most wised-up musicians, in fact – are willing participants in engineering themes and set-ups that serve to laugh at themselves, their media personalities, and spotlit lives. The effect that this has is to endear, to humble, and to humanize, and a spot-on self-deprecating performance can make serious money. Indeed, George Michael's *Outside* promo was sheer turnaround marketing genius.

The fact that there are very specific genres of music video allows for many opportunities to undermine expectations and create amusement by playing with them. Simple exaggerations create fine lines between serving a genre and exploiting it for humour. The finer this line, the more subtle – and perhaps more sophisticated – the humour will be; the more exaggerated, the more grotesque, accessible, and easily dismissed.

The Ridiculous

Madness made money out of it; the Beastie Boys still bang away at it. This is the total submission to the ridiculous. This is a visual gag that both applies itself to the set-ups and to the performances – so much so, that they become inextricable.

The huge neon warning sign is that you risk making the music redundant. If the music isn't taken seriously, then it is hard for an audience to buy into it – certainly in the long term. If the entire package is a gag, then it's a short-lived one. Jokes simply don't get any funnier every time you see them or every time you hear them.

The Unintentional

Serious musicians playing serious songs with serious visuals can often be the funniest thing that you're likely to see. Don't fall into this trap. It's easy on the day of the shoot for everyone to be overly serious. If this is what you actually shoot, though, you may end up with take-after-take of unrelenting sobriety. While this is often just dull, extreme exaggerations of committed stone-faced musicians can be unintentionally amusing.

This is the worst case of all humorous scenarios. If the music video is amusing by design then that is fine; if it is an accidental laugh-fest, then no-one will buy into it. Unintentional humour is as bad as a four-minute joke that isn't funny. It's embarrassing and a waste of time.

ABOVE LEFT: Smile…

ABOVE: Humour in the music video can be dry, or it can be bright, sparkly, and poppy. Interpreting it this way allows for the talent to take trips onto the other side: the appeal of the sexy.

A musician as a politician can be wearing on the ear and eye. The more blatant the display of politics, the more one questions whether they should be less party anthem and more party elect. It's your buck, though, and because music is a business, alienating audiences is the risk that political tracks and musicians make. This is why the pop genre (as the biggest generic business) isn't often overtly political. It is thinking about the revenue and not the revolution.

Of course, the most honest way to preach or externalize *and* take your money for a cause is the charity record. Governments around the world have stood back and watched in amazement at the power of politics in music. People are people, some of them are musicians, many are the buying public, and music can make even the most suspect causes sound worthwhile.

Opinions are largely the privilege of personalities, and in order to be able to express them, one might have to venture out of the box. Expressing soap-box politics can be that one risk too far for a musician's career. Alternatively, it can also be the publicity drive and tabloid drivel that works for a cause, just as much as it works for the musician. From the Boomtown Rats ripping up a picture of Olivia Newton-John and John Travolta, to Sinead O'Connor doing the same with the Pope's; from Madonna and Britney's kiss, to Pearl Jam and the Dixie Chicks riding anti-war bandwagons. Using a profile can be misjudged and can backfire, but it can also earn respect. Respect, though, does not necessarily equate with sales.

Lyrics provide the biggest outlet for social, sexual, and personal politics. Saturation point is reached where an artist becomes almost a spokesperson: Howard Jones for vegetarianism, Bono for third world debt, Alanis Morissette for bad relationships, Billy Bragg for socialism, Madonna for polymorphous sexuality, and Michael Jackson for the entire state of the world today.

Emphasizing the political content of the lyric can be achieved through the performance, or through the music video. The music video becomes a loud speaker for their opinions, just in case anyone should not be listening. If it is through the music video, it may be that the politics aren't a translation, but the externalization of the director's personal politics. Usually, though, a political music video will accompany political lyrics – and even more commonly, it will go about it literally rather than metaphorically.

Politics, like fashion, comes and goes in waves. The times, they really are a-changin' and music genre often reflects it, from the hip sixties' perspective of making love, not war, to punk anarchy encouraging us to riot against establishmentarianism, to the material world of pecuniarism in the eighties. In the contemporary music world, these types of statements continue to be made. George Michael puts Bush in a bed with Blair, Marilyn Manson challenges America's sense of decency with provocative visuals, and – *bling! bling!* – no rapper can be taken seriously without ten grand's worth of gold in his mouth.

Today, even clothes have a political agenda – and the music video is more than happy to show them off, if not show them *taken* off.

9-11

STANDING DOWN: **POLITICS IN THE MUSIC VIDEO**

In the world demographic, artists and creatives are in the top band for political displays. It is not because they are any more political than anyone else; it is because their job involves externalizing the internal. Their thoughts and feelings on the state of things are a rich feeding ground for their work, whether a painting, a book, a movie, a song, or a music video.

***RIGHT:** Choosing to include a tattoo of a musician lays that individual politically bare. By proxy, this affects the tone of the video simply by making that choice. Whether or not a decision is made to create irony or emphasis beyond that point is just another of many choices in the edit.*

A Union Jack T-shirt, an Osama Bin Laden beard, a CND button – even the cutting of iconic hair. They all *say* something without the lyric necessarily hitting a listener over the head with a blunt opinion.

If not for social comment, clothes are just one of the many devices used as public displays of personal politics in the music video. Whether this is Madonna's combats in *American Pie* or George Michael – again – in his officer's uniform for *Outside*. It appears that T-shirts with slogans may be the *easy* way out…

The exhibition of a musician's personal politics becomes an exploration of *social* politics under the media magnifying glass, often by design. This serves to highlight the grey area of a marketing machine on overdrive.

Sexual politics are rife within many genres of music – even within popular music, a genre that usually eschews any other type of controversy in order to appeal to the larger demographic. This is because it isn't purely sexiness that sells, it is any other aspect of it. It's the girls-who-are-boys-who-like-boys-to-be-girls-who-do-boys-like-they're-girls-who-do-girls-like-they're-boys school of sexual politics. In the business and to its buyers, it's sexuality; to the sensual world, it's politics.

These are the exceptions—and they have artistic and budgetary implications. Your musicians may not like it, and they probably can't afford it.

When the music comes before the plot, the plot is either delivered with the participation of the musicians or without. Musicians aren't expected to be the greatest actors in the world by any means, but they *are* performers. The music video doesn't require dialog to be delivered, and there are plenty of performers that can perform physically. With a plot, this can be manipulated or perceived as part of it. And then it is acting.

ACTING UP: **PLOTS IN PROMOS**

Most music videos have a plot. It won't be Mission:Impossible *to understand it – in fact, if you don't understand it, you're probably looking too hard.*

There are two ways to handle a plot in the music video: either the music video comes first, or the plot. There are very few examples of the latter, although it's often not for the want of the director trying. A lot of successful directors start out in music video and use it as a springboard to creating Hollywood movies – these directors tend to use the music video as a way of fine-tuning their talent in preparation for writing, directing, and cutting narratives.

The blur between the movie and the music video is usually seen in the movie of the musical. Occasionally, though, it's seen in the music video. Spike Jonze's promo for Daft Punk's *Da Funk* plays the music as background incidental music to the very human, dialogue-driven shaggy dog story, and John Landis' *Thriller*, of course, plays the narrative as a movie reel in a can.

ABOVE: Acting within the music video can be a terrific way of freeing yourself from the convention of using the band themselves.

TOP RIGHT: Wrestling yourself out of the traditional visual wallpaper bag allows narrative and dialogue skills to shine – even if you choose to dip the sound. While this may not be the marketing showcase that the band or client have in mind, fight your corner. Because it is working against convention, it will get the video – and the band and track – noticed.

RIGHT: A lack of lines for your actors doesn't mean that you don't employ actors. A lack of lines means that the physical performance is completely vulnerable to scrutiny.

Without their participation, the plot will continue around a musician or band as they perform as-live or in sync. This is a music video that uses the musicians as a device to explain the story around them. This is a decision that has to be made first off, because it will generally mean hiring actors and progressing the shoot as two separate ventures. To explain the narrative, there will be a moment of interaction between the two basic set-ups.

That moment – or *few* moments – of interaction will require a performance from the musician, whether it is watching the narrative develop in front of them (emoting) or becoming involved (acting). If there is no point of interaction, the band are playing the track as the incidental soundtrack to the narrative, and we have come back full circle again.

Using the track as incidental music with sync inserts usually means that the narrative is following the lyric, literally or metaphorically. If there isn't sync, the track will often be perfect to use as music to drive a narrative – that is, to all intents and purposes, it *is* a soundtrack to cut your Hollywood teeth on.

If your lead – or, indeed, *all* your musicians— can happily and successfully perform, then they can straddle both the narrative and the sync. The music video allows for sync to continue almost as if it were a voice-over to the narrative that they themselves are involved with. It is the prerogative of the music video to break space and time, but it can also split personalities.

It is the sync vocal that means everything, though. By their very nature, leads perform. Getting them to turn lyrics into meaning for an insert narrative requires a display of emotion to make sense of the narrative placement. To get such a performance requires direction, even if it is getting the performer to revisit the lyric that they've sung countless times before. And good direction might even get you to Hollywood . . .

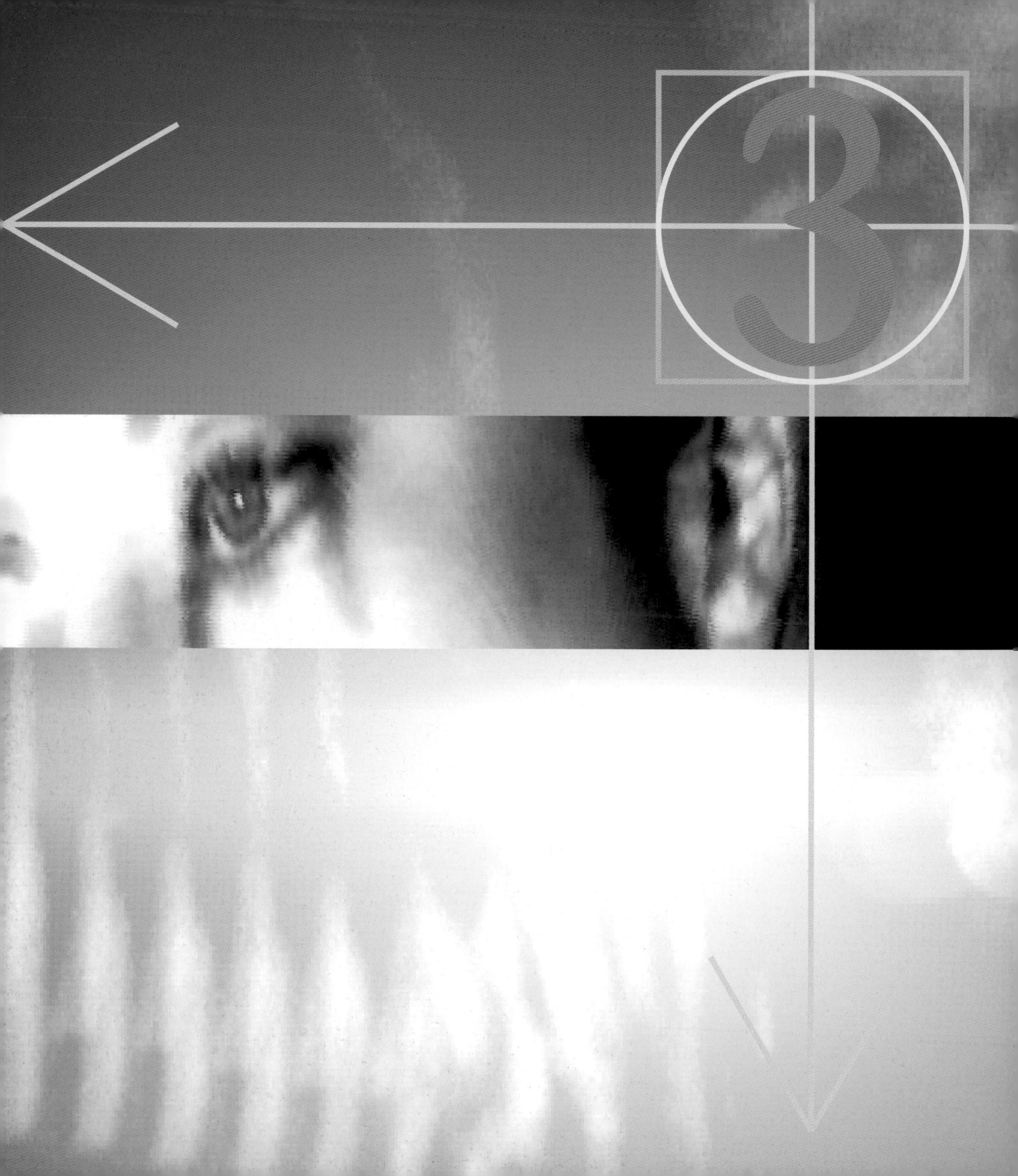
3

PRE-PRODUCTION: SINGING TO THE SAME TUNE

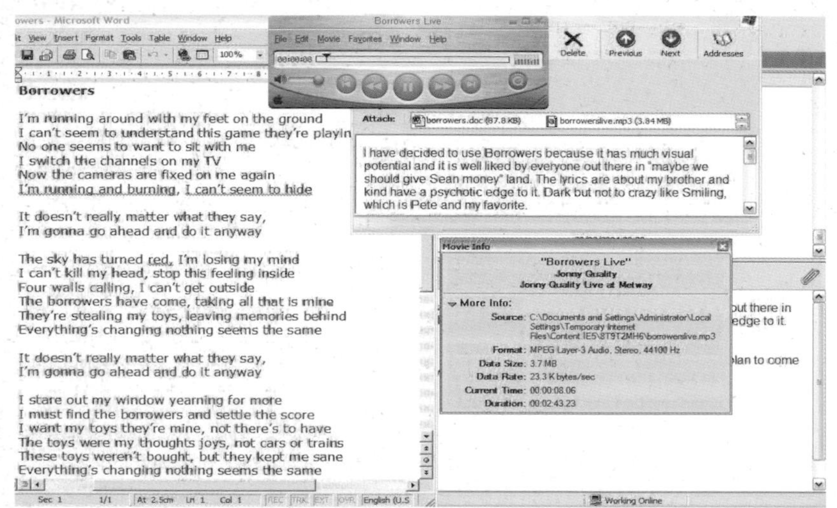

visual concept. The most memorable music videos contain that focus. Think of Richard Ashcroft bumping into pedestrians in *Bittersweet Symphony* or the embarrassing dancers in *Praise You*. Both of these are simple ideas taken from witnessing the real world.

If you are lucky, you've already got a lead singer or musician who is a natural performer, and you can use their camera-friendly personality for inspiration. Björk can dance on a truck and she's electric; Madonna can work both pseudo silver-screen and blue screen and be captivating. If you want your lead to carry the video, try projecting an emotion or personality. Alanis Morissette embodies multiple personalities for *Ironic*, and Robert Smith becomes a happy claustrophobic in *Close To Me*.

START UP: FINDING THE RIGHT CONCEPT

Stephen King once likened the empty page to the search for a hole into which to dive. The empty page waiting for ideas will always be like this, unless you approach it armed.

ABOVE: It's impossible to formulate any idea unless you have all the right information at your fingertips. This is the track, the lyric, and any requests that the musicians might have with regard to the marketing. If you want a background to the lyric to understand with a greater depth, ask for it. Sometimes this is exactly the seed that you need.

The best ideas come from external influences. Ideas don't come from within; they *develop* within. You won't have an idea if you don't get out into the world and experience that one thing that can germinate into the concept. If you don't have that seed, give yourself a day out; meet people, be a barfly, get into the countryside – whatever you need to do to get it. Just don't get it from MTV.

Different locations can often provide the perfect inspiration. Natural landscapes, subways, trains, rooftops, theatres – any location will have a mood that can be used straight, ironically, fearfully, or in whatever way you wish to make sense or nonsense of a track by design.

The thing about getting ideas is that you really only need just the one. The script is written but the visuals need to hang together on the thread of a

There's also the flipside of life: life's a musical in *Oh So Quiet*, rooms have moving floors in *Virtual Insanity* and the world is under water in Portishead's *Only You*.

People, emotions, situations, locations: all of these encourage the creative to find that one thread for the video. If you're finding it harder than you might imagine to marry the visuals with the track, forget about the track altogether. Find a person, a situation, a location that interests you and then find a way of working it into the track.

Bittersweet Symphony isn't about bumping into people. It's about being trapped in life. What the video does have is a consolidation with 'I'll take you down the only road I've ever been down', a repeated line that seals the song and visuals.

That one idea keeps the visual focus. The essential step from there is to create the crucial entertainment factor. The one closed frame sequence in *Praise You* is enthralling because the viewer can't

LEFT: When you meet the musicians, distance yourself enough to observe their individual personalities and the ones that they use when interacting within the band. Often, these identities are very different – conflicting even – and can offer new frameworks to support and propel your idea.

quite believe what they are watching. This is the exception that proves the rule. Keeping the interest level up usually means pushing this focus. This can be done by progressing the story (*Coffee And TV*), changing the location (*Ray Of Light*), embellishing the dance (*Weapon Of Choice*) – anything that ups the ante and draws to a natural conclusion with the song. The song will build; build with it.

There is one other place to find ideas that won't necessarily cost you five beers, lattes, or gallons of gas: it's your edit. A lot of videos hang the hook on an effect or a transition. While this may sound like a technical cop-out, such ideas are usually conceived in combination with a camera move or lens on set. A lot of these themes are gained through experience of shooting and editing. A lot of them are also the result of simply experimenting.

Morphing transitions used within frames, fast movement on [illegible] backgrounds, long slow-mo mixes with massive telephoto depths of field, constant camera zooms coupled with continuous DVEs in the edit – all of these things can work together to become a central idea or theme for your visual production. The most successful ideas are obviously going to be those that enhance or work well alongside the meaning of the lyric or music. Michael Jackson's *Black And White* morphing proposes (no matter how tritely) that on a fundamental level we are really all the same.

Whatever you settle on for an idea, always keep some rough budget at the back of your mind. There really is no point in pursuing ideas that are outside your financial parameters. Money is really spent when it comes to locations, sets, and live effects. Try to steer away from anything you've seen, or find a different slant if you are constantly drawn to a certain idea. Rap with fisheye lenses and flash bulbs has been done to death; try taking visual themes from one genre of music to another and produce something new and exciting in the process.

MEETING UP: **SINGING FROM THE SAME SONGSHEET**

The great thing about meeting up is that it's free – or so you'd think. But time is money and money is time, and the only way of actually addressing meetings is that you will be saving money by spending time.

Meeting with a band, singer, or musician regularly is incredibly important to avoid time wastage. Things change very quickly with temperamental creatives; they evolve organically or change by whim and the last thing that the video director wants to find is that the song is longer, the words are different, the concept has changed or the entire track has been ditched in favour of a new favourite. These things happen.

It is often the lead singer that speaks on behalf of the band. Whoever the authority figure turns out to be is the one with whom you want to engage. While the writer may have their own ideas as to what the song is about, it's the interpretation by the whole band that matters to you. From there, the video is going to be *your* own interpretation.

Your interpretation of the song is the one that sells the tune, and that is the one that everybody has to be happy with. This means that meeting with the talent is not only so that you can be happy enough that things haven't moved on without you, but that you can determine that the talent understands what you have in mind.

In order to accomplish this, you must conduct yourself with a certain level of authority; this implies that you know the right way to sell the song. The differentiation between yourself and the other creatives at meetings is that it is your skills in visuals and marketing that are your value and the reason that you are involved. You are not expected to mess with the track, just as the talent is not required to undertake the shoot.

Getting this balance right is the key to a smooth shoot and edit. Unfortunately, creatives are not the kind of people that like to be told what to do – even if they employed you to make the video. Therefore, your level of assertion will keep the focus, time, and budget under control. Take charge.

***ABOVE:** Discussing the video with the band is not just saved until the shoot. Prepare the musicians as to what they can realistically expect to be doing on the day. On the day of the shoot, you are simply detailing what they already know in order that the shot works.*

***LEFT:** Even musicians prepare themselves for shoots, and places of tedious captivity (like the hairdressers) can provide perfect locations for last-minute and time-saving discussions of detail.*

This process doesn't just apply during pre-production and production. Post-production is one of the most time-consuming, budget-busting parts of any music video because it's make or break time. The aware, listening, assertive personality that you've adopted will pay off in post-production because you'll need personal space and a certain amount of patient isolation.

Intrusiveness in post is a nightmare. Any distraction to the precise cutting against a beat, effects, graphics, or complex editing, isn't going to give either yourself or the band a product that they'll be totally satisfied with. Again, this is something that they have to understand. They should only see a cut when you are happy with it.

GETTING IN EARLY

Early meetings should be treated like a pitch. Represent your idea for a video with a creative and an executive. Meet beforehand to discuss strategies for winning over with your concept. Double-acts work well – one to be the black-clad reluctant artist, and the other to act as hard-nosed, practical, and occasionally toady negotiator.

HOW IT SHOULD GO

- > You are asked to make a video for a track
- > You listen to the track and study the lyric
- > You ask the musician for any particular elements or feel that they'd like to create
- > You interpret and incorporate these ideas or mood into your storyboard
- > You show and tell and discuss in a meeting
- > The concept evolves
- > You redraft the storyboard or script
- > Repeat no more than twice
- > Prepare for production

ABOVE RIGHT: Getting the details of the day's shoot out of the way enables the musicians to simply get on with the music.

The relationship that you have with the band, musician, or singer is therefore very delicate. Even if you only scribble up some kind of contractual understanding of your job description and its parameters, then it might keep you from storming off the set later. This might sound over-dramatic, but it happens when creatives from different media work together within a sub-section of their talents. Worse still, while everyone's a director – if not a critic – *not* everyone's a musician.

There's still plenty of scope for disagreement when shooting a music video, though, and you will require your own conviction and the courage to assert yourself to individuals and the group as a whole. A musician or band might well have a fanciful whim about shooting on film, sound stages, locations, or marketing strategies. These kinds of production issues are entirely down to whoever is controlling the budget – usually, the producer. If the musicians are paying: fine. If not, there are plenty of ways to spend money, but finding the right distribution, making compromises, and creating good, sensible production value is outside their remit.

To make your point at meetings, always come armed with the right weapons. If you're the director, bring an example of whatever idea you might feel strongly about. It might be that you want them to understand a thematic video effect, a grading that shows the mood or an in-camera transition that threads the video. These might exist in a previous production or you might just have to knock up a quick demonstration with your DV cam and home-edit the result.

You might want to bring a latex alien, an electric blue frightwig, or a photo of a nearby beach: anything that can help describe your ideas and make a musician realize that you are, in fact, serious.

Effective communication is the doorway to success, but it won't open without passion, sincerity, confidence, and some assurance of your creativity.

WORD UP: DEVELOPING THE CONCEPT THROUGH LYRIC

If the track that you're working with has lyrics, you'll be that much closer to nailing the concept for the video. In effect, the script has already been written….

Sometimes, lyrics are uninspired – and in turn, uninspiring. Sometimes they are clumsy and obvious. Sometimes, they're laughable, and sometimes the songwriters are so full of themselves that it's impossible to extract any kind of visual interpretation. If any of these are the case with the track that you're trying to work with, opt to work with the music instead.

If you do find the lyric inspiring – or at least workable – you're two steps ahead of the game. Examining and extracting meaning is the first thing to do if you didn't write the words yourself. If you're not the writer, it's a lot easier to be objective about visualizing the track. The audience for the video will have little or no insight into the mind of the writer and your objectivity allows you to have their perspective, fresh to the track. Because this *is* such a benefit, try to formulate your own ideas before the writer inevitably tells you where their inspiration came from.

Lyrics can be prose or poetry, written well or badly. Whichever way they are written, they often require some reading between the lines to find something that's going to help you visualize. The biggest mistake made in contemporary music video is to portray what is being sung: show and tell, if you

Literal interpretations are not just the movements of the unimaginative. It's very hard to work a video to a track that tells a story. To be literary, look at Kate Bush's iconic swirlings in Keef's *Wuthering Heights* promo. When an artist is telling their story in first person singular, options other than telling it how it is to them become fewer. To a creative, this is a healthy challenge. Lady Luck is working her charm if you have a visual artist who can simply perform for the camera (Sinéad O'Connor: *Nothing Compares 2 U*; Annie Lennox: *Julia*).

The way to respond to any lyric challenge is to break it down. Look at each verse and find the themes. Writing these down helps no end in finding the right mood for the piece. What this doesn't mean is that the themes dictate the mood – you may decide to create irony by doing the opposite. Fun themes or dance tracks may need something hard to take the edge off, just as fluffy bunnies make Marilyn Manson Satan's plaything.

Once you've found the themes that you like, pick out individual elements – words, phrases, adjectives – from the verses that are evocative. Think laterally, not obviously. The challenge, again, is always the most throwaway of lyrics. While 'ooh, I love you baby' probably won't conjure up ideas, 'I believe' can be perceived metaphorically, which is to your advantage. Skewing perspective on the track can often add depth.

The chorus is repeated often enough to make the hook. This doesn't mean that the visuals have to follow suit. A chorus can also become a dumping ground for non-specific lyrics. To avoid outstaying its welcome, it may be asinine, or it may contain the main theme. And this is why you should not concentrate on it until the end.

Not bowing to the obvious is the practice of leaving deconstruction of the chorus until last. Even if you decide that the chorus dictates the visuals, working on the verses first will always enrich it. The example shows a chorus that could be read in different ways: childishness, arrogance, and resolve. Because of the repetition of the chorus, this indicates that the singer could progress through these attitudes throughout the video, and a thread to the visuals comes to light.

Finally, the script may already have been written, but there are some brave directors out there with Hollywood ideas above their station who attempt to add to it. If you feel that dialogue needs to be added to make sense of the visuals that you have in mind, sell the idea to the musicians. A prologue and epilogue can sometimes lift a music video into a rather more epic state. It's not unusual now to see a video nestling within a short movie – *Thriller* certainly helped that idea along.

If you want to elevate your status as more than just a music video director, then by all means try it. Just don't make your mini-movie better than the music and the visuals....

Borrowers

I'm running around with my feet on the ground
I can't seem to understand this game they're playing
No one seems to want to sit with me
I switch the channels on my TV
Now the cameras are fixed on me again
I'm running and burning, I can't seem to hide

It doesn't really matter what they say,
I'm gonna go ahead and do it anyway

The sky has turned red, I'm losing my mind
I can't kill my head, stop this feeling inside
Four walls calling, I can't get outside
The borrowers have come, taking all that is mine
They're stealing my toys, leaving memories behind
Everything's changing nothing seems the same

It doesn't really matter what they say,
I'm gonna go ahead and do it anyway

I stare out my window yearning for more
I must find the borrowers and settle the score
I want my toys they're mine, not there's to have
The toys were my thoughts, joys, not cars or trains
These toys weren't bought, but they kept me sane
Everything's changing nothing seems the same

It doesn't really matter what they say,
I'm gonna go ahead and do it anyway

Written and Arranged by: Jonny Quality
10-26-03

ABOVE: Get a hard copy of the lyrics and carry them around with you. Read them in different locations and environments – even get other people to read them to you. Context, relativity, and subjectivity are the best places to find alternative meaning in words.

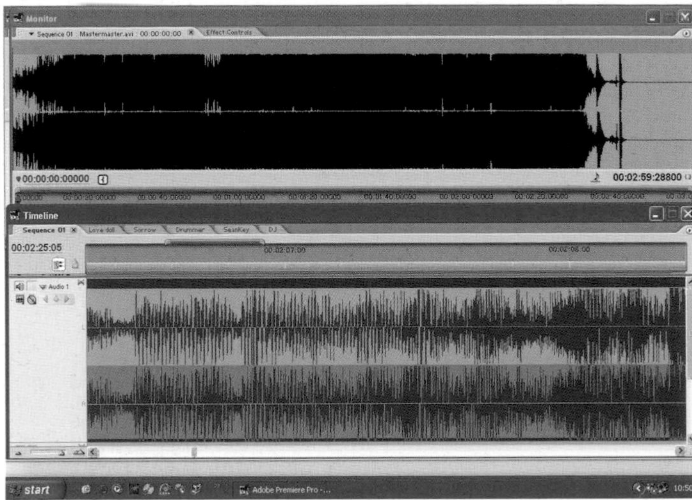

LEFT: Changes in dynamic range are also a good clue as to how your concept should work. Tracks like Smells Like Teen Spirit *or Lamb's* B-Line *both have relatively quiet verses and a really LOUD chorus, and the videos to each make dramatic use of them.*

NOTE DOWN: **DEVELOPING THE CONCEPT THROUGH MUSIC**

Without the music, you won't be making a music video. It sounds logical, but it is important to understand that the music itself is as essential as the lyric in determining the idea – or at least how the idea is treated.

Music is an emotional experience: it makes us *feel*. Whether romantic, angry, energetic, scared, hateful, sad, delirious – they're all feelings, and being true to the track requires careful consideration about what to show visually.

The way that composers and musicians create musical emotion is through the knowledge of what specific chords, keys, key changes, dynamic range, and beats evoke. The cynical side of this is that it is contrived and shallow, and if you buy it, it's through emotional blackmail. A lot of successful producers know how to manipulate a track and consumers with a particular trademark sound. The other side is that the track is written from the heart to inspire the same emotion in the listener.

Lyrics only detail the emotion. Music forms the landscape and boundaries for the singer's emotiveness. Strip the lyric away and the reverb choral harmonies in 10CC's *I'm Not In Love* warn any director away from a fast-cut Ibiza sweat-a-thon. Likewise, the nerve-shredding clangs, the minor key, and the *Friday The 13th* samples in Soft Cell's *Martin* isn't a cue for a Jennifer Lopez-style soft-focus bootyromp. The music communicates the right mood for the visuals, and if it doesn't help pinpoint your idea, it certainly narrows the field.

The mood in which to convey the idea is important to the band. They will want you to emulate the mood of the song to instill the intended feeling. If it's a dance track, they might want clubbers; if it's a ballad, they'll want the singer emoting. The music is helping you to define what you *can* show.

All music has a rhythm, and most music has a beat that emphasizes that rhythm. Beats often change throughout the duration of the track either in volume, instrument, or speed. This change enables you to progress your video – to build-up, to pare-down, or to change tack.

The instruments used in the track are the most obvious hint to your idea. No matter how obvious, always consider what might happen if – for example – you don't incorporate some Indian cultural influence in the visuals while there is a sitar featured on the track. A music video audience is virtually the same as a movie audience. They want to feel rewarded. Doing the obvious isn't always a question of pandering or non-creativity: it's doing what's *right* for the track.

The key in which the song is written is really the key to the mood of your video. Most songs are in major keys – so much so that it's only when they come in a minor key that listeners sit up and notice. 50 Cent's *In Da Club* has an ominous, relentless, threat to it that was wasted in the slowmo dance visuals. This is the kind of gift that you really don't want to ignore. Key changes, too, not only take a listener from lightness to dark in the music, but act as a fantastic opportunity for a director to marry with the visuals.

Reverb, audio effects, and EQ are the polishing to achieve the mood of the track in isolation. It is the mood that the producer wishes to convey. Try to hear all of these. If the music plays as if in a hall, a grander or subterranean theme will work with it. If it's a compressed sound, consider a claustrophobic location. Producers and engineers work to get the sound that they want. When they experiment, it's in your creative favour. These tracks are show-jumpers – don't look 'em in the mouth.

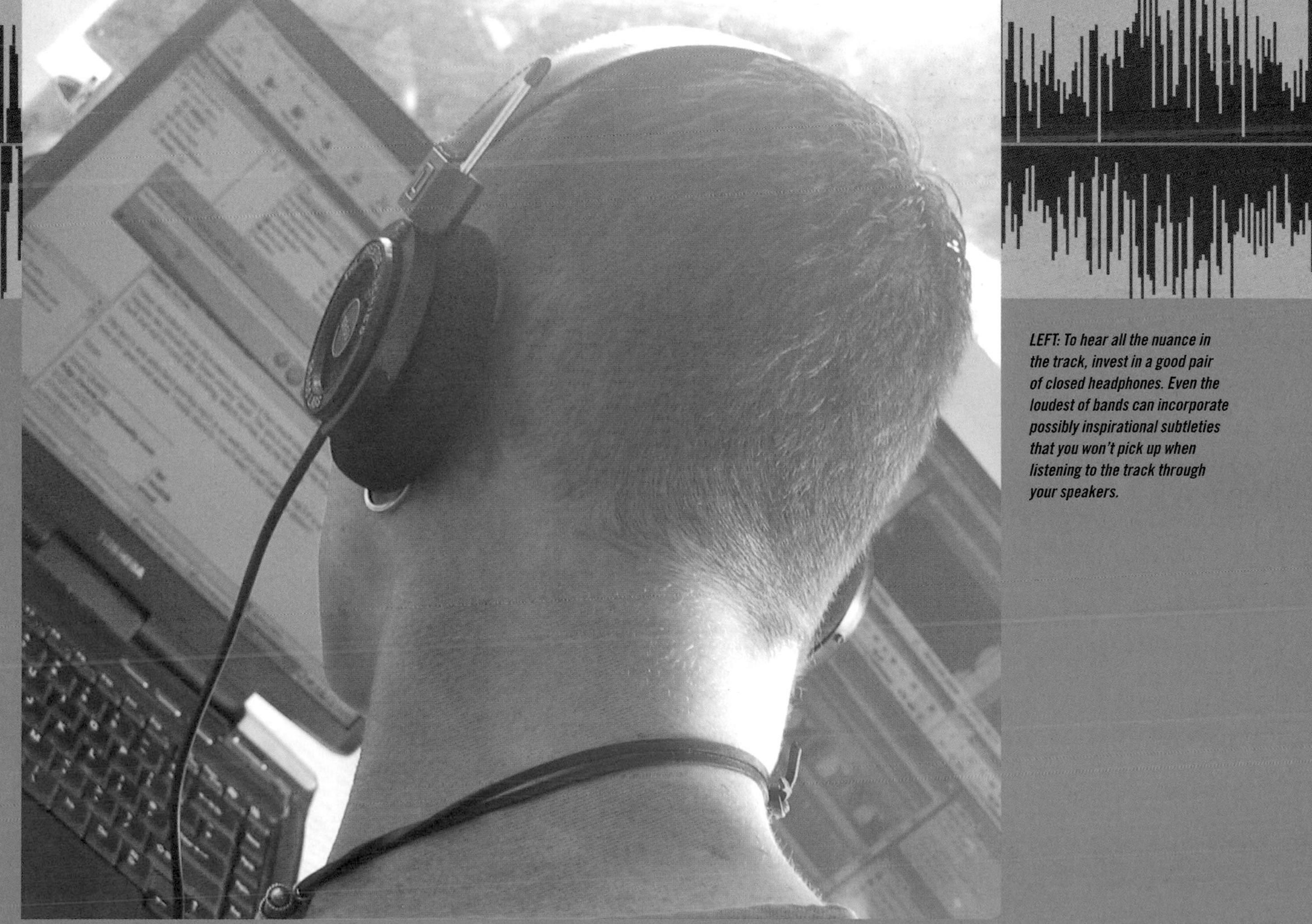

LEFT: To hear all the nuance in the track, invest in a good pair of closed headphones. Even the loudest of bands can incorporate possibly inspirational subtleties that you won't pick up when listening to the track through your speakers.

This notion of storytelling is based upon the passage of time. Time is the fourth dimension, the one huge advantage that time-based media (film, video, television, animation, Web media) has over others. The difference between real time and time in media is the ability that art has to change it, whether compressing or protracting it through transitions and cuts from one scene to another.

The fundamental Hollywood narrative structure works as beginning, middle, and end, with one common, linear story thread. Conversely, music video works often as simply a series of individual, possibly unrelated, set-ups, and it is these set-ups that will form the basis to your storyboard.

LEFT: The Director checks his storyboard to make sure the video is progressing the narrative as it should, whether it follows a chronological sequencing of events or not.

DRAWING UP: **STORYBOARDS**

The difference between storyboards for movies and storyboards for music videos is that musical images can break all logical laws of space and time. Once you've finished your storyboard, it may not make any rational sense at all in the traditional language of storytelling.

Time is the one thing that your music storyboard is dependent upon. Time, in this sense, is usually the duration of the video and the beats per minute, unless you have a prologue, epilogue, or musical break. The length of the song acts as an obvious city limit to the visuals, which means that the duration of the song is the amount of time that you have in which to tell your story.

To put it another way, everything has a story. Once you've got together the themes and visual ideas to your video, they'll tell a story too. It may not be a conventional narrative but it *will* be about something. Even if you're cutting together a live gig, the story is about the gig from the start of the song to the end of it.

If your music video is not based on a conventional narrative using the language of cinema (a dissolve = time passing, a cut = what happened next, etc.), it *transcends time*. That is to say that if you have a series of different shots with musicians or singers in different locations doing different things, there is no logical progression of time bar the track itself.

If you look at a lot of music videos, this is massively representational: different events in disparate surroundings with disconnected people. While a storyboard for a narrative or time-sequential film or video is useful, a storyboard for a time non-specific video is essential.

The reason is that logical humans fill in the gaps to a narrative. They're programmed to do this. When something defies logic, some kind of visual description of order is needed for *you* to understand, let alone anyone else that needs to approve your idea.

RIGHT: The primary function of the storyboard is for use on set. It represents all of your ideas as images and text and, thus, there is no real need to spend a lot of money on the software. Simple boxes will do.

The storyboard is the closest model you have to the finished video. If it is a non-narrative music video, you can muddle the images around to your satisfaction, just as you would cut and paste in an edit.

Storyboards, although requisite for approval by others, are fundamentally for you to use on set. They are there to represent all of your ideas as images and text. There's no real need to spend money on storyboarding software – start by just drawing boxes, roughly to your ratio – to fill a page (with enough room for notes). This is quick, spontaneous stuff, not a laboured colouring-in job. Your images are sometimes dictated by lyric, sometimes by music – and this is what your notations should inform.

GET BUSY WITH...

>Stage directions
>Wardrobe, make-up, and props
>Camera directions
>Lighting

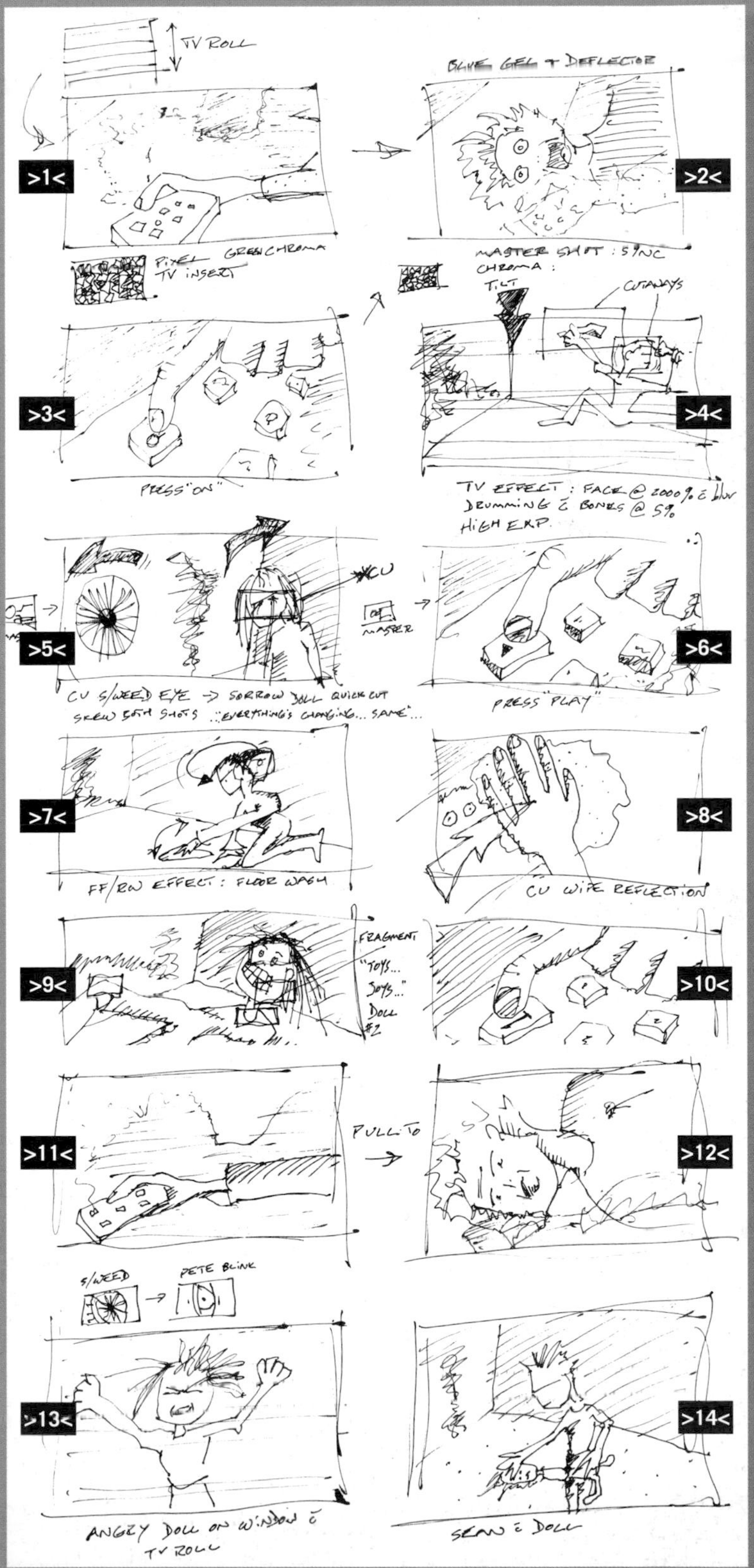

If there's a limited time element to certain sections (think *Bohemian Rhapsody* or prog rock), then put it in. When you drag out your storyboard on the shoot, you'll want to know just how long you have to drag out a shot.

Any of these are extra definition to what makes that shot – useful for you, useful for the client. Don't be afraid of pen and ink. Work and rework, cross things out, throw things away. It's just pen and ink. The important thing is what's in your head, and it's equally important that you get it down before you go and forget it. After that, you can eliminate and embellish as the storyboard progresses.

At the end of the scribble-a-thon, you'll have something that is as close to the edit as you'll get until you get to the edit. Treasure it – it's going to save your skin.

>1<

>2<

>3<

>4<

>5<

>6<

>7<

>8<

>9<

1>13: A vision is the future of your music video. That doesn't mean to say that you have to be a prophet to profit, though. Experience is the one thing that will stop your vision being lost In the shoot credit.

>10<

>11<

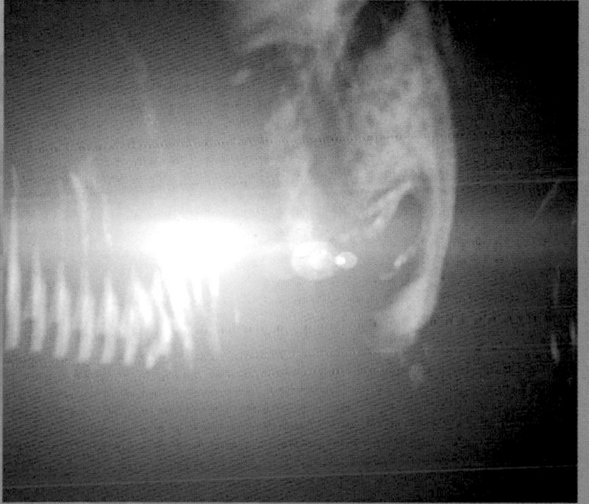

>12<

>13<

STRIKE STRIKE STRIKE

A shooting schedule is a realistic pre-shoot diarizing of how you anticipate your shoot day. In it, you'll have the names of every single individual involved in the shoot, their contact numbers, what they need to bring, what they need to use on set and when and where they have to be at any given time. Think of it as a housekeeping rota and you won't be far off the kind of barked orders that it represents.

While you are writing it up, base the order of set-ups on what is easier and quicker to rig and de-rig, and be sure to consider when participants are available or freed up from what they are doing so that they can assist. Schedules are logical, and on paper they look simple. The shooting experience can be the complete opposite and it is therefore crucial that contingency is built into the schedule for overruns.

THE SHOOTING SCHEDULE

For an actor, this might read:

> Jane Lesley, Doll #4, Scene 1/02

> Think *Sixties Texan Barbie*

> Supplied wardrobe: Blonde wig, red ribbon

> Bring: Knee-high boots, sixties Twiggy dress

> Supplied make-up: Light foundation, glycerine spray, false blue eyelashes, white eyeliner, pixie glitter

> Cushion supplied for support in position

> DO NOT WEAR GREEN

WRITE UP: **SHOOTING SCHEDULES**

Putting together a shooting schedule is a fundamental task to ensure that everyone knows what they are doing on the day, and that everything runs as smoothly as possible. What you want to avoid is having something go wrong, whether that means someone turning up late or at the wrong location. The best way to counter this is to keep your crew in the loop with all the details they need so that they can happily get on with their job.

Only by experience will you learn that you *will* get stuck behind a combine harvester on the way to pick someone up, you *will* have to run around the shops for an outstanding prop, at least one person *will* be late, one will not be able to find the location (always enclose a map), one will be let down by public transport, and one will run out of gas. It's all a bit like a car accident: no matter how careful you think you are, it's everyone and everything else that's out to get you…

The shooting schedule for the first day should be sent to each member of cast and crew not much more, and certainly not much less, than two days before the shoot itself. If you're shooting for two or three days, give them the other shooting schedules at the end of the day on their first shoot. They are not a huge secret, but don't give them to clients or facilitators if you can avoid it. These people will have far too much information than they will ever need, and they will hold you to your stated times.

The shooting schedule isn't a contract, but it is useful for everyone involved on set. When directing, there'll be many requests, queries and demands upon you while you're trying to work out your shot. Eliminating wardrobe and make-up supervision is one of the things that may help. Allowing crew and talent to get on with their job responsibly is something that they themselves would probably prefer to do anyway without you hovering over them. For each member of the cast and crew, you should take the time to draft up a memorandum of particulars and attach each with the shooting schedule. Putting the parameters in writing lets them do this without worry.

The same is true of production design and props. Tell them what they're bringing, what you're bringing, and what's already there. The schedule, opposite, had a set that was leisurely prepared the previous day. If you're dressing your set on the day, get your production designer, lighting, audio, and camera in early to negotiate between themselves the practicalities of shooting angles and directions, without interference.

All of these individual memoranda are for yourself as well, but take a little extra time to ensure that you're not the one who lets people down by making a few notes for yourself. The idea of schedules is that you stick to them, or you make logical changes and adjustments on the day.

SHOOTING SCHEDULE

CREW		MOBILE NUMBER
Production:	Jonny Quality, *The Borrowers*	
Director:	Ed Cooper	
Producer:	Clea Smith	
Camera and Lighting:	Tommy Hanover	
Wardrobe and Make-up:	Kathryn Fleet	
Audio and Sync:	Sean Moody	
Stills:	Ed/Sean	

CAST/TALENT		MOBILE NUMBER
Jonny	Guitar	
Pete	Singer	
Nick	DJ	
Steve	Drums	
Jane Lesley	actor	
Chloe	actor	
Clea	actor	

RV AND SET 1 LOCATION: BASEMENT FLAT AND CELLAR, 10 SUSSEX GARDENS
PARKING: 4-HOUR BAYS and RESIDENT H PERMITS; 3 DISABLED BAYS; VOUCHERS FOR ENTIRE DAY AVAILABLE FROM PRODUCER

RV	Event	Talent	Art Department	Camera	Lighting	Audio
09:00	Ed to pick up Kath from home					
09:30	Ed to pick up Clea from office			RV Set 1	RV Set 1	RV Set 1
10:00	RV: Set 1 Clea: Parking permits	Pete	Make-up and wardrobe Prop: Sneezeweed	Set-up for Sneezeweed 0.7 telephoto Mini-tripod Lock-off	Set-up for Sneezeweed Green Screen Spot Backlight	N/A
11:00	Shoot Master Shot: Set-up 1/01	Pete Jane	Jane: Make-up and wardrobe Remote Control	As above for split-screen	As above for split-screen	10% speed audio
12:00	SET-UP 1/05 EXTERIOR SET 1 Shoot Doll #1: Sorrow	Jane		Wide-angle	Spot Backlight	N/A
12:30		LUNCH	LUNCH			LUNCH
13:00	CONTINGENCY			LUNCH	LUNCH	
13:30	Steve RV: Set 1	Steve	Make-up and wardrobe			
14:00	SET-UP Shoot Steve Nick RV: Set 1	Steve Nick	Nick: Make-up and wardrobe Props: Bones	Wide-angle Tripod: Lock-off	Spot Fill	5% speed audio
14:30	SET-UP 1/03 Shoot Nick	Nick Clea	Clea: Make-up and wardrobe Prop: Blonde wig	Wide-angle Tripod: Lock-off	Spot Backlight	N/A
15:00	SET-UP 1/06 Shoot Doll #2: Hate	Clea Chloe	Chloe: Make-up and wardrobe	SHOT REVERSED Wide-angle	Spot Hand talent	N/A
15:30	SET-UP 1/07 Shoot Doll #3: Love	Chloe Sean Jane	Jane, Sean: Make-up and wardrobe Prop: Mirror	Wide-angle Tripod: Lock-off	Spot Fill Blue gel Hand talent	N/A
16:00	CONTINGENCY					
16:30	SET-UP 1/02 Shoot Pay-off Chroma	Sean Jane		Wide-angle Tripod: Lock-off	Spot Backlight Green Screen	100% audio
17:30	WRAP			STRIKE	STRIKE	STRIKE

When you're budgeting for your music video, total in all of those who have given their time for free – and how much of their time they have given. They should at least be on your budget sheet even if there's no sum next to their name. Certainly, if somebody else is forking out or you anticipate claiming back, there needs to be a record of whom has given what amount of time and is not asking for immediate payment. If there are eventual profits to be made, these are the people who are probably in line for receiving some financial gratitude. And this is another reason why you should be professional enough to have contracts: things can get very sticky, bitter, and sometimes litigious, if intangible fame and eventual fortune transpire.

In order to make sure that you've got everything listed and accounted for, prepare a top sheet. This is a master sheet that tallies totals. Your top sheet should incorporate the basics of pre-production, production, and post-production, and look a little like the example provided on the facing page. The sheets underneath should contain a breakdown of all of these fundamentals, with spaces to calculate the rate of pay, the number of days spent on it, the number of people involved on each facet of the process, and of course, the total cost.

The rate and the number of days work like a timesheet, and should be negotiated and allocated prior to production or post-production. Your contingency budget needs to be larger than you might imagine. Try 20% of your total budget and then throw in a bit more just in case.

Your budget should be one of the first things you do, given a green light. Casting your mind back to try and remember who's done what and when, for how long, can be an absolute nightmare, if not impossible. What you are trying to do is to limit distribution and allocation to every element therein from the start. This is going to help you a lot.

Your budget is working completely in association with time, and with production values. This means being realistic (shooting can or always will take longer than you've conceived), and being prudent. Saving money isn't hard.

COUNTING UP: **BUDGETING**

No matter if your band, singer, musician, or DJ, and yourself, have given time without charge, always bear in mind that nothing is free. Free time is something that people have when they could otherwise be earning money. Multiply this 'free' time by the numbers in your crew and anyone who's helping in some way, and it's actually quite costly. Time and budget are absolutely inextricable.

ABOVE LEFT: Working out your financial constraints can keep you on your budgetary toes.

SAVING CASH

Moneysaving tips:

- **Offer credit or acknowledgment rather than money**
- **Download shareware rather than purchasing software**
- **Change your script to use free locations and props you've already got**
- **Avoid multiple locations and find one that can be used many times**
- **Avoid writing complicated camera moves into the script**
- **Get as many people in a car as you can**
- **Borrow make-up and wardrobe from your most flamboyant friends**
- **Made a saving? Throw it into food, rehearsals, and safety. If you've got a happy crew and talent, they'll work and keep their enthusiasm longer.**

RIGHT: Your budget top sheet contains the block of essential parts that comprise the creation of your music video. Ideally, you should just be able to glance over at this and understand exactly what you aim to spend – and what you have spent – on what.

MASTER SHEET

ITEM	FEES	EXPENSES	TOTAL
Development			
Rights and licenses			
Producer			
Director			
Script			
Band			
Other talent			
Crew			
Travel and location			
Props and wardrobe			
Sets/Soundstage			
Kit purchase/rental			
Tape			
Insurance			
Edit			
Post audio			
Selling			
Marketing			
Contingency			

RIGHT: The reams of paper that you have underneath your top sheet are the breakdown of all of those parts defined on the top sheet. All of these must be updated whenever necessary to represent the figures in the top sheet.

UNDER SHEET

ITEM	RATE	DAYS	NUMBER	TOTAL
Stationery				
Website				
Business plan				
Press release				
Photocopying				
Couriers and postage				
Office overheads				
Phone bills				
Software				
Hardware				
Legal				
Administration				

If you are involved in a management structure, you will need to ensure that – as part of this business – you have some kind of contract. 'You' is yourself, your crew, and any post talent or facilities for which you will be directly responsible.

This contract has to be better than just a verbal agreement, and it has to incorporate more than just your time, figures, and budget. There must be some written agreement that defines the limits of your time, budget, and responsibilities. If there is no agreement, you may well end up cutting and re-cutting at your own expense until your client (management or musician) is happy with their product.

DOWN BY LAW: **LEGAL BROADCAST, CONTRACTS, AND MUSIC COPYRIGHT ISSUES**

Music and music video is a business. The musicians want to make money out of what they do, and so do you. Any label or management attached have exactly the same interest: they want to make money (but more of it).

Official contracts are full of indemnities and rights of termination. If you are given a contract, it is *your* right to make amendments as you see fit. Usage of grey area 'as-necessaries' and 'reasonables' are often not that useful at all unless *you* define what is your job and what is a re-edit, or an extraneous cost, or just a waste of time.

If there is no management, but simply yourself and the band, there is still no excuse for not determining roles, hierarchies, responsibilities, timing, budget, and the parameters of each in writing before you begin. There are three common ways of being paid for a video. The first is direct payment for the job that you do. It is good practice that this is an advance, a mid-term, and a pay-off. The second way is *in deference*. This means that you won't get paid until the product that you create helps to make money to pay you. In this case, the music video is as speculative as the music itself.

In this situation, there is no telling *when* the music will start to make money. Market value and interest can change dramatically – and a rock track that you've made the video for may well not be the flavour of the month, or indeed, the millennium. That doesn't mean to say that things don't change. They do – and often very quickly in the fickle world of pop.

Musicians that are interested in their own music as a business should be using a point-awarding system for their percentage of any profit. For the sake of the music video and its purpose as a tool to showcase their talent, you should have the opportunity with a deferred contract to be part of this. Instead of figures, the point system works as percentage of contribution for the track.

Your points for the track are made by agreement with the musicians, and whenever the track pays out (sales and royalties), you will get your percentage sum.

The third way is the combination of these. This is a one-off payment *and* royalties. Of course, your percentage here will be less – and it's often a strategic battle between yourself and the client to anticipate what makes them – or you – better off in the long run.

If there is no agreement with the musicians, you can find yourself in a power game. You may either be 'the weakest link' and leave with nothing, or at the most, achieve nothing more than an academic stalemate. It doesn't have to be this way, of course, but should a band or musician start to make money out of their talent, it might be to do with your video.

Conversely, if you decide that *you* want to use the video or stills for public exhibition, you need to have negotiated grant of rights to the material, the music, and the performances for exploitation for your own gain.

This is exactly the same slant that you need to take with a release form for anyone appearing in your music video. You cannot safely use their appearance (or *likeness*) without one. The 15-minute-fame seeking public, though, are easier to please and you may find that they are quite happy to be exploited.

THIS IS HOW THE PER-TRACK POINT SYSTEM WORKS AMONGST MUSICIANS

	MUSO 1	MUSO 2	MUSO 3	MUSO 4
Arrangement and production (40%)				40
Music (20%)	5	5	5	5
Lyrics (20%)	10		10	
Hook (20%)			20	
Total	15	5	35	45

4

PRE-PRODUCTION: FUNKIN' TECHNO & ALL THAT JAZZ

MEASURING UP: SCREEN RATIO

Aspect Ratio is the proportion of your music video on the horizontal versus the vertical axis. There are various terms for various ratios, and different amounts of pixels by pixels with PAL or NTSC. Pixels for digital video are not square, unlike pixels for graphics. Therefore the pixels on your CCDs in your camera relate to the dimensions of either 4:3 or 16:9 television output.

The ratios of 4:3 and 16:9 are convenient approximations. Between the DV camera and the output medium, there are also other approximations being made, such as the amount of active versus non-active pixels. Active pixels are the ones that you won't lose from vision when you are viewing your finished edit on another source.

Your decision regarding how to shoot your music video should be based on how you expect your product to be seen – and while European standards are very much weighted towards widescreen presentation, whereas NTSC-users won't find them *as* common. The thing about music videos in particular is that they are not made for longevity: they are made to sell the song here and now. For this reason, there's no point in speculating whether or not your potential viewers will have High Definition Television in the future; it's what they use now that counts.

4:3 Ratio

On output, this is Standard Definition Television (SDTV), and 'standard' for low- to middle-market televisions and DV cameras. If you are shooting on the PAL standard, then it's 720 pixels wide and 576 pixels high. If you're shooting on the NTSC standard, then it's still 720 pixels wide, but this time only 480 pixels high. Either way, this ratio is otherwise denominated as 1.33:1.

When recording 4:3 and playing out on a 4:3 television, a column of eight pixels on either side of the image is removed to fit the display.

16:9 Ratio

This is captured and presented as 'widescreen' with a proportion that maintains the image height (576 or 480 pixels) – and, critically, the same number of pixels, but extends the width of the image. Ultimately, this lowers the resolution slightly on the x-axis to present an image ratio of 16:9.

LEFT: Non-true 16:9 crops an image at the top and bottom of the frame and blows it up to fill a 16:9 ratio.

ABOVE LEFT: An anamorphic lens squeezes the image on to a 4:3 CCD...

ABOVE RIGHT ...which can then be read in the edit as a correctly proportioned and high-resolution 16:9 ratio frame when it is stretched out again.

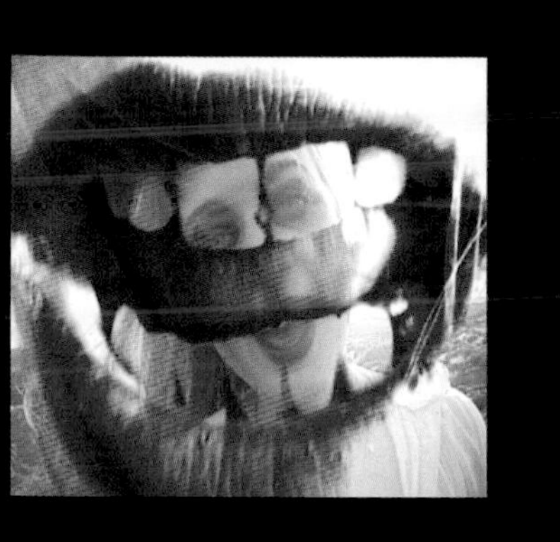

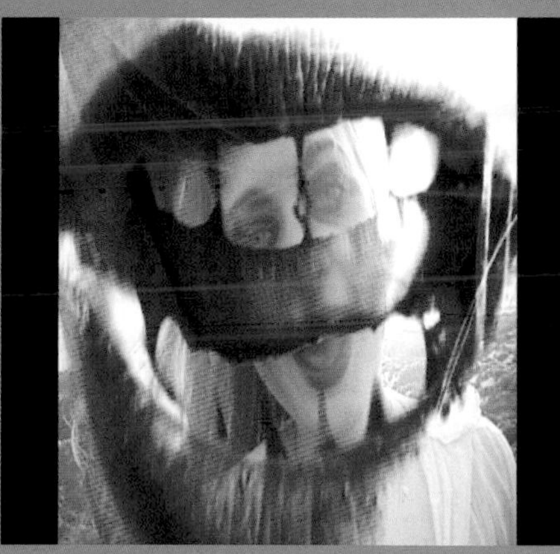

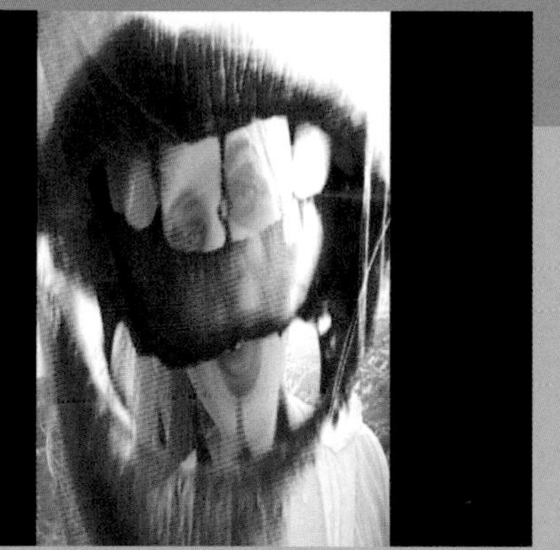

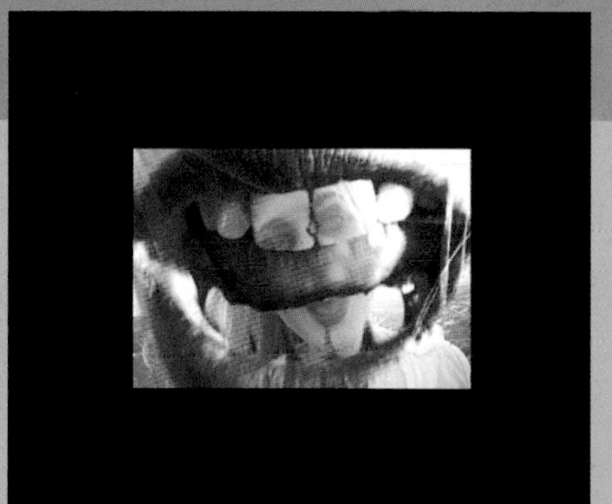

High Definition Television (HDTV)

HDTV is output to high-resolution digital televisions with the benefit of increased resolution and truer colour. High-definition images are becoming a high-end consumer reality for both recording (DV Camera) and output (HDTV). High Definition Video uses MPEG-2 to compress and is native 16:9, which means that it doesn't re-stretch pixels to fit widescreen ratio. Roughly doubling the amount of pixels from standard definition on both the vertical and the horizontal lines, HDTV comes in three formats.

To reap the visual rewards of HDTV, you'll need to shoot HD DV. High Definition digital video cameras can be extremely expensive. Manufacturers, though, want to progress the format and are beginning to produce more budget-friendly models using the 720p format. If you invest, make sure that you maximize compatibility with an option to shoot in *non* HD, and ensure there is analogue output for versatility.

The essential part of HDTV is progressive scanning. Most DVCs record with interlaced scanning – a method that has long been favoured with analogue recording and playback. This means that the vertical scanning process captures one half of the image every 1/50 second (PAL) or 1/60 second (NTSC). These 'halves' are fields, and a combined image forms a frame every 1/25 or 1/30 of a second. While interlaced scanning blends motion well this way, it is also lowering the resolution to each moving object captured.

High Definition using progressive scanning captures and delivers information frame by frame. For editing on an NLE, it becomes easier to frame match. The drawback is that the delivery flicker often makes viewing tiring, although there is little chance of that in your four-minute music promo.

PIXELS	
720p	1280 x 720 pixels progressive scanning
1080i	1920 x 1080 pixels interlaced scanning
1080p	1920 x 1080 pixels progressive scanning

***ALL IMAGES:** The ratio that you choose to shoot with and that which you choose to edit with, is a choice that affects how your music video and your musicians will be seen and perceived. Stretching images deliberately on the vertical axis is often undertaken to streamline the talent, but it can also be used as an affect in itself. Images seen through props such as hi-ball glasses or reflected in the back of spoons, can be quite easily effected by experimenting with your shoot and edit ratios – and more importantly, without losing resolution.*

Shooting *anamorphic* widescreen uses a codec or anamorphic lens converter to squeeze the horizontals on to the 4:3 CCD. The information is added to the data and reinterpreted in the NLE (Non-Linear Editor). In the NLE, the data is understood using the codec for 16:9 settings, and the image is stretched back to its captured proportions.

The way that widescreen televisions cope with a 16:9 DV image is to reinterpret the signal to fill the screen. A 4:3 image played on a widescreen TV will be stretched to fill the width: 'smart' stretched to cut off the top and bottom slightly, or have black bands running down each side of the image. Conversely, a 16:9 image on a 4:3 television will have black bands at the top and bottom with the image mid-screen.

A common problem with lower-end DV cameras is the purporting of 16:9 – and the lack of it. While true 16:9 takes the image to the CCD in a widescreen ratio, untrue 16:9 uses a 4:3 image and blacks out rows of pixels at the top and bottom of the picture.

STOCKING UP: **VIDEO VERSUS FILM**

The film versus video debate still reigns supreme in the music video industry. This book is geared towards DV-users. Shooting on film calls for a different approach – not least, a more professional one. And the reason for this is that shooting film has dramatic effects on your time and budget.

TOP: Film, as an analogue medium with infinite values can always capture skin tone with a lot more subtlety and conceived beauty than digital video ever can.

The quality of film is without a doubt something that video cannot emulate – and vice versa – and this is what makes both media unique and polarizes the debate. Their similarities are that both use light to describe a sequence of images that run over time to create an illusion of movement. How they use light is where the two media diverge.

Film exposes a negative. That is to say that against a photosensitive surface (silver-coated celluloid), changing light (source, reflection, absorption, deflection) hits the rolling celluloid and burns the silver to the strength of the light from each part of the frame. Therefore, any light areas will be dark and any dark areas light. This creates the negative that is processed to become a positive.

Film is an analogue medium that represents an analogue world. The image is a visible, scratchable, finite representation of the real world. As a tangible representation, it can be cut together physically by taping bits of image motion together. To create a mix or dissolve, two images can be put on top of each other, matching up the sprocket holes. This is a *linear edit*, working tangibly and sequentially. It's also the time-consuming version of moviemaking that tradition has created and purists still swear by.

However, it's not an economical or practical process. Film is expensive, time is always expensive and celluloid is subject to fingerprints, scratches, and burns. Over time, handling, shipping, and storage can also become complicated, troublesome, and expensive issues.

Telecine is the procedure for transferring film to digital video for use in an NLE. This means that you can have all the benefits of shooting film combined with those of working in a non-linear environment. Not only does this free up time and possibilities through image manipulation and working non-sequentially, it also takes film to a non-degenerative format.

Analogue formats degenerate. Film processing degrades both colour and contrast, and an analogue recording of an image will always be a degraded representation. Way down the line, the image becomes unrecognizable. With digital, a 0 is always a 0 and a 1 is always a 1. There is no change in image or quality.

The 'look' of film in a digital environment is an approximation of the original film footage. Because high-definition digital video is so good at representing an image, it shows every fault in an analogue image: dust, scratches, flaring. That's the resolution, but the quality of infinite chrominance and luminance levels are compromised by a DV's permissible (256,000,000) values. Therefore, between processing and digitization, the difference can be significant. Luckily, NLEs are built to manipulate images to the *n*th degree and film approximation can be utilized to create fantastic pictures.

Video's 'trueness' to reality is down to its use of fields – twice the amount of frames per second. This creates a smoothness that film (at 24fps) doesn't have – a faithfulness of motion as perceived by the eye in an analogue world. It is precisely this that discouraged moviemakers to venture into its realm. And once consumers got their hands on this format, the prices dropped.

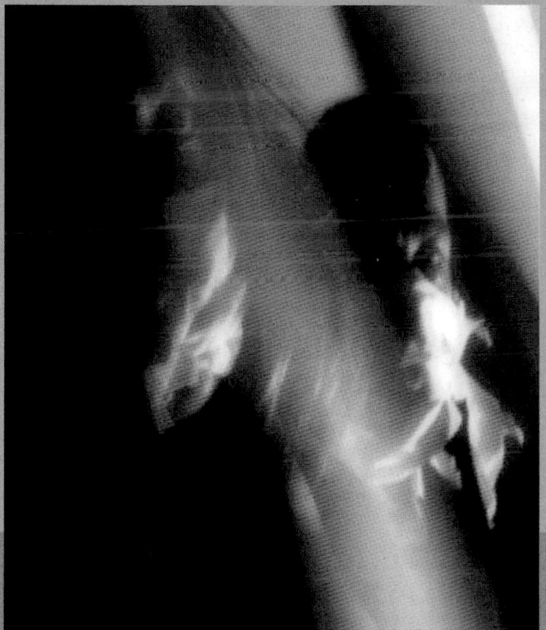

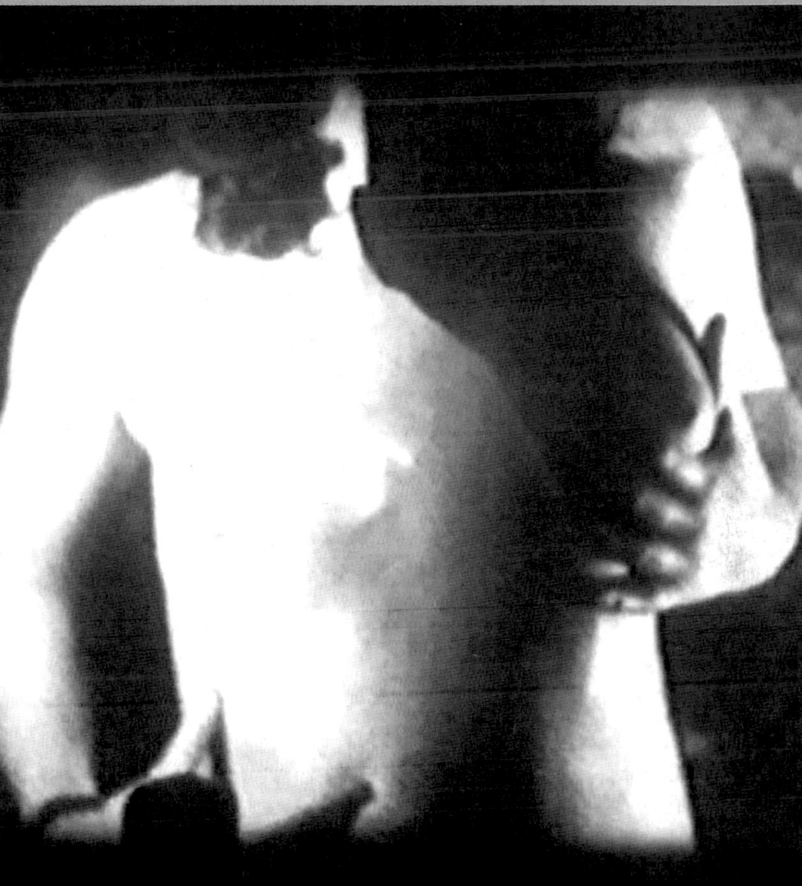

ABOVE: With the right light and the right grade, a 24p progressive DV shoot can get somewhere close to the effect of film, creating a familiar broadcast is-it-or-isn't-it? effect.

RIGHT: Effects in film are a much more long-winded business if you are accomplishing them optically. The beauty of the NLE is that it can take film, and take the pain away....

Music video, though, was the first television genre to embrace it and progress it. Bands used it because it was cheap and easy. The industry championed its use and progressed it and has never looked back. Moviemaking has been slow to understand how it can be used, but both *The Last Broadcast* and *The Blair Witch Project* got to grips with this cheap, easy, and hands-on format. The use of video in movies now describes 'reality': the hyperreal or the gritty.

This is not the case with music videos, as a rule. They are not using the format to try to make an audience believe in what they see on screen. Therefore, video-makers have had to find a way to use the format without the audience merely thinking that what they are watching is cheap.

And this has been done with ideas.

Indeed, pushing the boundaries of reality is what digital video does best. Coupled with your own creativity, the format's parameters are only made visible by the boring things in life: client approval, contractual obligation, broadcast limits. Choosing to shoot on digital video, therefore, is not necessarily the poor man's option. Instead, it allows you to experiment cheaply and relatively quickly in ways that will give you immediate, truer results.

This doesn't mean to advocate an exclusive pact with the digital devil. Try using film to contrast with the crisp video. This creates different worlds: heaven versus hell; dream versus reality; incorporated versus separateness. Remember that it's the *use* of your chosen format that creates the video – and not the format itself.

Once you've decided what format (or combination thereof) is going to give you the best results in your allocated time and within the limits of your budget, it's the manipulation of the ideas that will make sense of your choices. This process happens back in the analogue world with a just a pen, some paper and a sixteen imagination.

If you are privileged to have an effective, persuasive, won't-take-no-for-an-answer type in your ensemble, use them as producer. This will then allow the director to focus on creative writing and directing within the time and budget parameters that the producer allows them.

Camera

If the director is going to juggle any other role in a low-budget music video, it's likely that they'll work as camera op. This is not a bad thing. A director who knows what they want to see on-screen will tend to opt for this not only because of lack of crew, but because it's the only way that they feel confident that they will get what they want.

ROLE-ING UP: **CREW**

Getting your team together in order to make your music video is a process of judgment and juggling. Look at your storyboard and imagine shooting it: who are you going to need – bare minimum – to make it happen? Jobs can be shared and jobs can be merged, depending on who is doing what at what time on the day, and whether they would be prepared to do something else as well.

Remember, the focus is the video and getting it made. Whatever the size of your crew, just make sure that they are all working enthusiastically to the same agenda, schedule, and goal.

Producer, Writer, and Director

This is probably you. It's very possible with a short music video to act as producer, writer, and director, especially if you are working closely alongside the lead musician. In this respect, the lead can help with facilitating and chasing in pre-production, and can become a silent co-producer. A good relationship like this is no small weight off your shoulders.

The project is not going to work if you don't use both sides of your brain habitually. A producer's role is creative only to the extent of finding ways of spending money that can be shown UP THERE ON THE SCREEN. From there on in, it's a battle to get what you want, when you want it, to budget, and to time.

TOP: If you've got a member of the band just standing round, then make use of them. Involving musicians in your inconvenient, alien artistry can be interesting for them, and also prevent them from running off to the bar.

ABOVE LEFT: A producer who can act *and do make-up? Call in the Monopolies Commission. If you are using one multi-skilled person, remember that they can't be in the same place at the same time, thereby muting some of the demands that you might make.*

A director behind the viewfinder is given the benefit of working creatively as well as technically. In front of them, they have the actors to be directed as seen in the monitor; to the side of them they have the lighting op and the audio op to change and complement what they see in the monitor. And they make for a great shotlister this way.

There are variations on the director-as-camera op scenario, such as when the roles are not handled by the same person (obviously), or when a multi-camera set-up is being implemented. Two cameras can be operated simultaneously by the director if one is locked-off; three cameras need at least one other operator aside from the director-as-camera op.

If you are using an additional camera op, make sure that you've seen some examples of their work. The last thing you need at the end of a day is a tape full of crash zooms and auto-focus from the school of wedding videos.

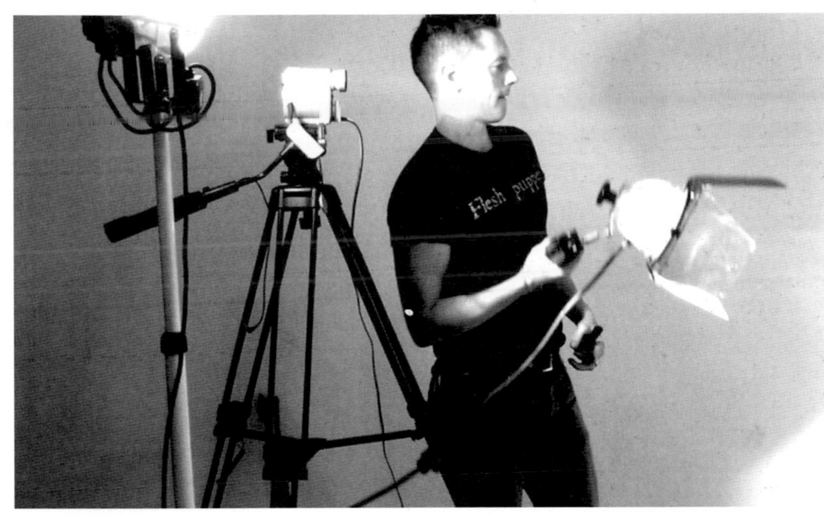

Having someone in charge of creating characters and personalities with make-up and wardrobe is another huge burden lifted. The joy of seeing someone emerge from make-up, confident, very different, and super-shootable can fuel your imagination and energize the set. This cannot be underestimated.

Production Designer and Props

When the corner of a warehouse transforms into a starship, or a drummer takes on a whole new character because he's holding chicken drumsticks, your set takes life. If you've got a space that just needs that extra touch, it's set dressing.

This is often a great way to employ your make-up and wardrobe artist in pre-production if you're pushed for crew. Pre-shoot mercy missions to find props to dress sets are best left to wardrobe because your musical clothes horses are probably going to be interacting with their background to some degree. Purposeful clashes in colours or aesthetic harmonizing is one of those things that can be influenced by the style of the track so *do* let them hear it before they hit the charity shops.

TOP: Lighting, like audio is often forgotten about until the shoot. It takes time to set up lighting, and it takes time to get it right. Make sure that your lighting op is in league with your camera op to sort it out whilst you get on with your direction.

ABOVE: Your stills op should be constantly on the go. If it's you, take shots during set-up and rehearsal. It'll help you understand and frame the shot that you're about to shoot.

ABOVE CENTRE: Your camera operator is 'make or break' for your music video. If it's not you, make sure that you're happy with the settings that they're using as well as the images that you can see.

ABOVE RIGHT: When shooting extras, use your producer or get an assistant director to help you organize. Large groups require entertainment and motivation to quell any 'us and them' pack mentality, which will kick in if you focus on the tech set-up.

Lighting

If you have a camera operative and you need to expand their role, always try to go for a lighting camera op. Lighting is the essence of your images and while you, as director, can be as creative as you like, a good lighting camera op will know how to balance light, speed, exposure, and depth of field to get you what you want quickly.

A separate lighting op should be a lighting designer. When the race is against you on set, a lighting op will have the time to make sure that the set is lit beautifully. The difference between the two is production value, and if your op can transform the set with a quick diffuser, gel, or reflector, it can make your music video much more appealing to the eye.

Make-up and Wardrobe

Don't dismiss these roles. Like lighting, the art department (and that includes production design, props, visual effects, etc.) adds professionalism.

Runners and Stills

With a small crew, these roles are often rolled into one. The idea is that the occasional snap will be taken when they're not out looking for lipstick or lattes. It's not a brilliant idea, though, as runners will never be there when you need a shot taken. Stills are very useful for publicity. If you think you can use your footage, think again. De-interlaced images come in at half the resolution, which sucks for press. If you can't employ both, employ stills. Anyone can run; few can take really good pictures.

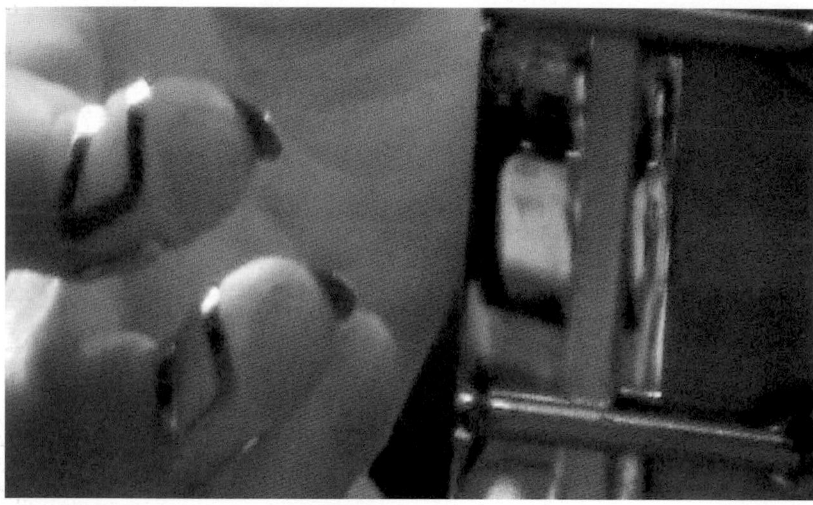
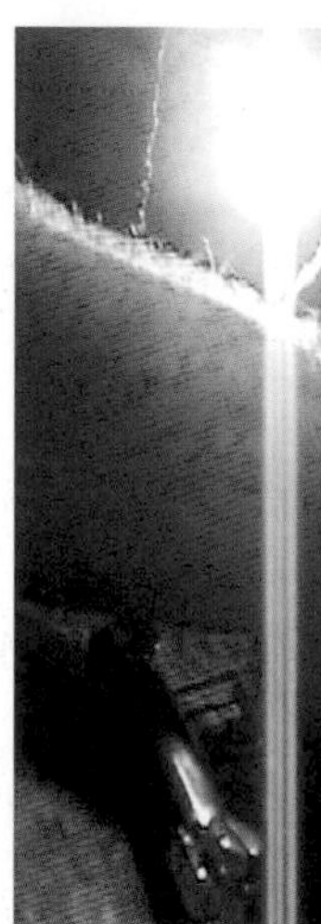

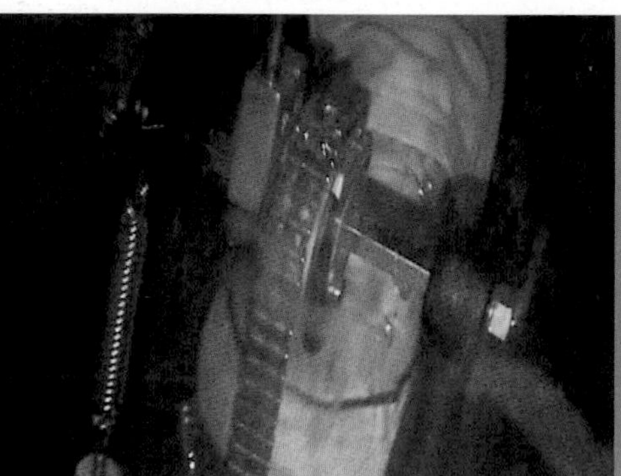

TUNING UP: **REHEARSING**

Your musicians will always be rehearsing. Any time that they are, you want to be there to saturation point. Know the tracks, know the themes, know the personalities of the band, how they move, where they move, how they interact. All of this information is ammunition both for your ideas and for constructing your shots.

If you are going to see a band or musician rehearse prior to your shoot, take your DV camera. This isn't just practice for how you might want to frame things on the shoot itself, it might be useful for you in the edit.

Rehearsals make great cutaways. On the day of the shoot, you may well find that you don't have enough time to get all the shots to fill the duration of the track. Close-ups of fingers on keyboards or strings, a drummer's cymbal or kickdrum, a singer's POV approaching the mic, or a flashing Fresnel lens can become essential tools. Think about the ways that you might need them. Is there an 8 bar that you need to fill? A transition from one scene to another? A flashback?

The most critical way that cutaways can be used is when the music video is to be taken from a live gig. Live gigs are notorious for being very difficult for getting exactly what you want because they are spanning two different objectives: getting a video out of it and getting an audience into it. The twain really never meet: you are either in their way, or they are in yours. Close-ups become the essence of making a live gig intimate in a way that long shots don't muster.

Don't worry about different lighting for close-ups: this can generally be fixed in a good NLE. If continuity matters, go for extreme close-ups avoiding the set, clothes, hair, or anything that is likely to be different on the day.

If a band or musicians are rehearsing on the same set they will play on for the live gig, try to get everything the same for the rehearsal. The musicians will get a technical run-through, usually on the day of the gig itself. If you have the power, try to insist that it becomes a dress rehearsal as well.

Dress rehearsals as technical run-throughs are perfect for medium shots and every position that you won't be able to get during the live gig. If it's a stage, get

***ABOVE LEFT>RIGHT** Shooting this rehearsal the night before the gig became an essential part of the edit. A long track (coming in at six minutes) needed some relief from the limited arena of the bar location. Using rehearsal footage is an excellent way to release a video from any claustrophobia or repetitiveness (see Filling Up: the 8 Bar, page 118).*

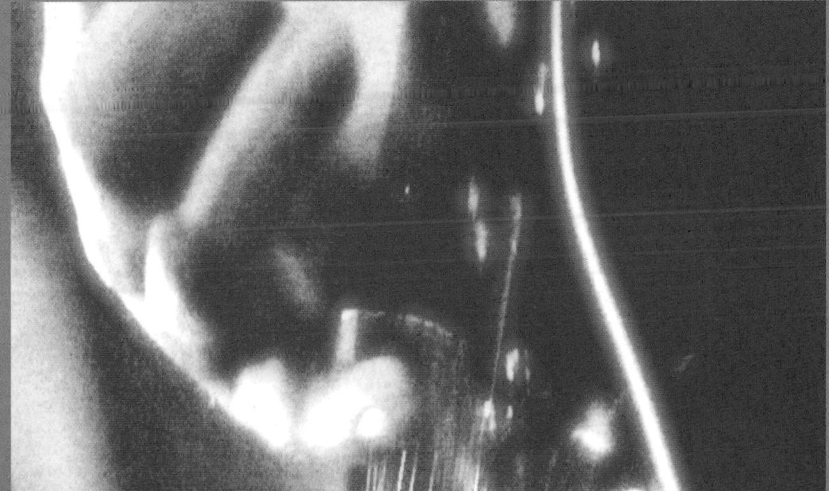

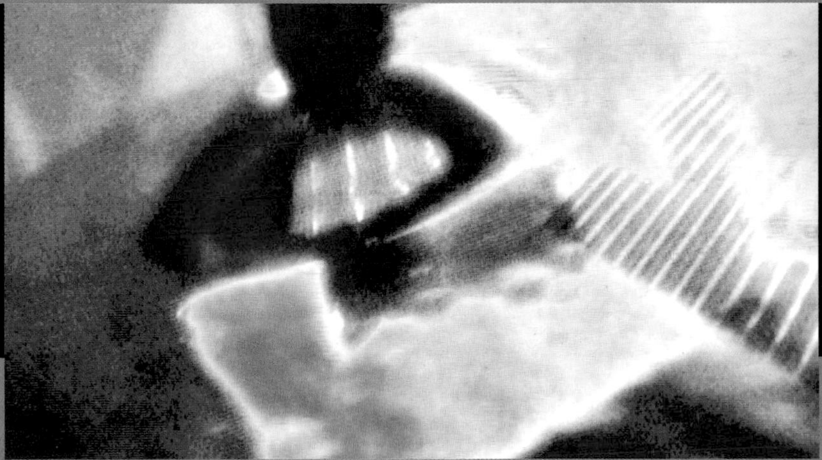

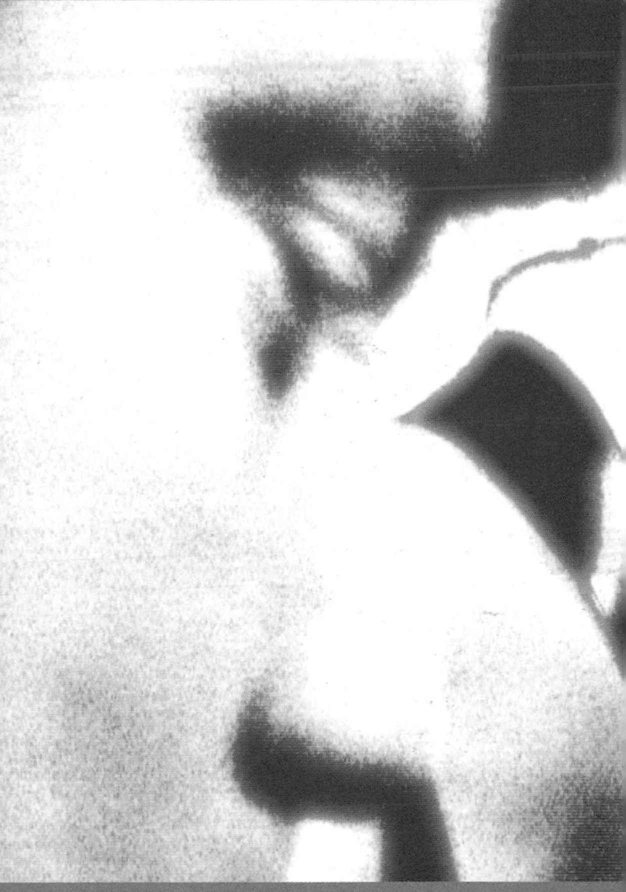

***ABOVE LEFT>RIGHT** Get up on stage during a sound check and get these kind of images. They'll be impossible at any other time and will allow you to break the barrier that you may well have when shooting a live gig. Intimate shots, close-ups, and reverse shots bring life to an as-live music video.*

to the back of it: it's very probable that you won't get reverse shots on the night. If you're worried about the lack of audience, try to position yourself so that you are shooting into the lights. Light flares not only obliterate most things beyond the mosh or orchestra pit, they can also look attractive and dynamic in edits.

When you are shooting reverse shots, cutaways, and POVs during rehearsals, always try to find a shot somewhere behind the lead or singer that simultaneously hides and shows their vocal talents. This might be the jaw moving or the Adam's apple working. In the edit, these kind of shots can be used as cutaways instead of cutting away to something entirely, and disorientingly, different. If it can work for news interviews, then it can certainly work for music videos...

If it is a technical rehearsal, take the whole of your crew. Don't let the gig be a total surprise. Without getting in the way, quietly work out with your crew just how you are going to tackle it: where the cameras are, where the lock-off is, where the audio feed is coming from and whether you have the right connections.

The other important person is your stills photographer. It's the stills photographer's ideal moment for getting what will be seen on the night. When the gig actually happens, they can concentrate on involving the audience in their work.

Scheduling rehearsals eliminates technical and creative challenges, and assures both the crew and the musicians that they can get a video out of their music as well as a gig. With that in mind, the show *can* go on...

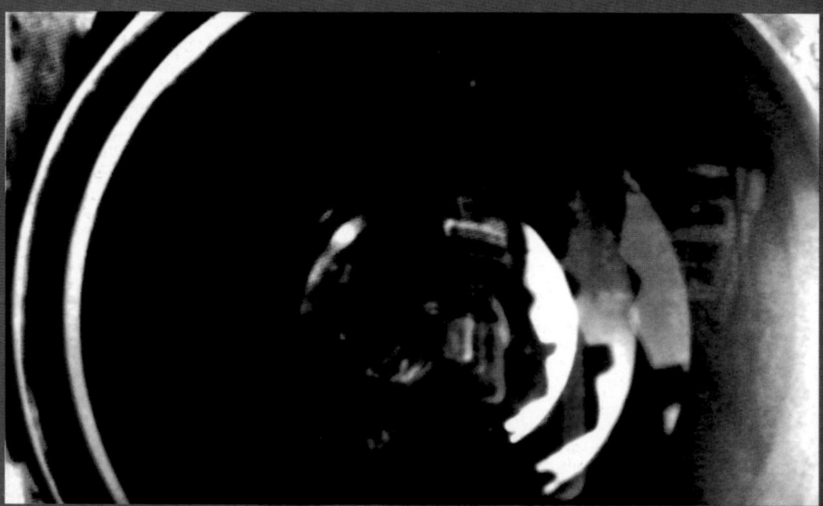

Screen ratio is covered elsewhere (*see page 66*), but make sure that the camera can frame to your requirements. For a music video, camera mics are not often useful, except for a sync guide track – but you'll end up with a standard cardioid that will be useful for anything else. A mic input *is* handy, though.

The most critical connections are a DV out and a DV in. Whether or not you think you would ever export back to DV is not an issue. You might, and if you haven't got one, you'll need to buy another camera. The DV camera operates using a four-pin FireWire connection. Sony call this *i-Link*, but don't let that confuse you – it's the same high-speed digital connection with the same jack.

GEARING UP: **THE KIT**

Because there don't have to be any limitations, making a music video can be as cheap or as expensive as you like. Production values aren't so much of an issue with the music video because sometimes you really do want it looking down, dirty, and downright cheap. With anarchic music, it would be hypocrisy to sell out.

There are a number of essentials that you will require even to go about creating cheap and nasty music videos, and a camera is only one of them.

The Camera

Your first goal is always to get the best pictures that you can. From there, you can degrade or lift as you want. The best pictures are often from 3CCD cameras that split red, green, and blue signals. 3CCD cameras will give you a *truer* representation of what you have shot. If you don't have three CCDs on your camera, or can't budget for one, don't jack in your project just yet. There are plenty of single-chip DV cameras around that are terrific in what they offer. Certainly Sony's *MegaPixel* cameras are pretty unnoticeable in chrominance quality.

***TOP:** The camera lens feeds the CCD with quality and quantity of light that represent the image. Without a good lens, your digital representation won't be faithful to the analogue world in front of it.*

***ABOVE LEFT:** Lights throw out different colours in different strengths. The subjects and objects that the lights hit absorb or reflect depending on the nature of their surface and of the surfaces around them.*

Don't worry about in-camera digital and picture effects. You'll get some anyway, but it's clean pictures that will help you more than anything else. Compensation for shooting in poor light won't be beneficial either because your lighting is integral to good pictures.

The Lighting

Lighting is the only way that your image quality can be controlled. Well-placed lighting can up your production values massively, so getting the right kit for the job is essential.

Light reads in temperature (degrees Kelvin). The way this translates into the lighting that you use is that between infrared and ultraviolet, there is a scale between hot and cold emissions. At the hotter end are tungsten lamps (like household bulbs). They throw out a reddish light. Halogens are cooler and DV reads them as a more yellow light. Fluorescent is green and should be approached with caution.

Daylight changes throughout the day, so if you are shooting outdoors, keep white-balancing on your camera (it is guaranteed to have one).

If you've got the budget for just one light, always make it a redhead. They're small, powerful, and give you a very balanced light either as a flood or – using barn doors – as a makeshift spot.

The Computer

Macs and Windows PCs both have the capability to run your edit software as long as they have the capacity. Slow, tedious edits are usually down to computers with lack of speed and full or fragmented hard drives. To avoid this, use more RAM (at least 512MB) and a larger hard drive (or drives).

The more you spend, the more effects and transitions you will get, and the probability that there will be some powerful realtime editing functions is greater. The whole package of video card and software relies on mathematics – and here we are again – in order to come up with the most accurate, the most versatile, and the quickest sums, it takes time, money, and expensive brains....

The Sound System

When working in your edit, the most important guide is the track itself. Make sure that you have a true surround sound system (subwoofer and satellites), set at a medium volume, bass and treble level at source and amp.

BELOW FAR LEFT: To enable smart edit decisions, make sure that you can hear your audio with enough depth. Subwoofers and small satellites allow for bass beats and treble detail to be distinguished easily on the desktop

The most important port you'll need is a six-pin FireWire. This will get all your images into the computer. Macs love FireWire – Apple invented it. Because PCs are an open architecture and used for so many things, Windows isn't always great at capturing video – and sometimes won't if you haven't updated your media tools. Either way, a PC is going to work a lot better for you with a video card installed. This will capture your clips as well as offering associated editing software.

The Editing Software

The editing software should define any video card that you purchase. Editing applications are graded in accordance with their price. Buy the best that you can get for your money, because most music videos are made in the edit.

The Drive

However you anticipate exporting your music video, you can only do it if you have the correct drive. DVD is probably the best way for you to go, but it's got to be +/- (a player to player difference) as well as *writeable*. This may sound obvious, but the cheaper varieties only allow for playback.

The Encoder

If you aim to have a DVD product or to put the video online, you'll need to have an encoder of some kind. This will convert your AVI into a DVD-friendly MPEG or a streaming file. Streaming media needs an application to tailor it for viewing on as many other computers as possible. A better encoder will usually let you get near to universal viewability without culling your quality.

ABOVE CENTRE: If you're purchasing software, look for any compatibility issues on-line before you buy. There are plenty of conflicts that aren't challenges, but problems. Good quality software often acknowledges, allows or even embraces other good quality software.

ABOVE RIGHT: Your encoder may well do things that you don't understand, but if you don't confuse it, it'll be your best friend when it comes to playback.

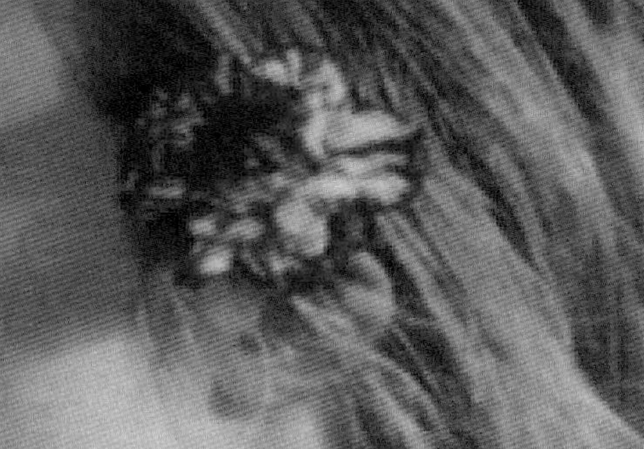

SHUTTING UP: LENSES AND APERTURE

Nothing works as hard and as readily when controlling light and focus than the human brain. It white balances, racks focus, restrains exposure, and adds any gain as it reads your mind.

***TOP LEFT & RIGHT:** An excess of light and the closure of aperture permits a properly exposed image with a small depth of field. The control of the image allows for racking of focus between two subjects, or foreground and background.*

The brains in DV cameras are the preset auto settings. They don't read your mind. Instead, they read the levels presented to them on input and make adjustments to a medium level. Indeed, everything about auto is average, middle-of-the-road, and – for the music video – very, very dull.

That doesn't mean that you need to shoot with entirely inappropriate settings that will ruin your image – but shooting clean doesn't always equate to shooting mean.

Controlling the levels of your image requires an immediate switch-off of your auto focus, your auto shutter, and your neutral density filter. These are all the elements that will allow you to get what you want for each set-up. If you have more than a consumer camera, you'll be lucky enough to be able to control aperture. If this is on auto, turn that off, too.

Auto controls – specifically auto-focus – constantly scan the image and readjust. The readjustments that are made use tiny servos in the camera. If these are left running, you will lose your battery power before you've got through the first morning. The real question is, though, how to get the image and exposure you really *want*.... The answer to this is usually with the depth of field for the shot.

A smaller depth of field allows for a more cinematic look. This enables you to shoot a subject with a background completely out of focus, or to pull focus between something in the foreground and something in the background. No matter what your set-up consists of, a camera lens operates with light to ensure that there is a greater amount of depth *behind* the subject than between the subject and the camera. This comes in handy when throwing any backing singers or landscape into a blur behind your in-focus vocalist.

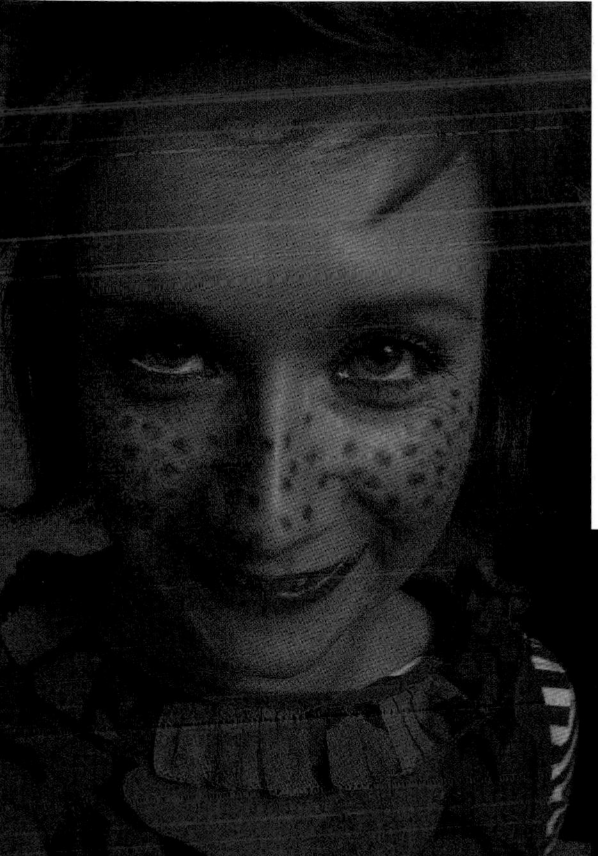

However, large depths of field are essential in the music video to create the believable. Miming artists will not be believed if they are knocked out of focus – and for this reason, greater depths of field allow a director to show this off. The fact is that if you've put a lot of effort into your set, wardrobe, and make-up, you will want to tread a fine line between overtness, revealing all, being discreet, and teasing. For this reason, using variant depths of field within the music video itself brings depth to the texture and rhythm of the video.

To create this smaller depth of field, distance the camera from the set-up as much as you can within your set. If you want your frame tighter, zoom in optically from that distance. The larger the wide-angle lens, the better this effect will *appear* to be. If you have a telephoto lens (400mm, say) the depth of field will appear far more readily. You will have to have strong lighting that keeps your scene lit while you stop down. Stopping down (a higher-numbered f-stop on your aperture) limits the amount of light while giving you a balanced picture. If you don't have aperture control, opt to use your neutral density filter manually as a compromise.

Larger depths of field flatten the image – and they tend to be exactly what consumer cameras find it hard to shake. Lower-end cameras are point and shoot, which is why they operate on auto by default. They grab everything in sight and try to put it in focus.

Try to have a selection of lenses at your disposal and play with them before you use them. If you're trying some out, take your camera to the store to make sure you've got the right thread or you'll need lens converters. Don't worry about filters unless they work specifically to create a concept that you have in mind. These should only be those that affect the light coming in through the lens – neutral densities, polarizing, or star filters, for example. Color or gradient filters aren't worth your money. Shoot clean, and you can add effects far more efficiently and effectively to your images in the edit.

MIKING UP: MICROPHONES AND SOUND RECORDING

Microphones and sound-recording on the set of a music video are a curious thing. On one hand, they can be essential; on the other, why on earth would you need them when your band is miming to a CD?

ABOVE LEFT: Ebullient performances are best left to lives, for risk of exposing as-lives for its mimed counterpart.

High-quality microphones can be outrageously expensive. It is therefore worthwhile considering whether you will actually be using them to capture sound, or simply as props.

Shooting for Sync

Obviously, if you're shooting live as live, your musicians will already be miked. If you're shooting as if your performers are synching live, though, you'll want to retain an element of realism to convince your audience that they are actually performing. They need mics.

The Microphone as a Prop

Your music video may not be shot as-live. It may just be that you want it to look authentic within the scope of a whiz-bang-zoom music video.

Authenticity is a noble idea in the face of the artificial video. What you are pulling your audience back from is that whatever is in the video, there is no manufacture with the musicians themselves. They can sing true and play live – they are, in effect, *real*. If this is what your band want to impress upon an audience, shooting them with microphones can help.

It's a fine line between success and failure. If you insult your audience, you lose credibility not only for the band but also for yourself. Because audiences *are* video-sophisticated, they will know that your musicians are not performing live. Your job is to create a video that will make them forget that they know this.

It's not an easy task, and you can't fool all of the people all the time. This is why the microphone in such situations should be regarded merely as a prop. Any success from there is a bonus. Tom Jones, Prince, and Robbie Williams have all played to a mic in videos that are absolutely not as-lives. Even the two lucky studs performing *The Macarena* gather round a boomed mic.

While a mic on a set can be utilized as a prop to offer a performer comfort and support, it has a hard time gaining any kind of credibility when used in neither as-lives or on sets. These are the painful recording studio music videos that document the recording of the track itself. It's hard to get it right when the video draws attention to the self-congratulatory celebration of the song, which tries to donate personalities to the musicians.

Microphones and headphones can be a real headache if they aren't part of the visual aesthetic. A DJ is a lot more convincing holding headphones, but finding ones that don't make him look like Mickey Mouse may mean not using the usual set. It's the same story with mics. If they aren't going to be functional on set, it won't matter if they work, only that they look as though they do and that they look good.

Headphones also obscure the talent. This is often why DJs simply have them around their neck in the music video. Microphones can obscure, but the right shot (slightly higher or to the left or right), the right mic (smaller, wind-cheater removed), manipulated expertly by the performer can leave the mouth free to sync.

Head-sets and wireless mics have made their stab at setting trends, but can look truly outdated. A quality wired mic is still the choice of the serious musician.

Headphones and mics? The occasional laugh and face-pull to the camera? It all begins to sound a little too Mariah Carey for comfort. Mics as props are best used with a safety blanket of humour. Don't take them seriously unless it's an as-live because you can guarantee that most of your audience won't.

Shooting for Sync

Sometimes you *do* have to worry that your mic is both functional and aesthetic, like when you are shooting for sync. Sync is sometimes used instead of the CD track in the edit. If this is what you are doing, it's going to be a complicated shoot. Your audio has to be as clean as your video: no pops, no interference, no background noise. Coupled with getting the pictures right, it's a longer shoot, with possibilities of pick-ups.

If this is the case – and it is for those as-lives where the gig isn't mimed – you ideally need to get the sync straight into the camera and on to tape. Your sync vocal or music played from your lead musician is the most important track that you'll have and you don't want to be synching it from a DAT or MD in the edit to your performer. This is best taken as you shoot the master shot.

Shooting live performances often results in the mic obscuring the singers' mouths. This is never a bad thing and should even be encouraged. It's hard enough getting coverage for live performances without a bank of cameras. Obscuring sync gives plenty of opportunity to use these shots for any part of the music video where the talent is singing and you haven't got the right shot. Go out of your way to get them if you can. It's always good practice to shoot the next song using indistinct shots, just remove the audio in the edit and employ them confidently.

If your performer is synching audio to be removed in the edit, it is probably to match for speed – slowmo or speed-up – in post. You can use your camera mic for this if you are close enough. For any other shots, boom them out of frame.

ABOVE LEFT: A mic can really turn somebody into A Somebody: a rock star. A mic on a stand – especially for a guitar/vocalist – can become their trusty, thrusting support, and transform their stance into the sexual domination of the frame.

ABOVE RIGHT: Shooting from below to the side that holds the mic will help – without resorting to any inauthenticity.

TOP RIGHT: Exposing your mime is something that you will always risk shooting from the side.

BELOW If the camera doesn't move, why not let the lighting add dynamism to the shot? This hand-held redhead uses a loosely covered blue gel to ripple a cold blue key on the subject's face, while the tungsten fill warms up the background.

LIGHTING UP LIGHTING

Most importantly, and at its most base level, it's the key to seeing an image.

The way that an image is recognized by your CCD(s) is because it is lit well. Landscape, objects, and subjects respond to light in two critical ways: they reflect and absorb.

The quality of light is measured in Lux (*lumens*). This is the amount of light for every square metre. The temperature of light is measured in degrees Kelvin. The combination of these two directly relate to what you are actually shooting.

All DV cameras have an automatic exposure setting. This opens or closes the shutter (in analogue terms) to let in more or less light. By doing this it compensates for too much or too little Lux in order to capture a balanced image. A balanced image (i.e. a correctly exposed one) shows a median of detail in the blacks and whites of the picture. Overexposure can be perceived by viewing the image with *zebras* on from your DV camera menu.

REFLECT AND ABSORB

How much an image reflects and absorbs depends on:

- **> Surface texture**
- **> Surface colour**
- **> Surrounding surfaces**
- **> The light source(s)**

ABOVE Chromakey lighting is always a juggling act between lighting the subject and avoiding background shadow. Again, what you are able to get away with is dependent on the flexibility of the software that you'll use to composite. If it is at all possible within your framing and with the size of the screen, get some distance between the subject and the background.

Taking the camera off automatic exposure is going to help you with your shoot. Not only does this mean that you can precisely tailor what an image shows and doesn't show, it will also help you to create the mood of your music video.

The mood of lighting relates to how the audience responds to the image. A darker image creates unease (it hides) and a lighter image creates reassurance (it shows). The black and white levels stored as data for each pixel denote which parts of the frame are dark and which are light.

Gamma is the level between black and white: the grey areas, the *balance*. Grey areas are the values that reveal form. Taking gamma values away from the image creates contrast – and this is a mood all of its own. High-contrast images stimulate a viewer because they are hyperreal. The world that we live in is full of gamma because we generally want to be reassured that we're not going to fall over something, drive into something, or not be able to read something.

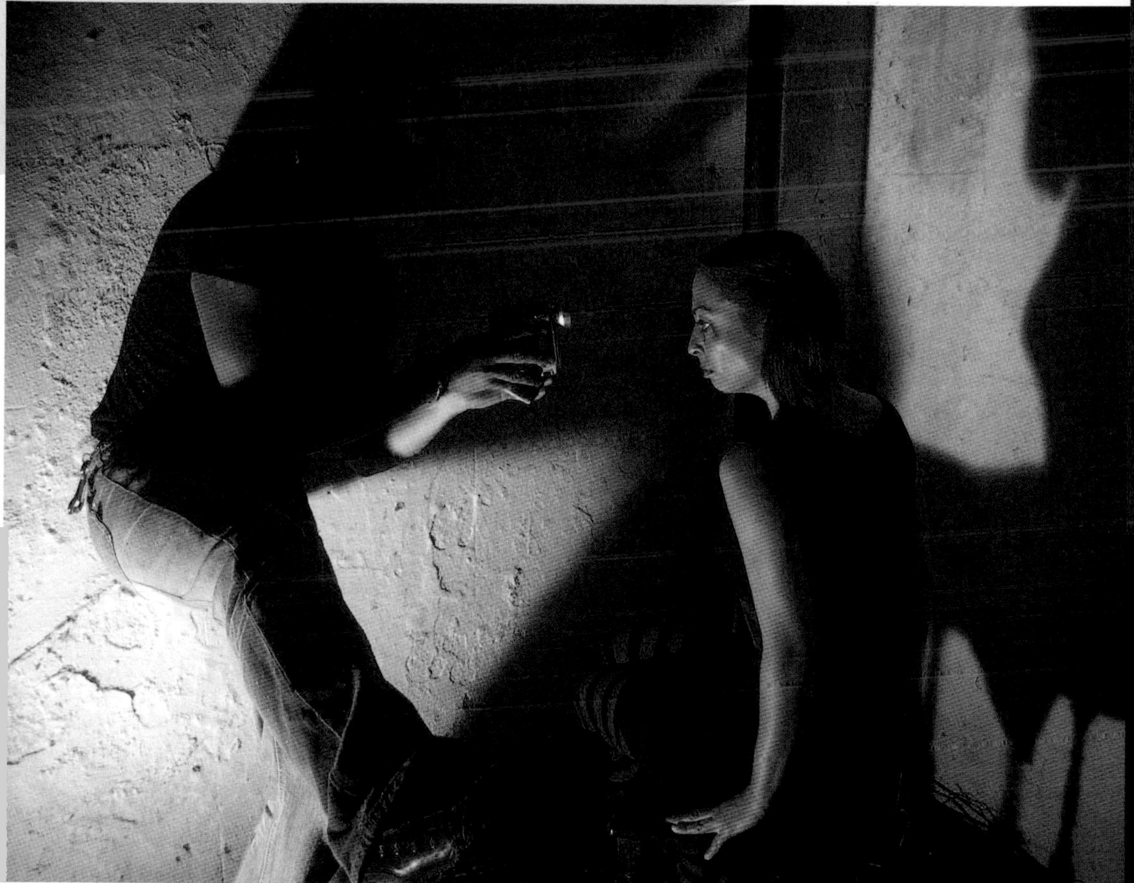

LEFT Single source lighting is the one-stop shop to contrast. Sharp highlights and steep fall-off into shadow can create striking images without the fuss of a complex set-up.

Human beings want as much information as is practically possible. In the real world, gamma values come from reflection and refraction. In daylight, the sun acts as a flood with which objects and subject react by absorption and reflection. At night, there are far less gamma values. Exteriors are often lit by single light sources, direct light that creates highlights by reflection, and shadow by obstruction: contrast.

The way to work this is by controlling the quantity, quality, and direction of the lights that you choose while still working within the parameters of light. Too little or too much doesn't just affect the visibility of the image in the edit, it dictates such things as whether it is legal for broadcast, whether there are artefacts on compression and image quality on your playback source.

The other companion to this is the *colour* of the light. Using the temperature of the light helps create the aesthetic of the image to work with the mood. If fluorescents work as an insipid green, flicker them with a high shutter speed to create menace. If tungsten backlights the image yellow, use a daylight key to hit the side of a face blue.

Know what your edit software is capable of before you start designing your lighting. Quick colour correction and black, white, and gamma level adjustment can make complicated lighting set-ups a waste of your shoot time. Sometimes, though, lighting can just destroy your image. Always remember that shooting clean and properly exposed is your first priority. Compensating in the edit for dim or overexposed lighting can reveal a lot more than just your image: it can reveal each and every horrible pixel.

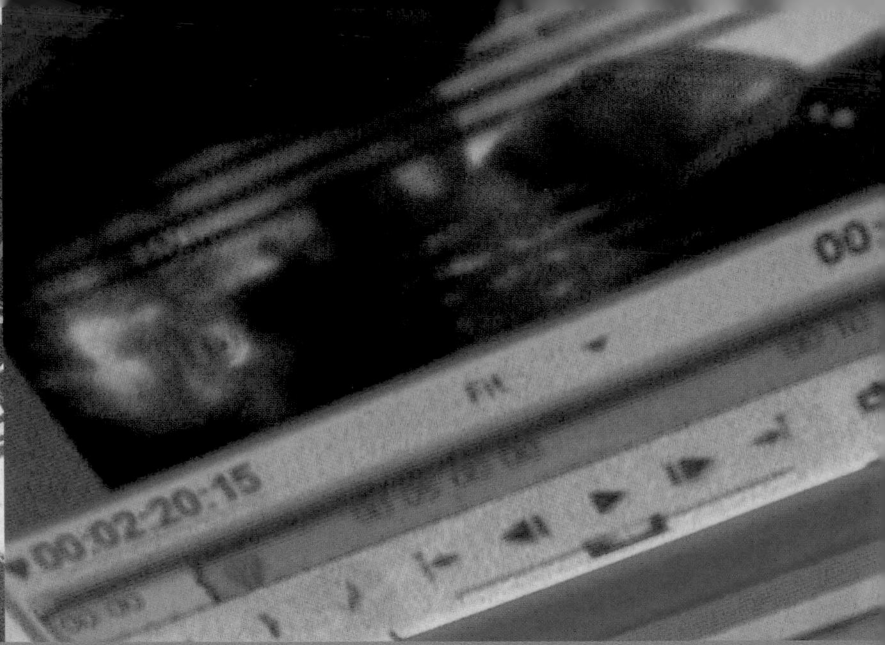

CHECKING UP: **CHECKLIST**

Before you start shooting, make a checklist. Checklists are there so that the producer can budget, so that the crew know their responsibilities, and so that you don't forget anything on the day.

No matter how organized you are, and no matter how good a memory you have, you'll be under a lot of pressure on the day of the shoot and you will forget things. The checklist allows you to keep up, and it reduces the amount of questions people will need to ask you throughout the day, thereby saving time.

TOP LEFT: Checklists should be taken seriously. Treat it like moving house, making sure that each item on the list relates to everything that you're taking out of the door and that comes onto set and off it.

TOP RIGHT: Successful checklists used in pre-production pay off by making post-production an entirely organized process, something backed up only by suitable cranial software…

RIGHT: This is the kind of list that you need to come up with for budgetary considerations, and to allocate responsibility in all aspects of your production.

PRODUCTION CHECKLIST

Production
- Shooting schedules
- Storyboard
- Scripts
- Sets
- Props
- Wardrobe
- Make-up
- Stills camera and film or laptop

Camera
- Camera
- Lenses
- Filters
- Tapestock
- AC power supply
- Batteries
- Battery charger
- Tripod
- Other mounts (dollies, rigs, Jlbs)
- Monitor

Lighting
- Backlights
- Spots
- Fill
- Barn doors/Fresnels/Gobos
- Spare bulbs
- C-stands w/Vlamps
- Backdrops (B/W roll/Chroma)
- Scrims (Diffusers)
- Reflectors
- Gels
- Dimmer
- 110 Volt adaptor
- Extension leads

Audio (props or practical)
- Music player (CD player/Laptop)
- Music source (CD track/Sequencer)

Cardioid In-Frame Mic
- Mic stand
- Shotgun mic
- Lavalier mics
- Mic furry
- Boom
- Mic and audio adaptors
- Headphones

Field Mixer
- Amp
- Speakers
- Mic, mixer and speaker cable

POST PRODUCTION

Hardware
- Computer
- Capture card

Monitor
- Speakers (satellites and sub)
- External hard drive
- Camera or player
- FireWire (or USB2)
- DVD burner

Software
- Capture/Edit application
- Effects plug-In/App
- Audio mixer
- Cleaner
- Encoder
- DVD authoring/Burning app
- Drivers

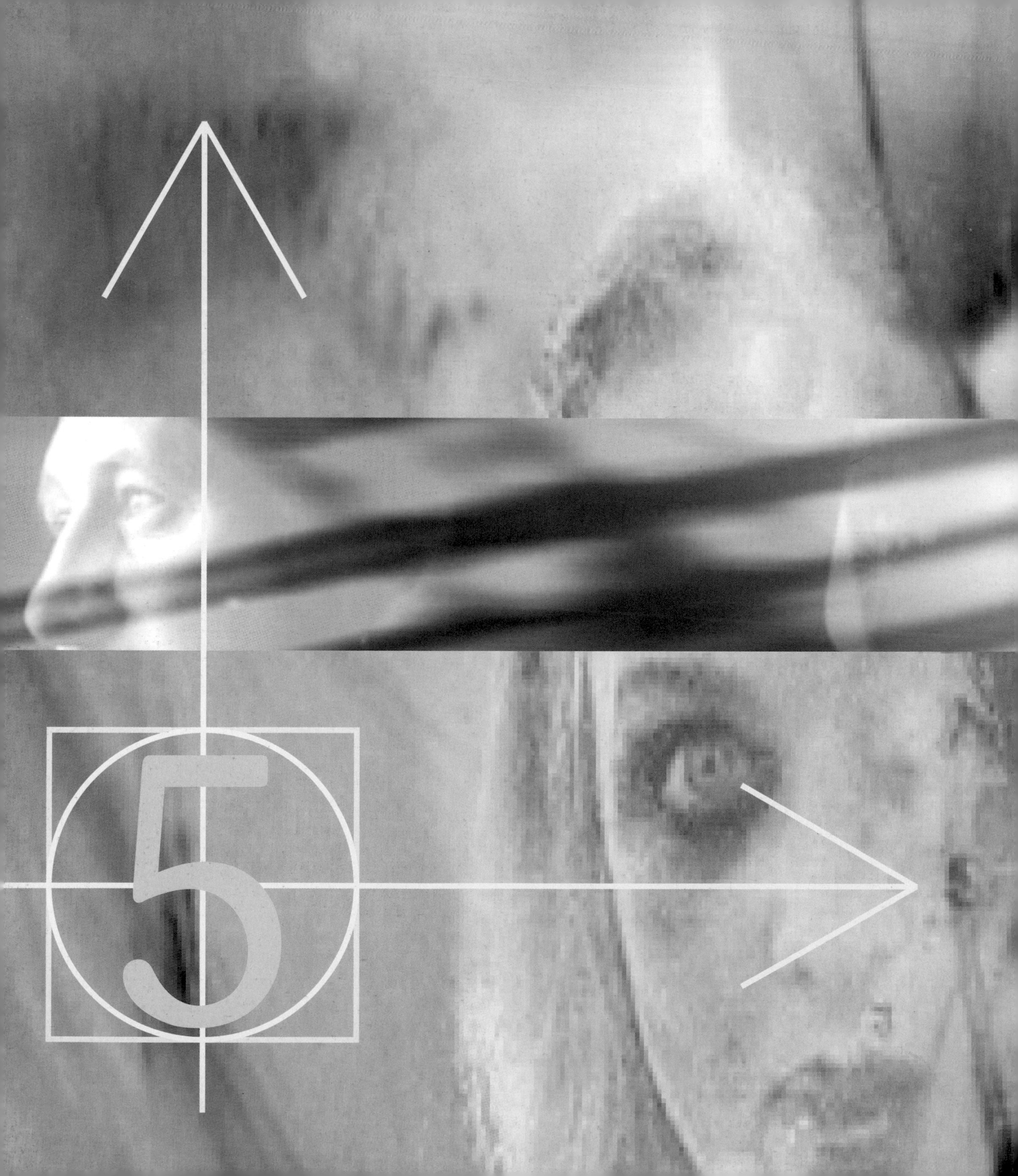
5

PRODUCTION:
BETWEEN ROCK
& A HARD PLACE

LEFT: The musicians will know each other a lot better than they know you. And while you are the outsider that has to crack the seal, be warned that there may be other agendas at play in the band itself. Look out for signs of current disputes or competitiveness and try to avoid conflict that wastes time. As director, you have the perfect right to ask band members to put aside differences and act *while on set.*

This will then give you time to turn your attention to your talent.

Musicians will need looking after if they are not used to making music videos. Don't let them interfere with what is happening on set, but get them into make-up and wardrobe as soon as you can. If they're not used to the experience of make-up, they're likely to find it terribly amusing.

WARMING UP: LIVE SETS

The day before your shoot is nearly as critical as the shoot day itself. You're not going to get the good night's sleep that you need unless you have peace of mind by being completely prepared.

Wake up at least half an hour earlier than you think necessary in the morning. You'll need it. When you get to the set or location, try to arrive loaded with enough coffee, tea, and breakfast (never forgetting a vegetarian option) to show that you mean business, but you're willing to muck in as well. Small gestures like this show that this is exactly what you are looking for in everybody else.

Once that's done, start directing. Direct your art department and your crew and get some enthusiasm going. If you give them specific instructions as to what you want and when you need it, you'll get the best out of them. Crew like assertiveness and respond to someone who knows what they are looking for. Don't put up with anyone that says something is a problem: always correct light-heartedly that it is a challenge.

CHECKLIST FOR SETTING UP

- **> Shooting schedules have been given to all cast and crew**
- **> All cast and crew have been called to ensure that they have no problems and that they know where they're going, what time they have to be there, and what they are bringing**
- **> All PRs or set/location facilitators have been called to remind them of your shoot and your requirements**
- **> All batteries have been charged**
- **> All kit, props, make-up, and wardrobe is by the door, ready to go**
- **> You've got a few copies of the script, storyboard, and shooting schedule**
- **> You've got a CD player and copies of the track on CD**
- **> You've got a laptop with the track on**
- **> You've got spare tapes**
- **> You've got spare batteries**
- **> You've got spare bulbs**
- **> Your vehicle is fuelled**
- **> Any tickets are pre-booked**
- **> There's cash in your wallet**

understand what they are doing in relation to your scribbled images. Distance crew and musicians as much as possible. The musicians should be reporting to you, as you are the one directing them. Any other relationships are going to waste your valuable time, and the last thing that you want is to feel left out of the equation. Never lose this anchor point or you will lose control of the set.

Give the musicians enough time to rehearse as you work on set-ups. Warming up not only means that they can get their timing and notes right for sync, but it also gives them a chance to take on their role within a band and their star personality in front of an audience – or in this instance, in front of the camera.

THE WORLD OF CLICHÉ

- **> A lot of musicians are heterosexual**
- **> A lot of make-up artists and wardrobe consultants are women**
- **> A lot of musicians are male**

If you don't keep a lid on things the result is often talent discomfort, peacock posturing, and time-consuming testosterone outbursts. This can happen on set as well, so do look out for it. If there are women around and you have 'susceptible' musicians on set, try to keep them apart. Macho behavior doesn't just waste time and money, it leads to bizarre performances on camera.

Back on set, try to have the musicians' tracks playing to get a suitable atmosphere. The track itself, if it is being used for sync, is going to be heard time and time again, so don't overplay it. It will, however, be useful for all crew and non-associated talent to hear it, to get a feel for what they are working with.

Keep your shooting schedule with you at all times, as well as your storyboard and script – they're indispensable and you will need to refer to them repeatedly. Working closely with your camera, lighting, and audio op, make sure that they

***ABOVE TOP:** A lot of things can happen with musicians in the make-up chair. Sometimes, they just become putty in your hands and resign themselves to the same. This is the perfect opportunity to put your requirements to them, however bizarre your directorial requests might be.*

***LEFT & ABOVE:** Lights, make-up, tight clothes, pressure – everything is against your talent from keeping their cool. Try and make their lives a little easier by preparing yourself to keep your own…*

Make sure that lunch happens as close to the scheduled time as possible. Don't miss out on it altogether just because you're behind time, or people will become disgruntled and obstinate. And while flowing caffeine is helpful at all times, enthusiasm does tend to flag somewhere in mid-afternoon. You may need to revitalize the set, so try not to blow it all first thing in the day.

When you're wrapping, let everybody know. Give yourselves a clap and a pat on the back and you might forget that everything went so badly by the time you turn up for the shoot the next day…

The reality of shooting is never quite what is anticipated. Whatever the shoot is like, it's one more day of experience in what can go wrong, what can be serendipitous, how talent can react – all of these things and many, many more. What is important is that you take with you on to the next shoot the knowledge of exactly what worked and how you can make it *better*.

ORDERING UP: **THE DIRECTOR ON SET**

The director on set has a responsibility to rein in the chaos before chaos reigns. Most actors and crew know that their day on set is going to consist of a lot of waiting for the resolution of technical, artistic, or practical challenges. Actors and inexperienced musicians are very different people, and impatience can breed ill-feeling and restlessness. This is something that you have to control.

A large part of the director's role is communication. Let your talent know why you're wrestling with the camera position or the lighting rig or your exposure settings if you sense some king of agitation. If this isn't contained, the worst case scenario is out and out mutiny, or at best, the talent returning from the pub, wasted and wasting your time.

If they are inexperienced, they shouldn't mind occupying themselves as runners – certainly for something that is in their benefit: the food and coffee run is a great way of entertaining a band while you set up the shot.

This isn't to say that all musicians are inherently incapable of behaving themselves; it's just that if *you* get frustrated at some point (which you probably will), you can guarantee that everybody else got to that point a couple of hours before.

When you arrive on set, you'll probably have a list of set-ups. These are the shots that you need to get the body of your music video in the can. You should be shooting your master shot first. This might incorporate all musicians or just the lead. Use this to get everybody into the spirit of the shoot. If you haven't had the time to rehearse, it's the perfect moment to run through the tune as an invigorating warm-up. You should be shooting the master shot twice anyway – the second take can be used for safety or just to give you some extra footage.

For the master shot, it's loose direction that you want. Let them find their own screen personality and positioning. After that comes the time that you'll want to give them directed parameters in which to work their stuff.

From that point onwards, your list of set-ups will need to be checked off in the order of practical and technical logistics. Your musicians should have the entire day with you if they are remotely serious

***ABOVE LEFT>RIGHT** On set, your job is largely entertaining – or at least, getting what you want done within time and making it a reasonably enjoyable experience. This is particularly important where no-one is being paid. You don't want a situation so fraught and grueling that no-one wants to work with you again.*

***OPPOSITE LEFT>RIGHT** Entertaining is one thing. Making life comfortable for your talent is another altogether. Whether this is providing physical support for them in order that long shots can be held...or emotional support by getting as dirty or as uncomfortable as you are asking your talent to be. Try to demonstrate movement or positions as much as you can. If you can't do them or hold them, don't expect anyone else to unless they're trained artists.*

about what they're doing. If there is a bit of cut and paste on their availability throughout the day, it'll force your hand in the order of set-ups depending on who you need for each.

The other thing that's going to alter the order of priorities is location availability. When you're sorting your shoot days, always try to remember that rendezvous, travel, set-up, shooting, striking, and relocation always take a lot longer than they/you should expect.

A producer should always keep an eye on time and budget. The shooting schedule can dictate both of these, but it's just a piece of paper. There has to be someone there who can rationally – and not emotionally – juggle overrun from one set-up to another. Shoots are a rag-tag bag of compromises, serendipity, success, and failure in the race to get the video made.

Above all, remember that even though you might not have all the shots that you wanted to achieve by Martini hour, music videos can be, and often are, made in the edit. Don't be disheartened by what you've managed in a day visually; the most important thing *always* is that your shots are in sync if they need to be, and that there's enough light to give you a properly exposed image. From that point on, anything's possible…

IDEAL ORDER FOR SET-UPS

- > Master shot
- > Cutaways from master shot
- > Longer shots
- > Cutaways from longer shots
- > Technical set-ups
- > Shorter shots
- > Cutaways from shorter shots
- > Messy shots
- > Cutaways from messy shots
- > Wrap, strike, and clear up

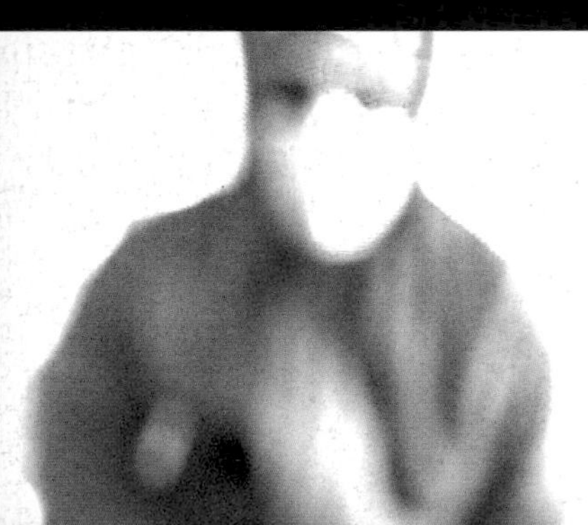

FACING UP: THE LEAD SINGER

By nature, lead singers are exhibitionists, willing to take the lead. They may well have gathered the band as a background against which they can show off. If you've got a lead singer that isn't particularly gregarious, it's probably because they can sing. Certainly, less physically attractive lead singers can always sing…

By default, a band tend to be occluded by the lead singer. You don't expect a lead to be located behind the band – and they never are. They're right in front, showing off, exuding the image and personality of the band. If there's any exception that proves this rule, it's the gregarious bass player that is trying to steal a little of the limelight themselves – in leopard skin pants. Come in, Manic Street Preachers, your time is up.

If you are working alongside convention, it's a hardcore necessity that any lead singer has enough personality or sex appeal – or both – to carry the video. As conventions go, however, it's a curse, and you are absolutely welcome to work against it as much as you can.

With the curse comes the blessing. A lead singer is your theme for your concept, a thread for your edit, a vocal shortcut to the band, a clothes horse, and an icon. They can be very useful tools if they respect you and your ideas as director. If your singer has a personality, find a way to use it. If he or she is particularly attractive, use that. If they don't have personality, it's your job to create it – just as it's your job to make them look exactly how you want them to look.

Start by working with what you've got. If there are any characteristics that you can see on a one-to-one basis that make them appealing, get your lead to focus on those. Cheekiness is a quality that often comes with exhibitionism. It can veer dangerously into tiresome annoyance, though, unless it's contained – and these traits can become a turn-off to an audience. All endearing qualities that can be revealed in four minutes of video have a vulgar side if not directed and contained. Sexy becomes sleazy, demure becomes dull, confident becomes conceited, cool becomes laughable, and attitude becomes annoying.

***LEFT:** Got a shy lead singer? Some leads' obvious nervousness or distraction reads in their faces during certain shots. If you need to use the shot rather than a cutaway, find a way to disguise inappropriate expressions. Sometimes, a simple effect – in this case, bleaching the singer out with maximum exposure and adding a blur in the edit – can be efficient and visually dramatic.*

***ABOVE LEFT:** The application of attitude can be directed, but an over-ebullient or enthusiastic lead singer actually needs direction to subdue exaggerated physical moves that can quickly become irritating to an audience.*

***ABOVE RIGHT:** The alternative to a lead singer who occludes his band, is the lead singer that is very much part of it. A band that support their lead singer with unified physical motion which matches their own identities, suggests a band that are very much in tune with each other: a happy marriage.*

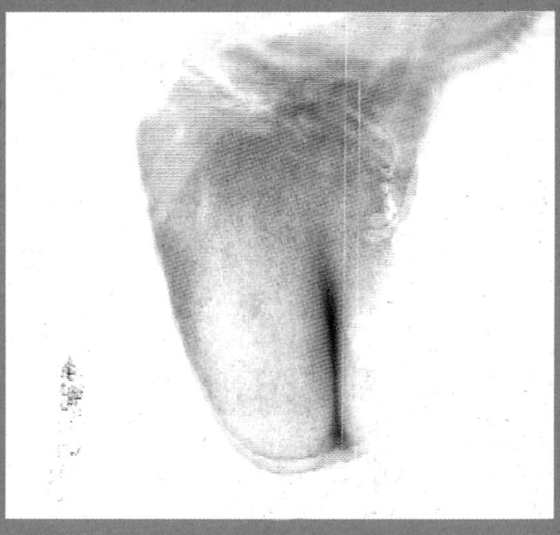

Understand that as a band – especially newly-formed bands – they're not only used to playing against a live audience, but are fighting between themselves to be noticed, and as a whole, to gain an Identity. The staged gig, just like theatre, offers up the challenge of creating distance between band and audience and the players may well have become used to exaggerating moves. Just as with theatrical facial expressions In cinema, this plays badly in a close-up, intimate, music video. Studio work is a different beast altogether from performing live.

***ABOVE, LEFT & BELOW:** Personality can be projected on to a lead singer with conflicting attributes. While make-up and flailing arms turn a would-be attractive lead into someone a little more dangerous, the contradiction of enhancing their projected personality with sexuality can create a much more complex individual with little effort*

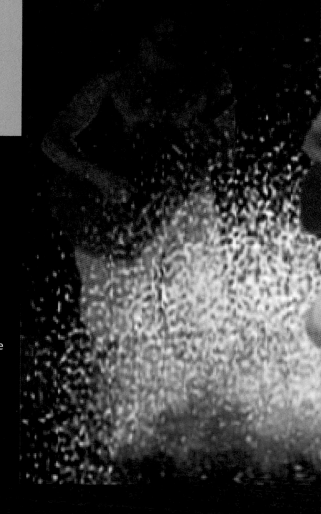

something else, and their whole performance – indeed the whole rehearsed-to-death track – will gain a new vitality.

A major problem with all leads is stone-faced seriousness (are those Manics waving or drowning out there?). Bands that understand that music is just business tend to be far less serious than those that think that it is important that their music be heard. It *is* just business. When you come to shoot, any poker faces need to be eradicated from the set, and it's worth your while to explain the real purpose of the video from the start to the lead singer. To the lead and to the band, the video might just be a means

ABOVE: Above all, the lead has to trust you as a director. Find those quiet moments when you can make them understand exactly what you want them to do and why. Everyone likes to be regarded as a special case, but leads tend to think they deserve it more than anyone else. And once they're on side, they will do pretty much anything...

If your singer isn't attractive and doesn't have any personality traits that you could possibly work on, then invent them. Some singers work a lot better when they are given a role to play. Attitude, confidence, coyness, and sexiness are all attributes that can be displayed without the singer actually having them. And don't forget that your singer *doesn't* have to be an actor.

Confidence and conceptual identity can often be boosted if your lead is playing a given part. Instead of asking the lead to be Justin Timberlake, give them a more interpretive role. Try offering up the persona of a 1930s' torch song singer, a Las Vegas showgirl, a hat-trick footballer back in the showers, an anti-war demonstrator caught in a riot.

Find a scenario or an individual that isn't too alien from the lead's own experience. What they'll be doing, as a matter of course, is translating the lyrics into physical movement and facial expression. Eliminate this, give them to an end – the end being serious stadium gigs with long guitar breaks and world-changing lyrics. The fact is that they won't be given the privilege of being this and doing this unless they understand that the nature of the business is not to change the world, but to entertain.

There is only a certain amount of leeway in everyone's life to afford the money and time for entertainment. The video is a grain of sand in the sandcastle of the band's catalogue on a beach of music in a desert of leisure activities – and dry land is only 30 percent of the living world. Perspective helps to eradicate artistic seriousness. Intelligence helps too.

The point, though, is not to dress your lead singer up as a bunny rabbit and tell them it's sexy, or to tell them to act like they're trying to control the DTs and it's cool. The point is to use the lead singer as a sounding board and way of communicating with the band as a whole, and to create a persona that isn't a fraud or a fake, but a physical incarnation of the band's concept or mission statement. You're a director and they've asked you to direct: do it.

***BELOW:** . . . yes, really,* anything . . .

BELOW: If you don't have anything specific for your band members to do, give them a line of sync for narrative gain. If this doesn't work for you, try giving them one of the lines of harmony as sync.

BACKING UP: **BACKGROUND TALENT**

While the lead singer or musician is the obvious leader and representation of the band, it may not be that they are the most important or significant talent. That job may well lie with one or a number of the other talent in the ensemble. This is the Noel/Liam dilemma: what do you do with them?

The shy, retiring, artistic members of the band often have a dichotomy of their own: they want to be seen, but then they don't particularly want to be seen either. This attitude is fairly typical of those that see music as music and not as audio-visual.

Performing doesn't come easy to those who have no interest in acting. Music is a business: it's serious. If you can imagine asking a pow-wow of executives to conga around the boardroom, you might be approaching the shoot in the right way. Better still, is to come equipped…with tactics…

If a musician can't be directed, then don't make them. There's something a little bit sad about Vince Clarke (Erasure) in a dress. Reluctance will often shine through in a background musician's performance, and bullying is hardly the way to win respect or future employment.

Background talent are good at what they do. This is why background singers usually sing and background musicians usually play their instruments. Taking them away from what they know if they are not a born performer leaves them not quite knowing what to do. If they are willing to try something different – to be *directed* – then find something that is not a million miles from what they do usually. This might mean replacing their instrument with something else. Non-performers can be pretty good with props, and it keeps them amused and focused.

If you've got your background talent comfortable with what they're doing, but are still having problems getting what you want from them, there are other methods to get what you want. The easlest one is editorial, keeping cutaways to the individual short and sweet. You may be shooting to a large ratio, but somewhere in the take will be a few appropriate moments.

ABOVE LEFT Giving a DJ a wig to wipe the floor instead of his usual decks creates natural movement with an unnatural tool. While this eliminates physical awkwardness by giving a musician something he can do, it doesn't necessarily negate facial embarrassment.

ABOVE RIGHT: Adding a hat not only makes the DJ feel disguised – invisible, even – it also helps hide any residual mortification.

ABOVE There's always a joker in a band. This is the talent that likes to show off in company. Do yourself a favour and get everyone that they like to show off for off the set. The fear of being alone with a serious crew and a camera can quite easily turn a peacock to a bunny in headlights.

Another technique is to shoot, zoomed tight, from a distance. This avoids the confrontational lens, which some musicians may find off-putting. Shooting under the guise of camera positioning while they rehearse is a good way to get a more natural performance.

Overexposure can bleach out expressions of nervousness and anxiety, as can defocusing. Video effects in the edit can help this along in an effectively stylish manner.

The alternative is to employ any whiff of embarrassment to your advantage. This is patented as the Chris Lowe (Pet Shop Boys) Effect, and serves to create a healthy contrast between the lead and the band: if the background talent is motionless and *emotion*less, the lead doesn't have to over-bake their performance to raise the interest level. Sometimes actually directing them to play down, dumb, or dull is the icing on the cake for the take.

Think about transvestites…go on… The personal philosophy behind cross-dressing is that a different shell creates a different core personality. In effect, it's an excuse for getting away with things that you wouldn't normally do. It's like going on holiday. A different wardrobe for background talent can have that same effect. Finding something that they like, that makes them feel different (sexy, aggressive, ridiculous) can work wonders for their performance in the same way that it can for the lead. If the performance of the background talent counts for screen-time, consider spending as much time on creating a new personality for them as you would spend on your lead.

Whatever you do, make sure that you don't abandon them or their feelings on set. If they've got an idea, it's probably worth pursuing to get the best performance out of them because *they'll* want to make it work. Direct them yourself: don't let the lead reinterpret your requirements. They're people too…

Hair and make-up is integral to the music video, as it helps to create the image of the band or of the artist. The problem is always that while a female talent usually (and often begrudgingly) sells herself visually, her male counterpart wrongly believes that a shave is enough.

As far as the director is concerned, all talent on screen should be made up and dressed or they shouldn't grace the frame. The music video *is* contrived and superficial and how somebody looks is exactly that. As such, it's actually less evil than the marketing juggernaut because it is part of the artistic structure and aesthetics of the promo.

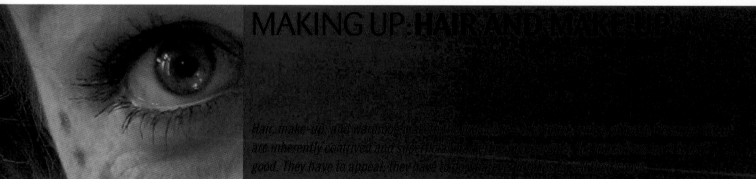

MAKING UP: HAIR AND MAKE-UP

Hair, make-up, and wardrobe maketh the musician – the music video, at least. Because videos are inherently contrived and superficial marketing instruments, the musicians have to look good. They have to appeal; they have to do whatever it takes to sell their songs.

There are two types of make-up for the music video. On one hand, there is the make-up that makes the musician, or that the musician brings to the shoot. This is the Gene Simmons black lightning eye make-up, or Adam Ant's white nasal stripe, Liza Minnelli's mascara, or even Freddie Mercury's moustache. If these sound horribly outdated, it's because devices change or become more subtle. Perhaps more importantly, they *have* to change and be subtle in order *not* to be outdated. The fact is that the 'look' of talent remains within certain parameters while riding the tide of trends. It's the Madonna syndrome. The director may not have any control or say over such iconic make-up. If it is how the talent wishes to define themselves, it should be worked into the video.

The other type of lipstick, powder, and paint is that which the director brings to the shoot. This is make-up applied to create the look of the talent that locates them in the video's landscape, thematically, dramatically, or attractively. In effect, you are giving them a visual personality and a *raison d'etre*. These following are the ways that make-up is applied and controlled within the music video:

The Good

This is the kind of make-up that turns your everywoman or man into the sexiest person on the planet. Beauty-enhancing make-up is the most dependent on trends and fashion. Your talent can be made up to look stunning, but if the blusher says more about obsolescence than it does about their cheekbones, it's wrong, wrong, wrong.

Make-up artists know how to get the best out of a face. All visual artists, including the director, should be able to look at a face objectively and see where enhancement and concealment make that person more attractive. If necessary, simply direct someone familiar with make-up application to undertake your instruction.

***ABOVE** The conventional face of hi-art, lo-budget music video is DIY – and it goes for make-up too. Only let this happen if they know what they are doing. If you've got a whole band of male talent applying their own, you'll probably have to wipe it off and start again. It's a waste of useful time.*

Making talent more attractive is based mostly on primal instincts. Alluring eyes are primarily hooded (eyeshadow), younger eyes are wider (white eyeliner), handsome cheekbones are shadowed (blusher), sexy lips are fuller in men and positively engorged in women (lipstick). Make sure that you have all of the bare essentials on hand to make your talent look good as quickly as possible by incorporating these products and techniques. Always have face powder on-hand, too: hot lights always strip make-up – and while perspiration might be the physical visual element that you want to capture in the scene, it should be simulated with glycerine or oil, and never be the real thing.

The rough and ready also means that you have to prepare the talent for the shoot. If you're not starting with a blank canvas, you've got to let them know. Critically, with male talent, this means letting them know days before whether you want them to arrive shaven or unshaven. Remember that working make-up around stubble for close-ups is a tough job for any applicator.

The Ugly

Back to icons. This is where the differentiation between the musician as an individual and the musician as a video personality begins to blur. Does Marilyn Manson wear unmatching, oddly-coloured contact lenses when he goes down to the supermarket? Does Robert Smith (The Cure) wear his bleeding Barbara Cartland lipstick in bed?

Designer Ugly, though, is not just for icons. It can establish the nature of the musician in the video landscape. Does Christina Aguilera always look like a heroin addict…? No, it just makes sense that she does for *Beautiful*.

The process of uglification is not to make stars look 'naturally attractive'. The likelihood is that you won't be working with such a celebrity and they won't be known for being God's Gift to the libido. This kind of uglification therefore becomes redundant. Using distressing looks helps you to create an unforgettable icon – and a video personality that burns the retina.

Always keep pretentiousness in check, no matter how willing your individual performer may be. Remember this: Vanessa Mae with make-up and hair supplied by the Prodigy's Keith Flint won't start any fires.

BELOW LEFT The make-up artist doesn't just go home after tarting up your talent. They are needed on set immediately before every shot. A full, fine brush and anti-glare powder will take the edge off their extremities under the lights.

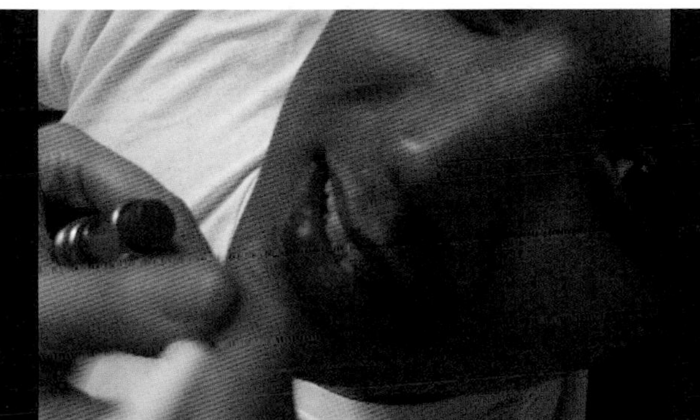

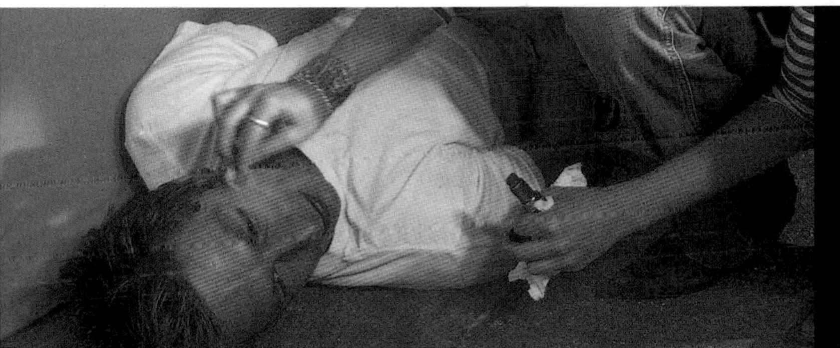

ABOVE: No-one has the same coloured skin, so come prepared. Did you know that the drummer has just got back from five weeks in Botswana? If in doubt, you can always mix light and dark foundations. Don't just have a medium beige and hope for the best…

The Bad

'Bad' make-up is essential for creating a visual representation of rock, grunge, punk, or any loud or dissonant sound. This is where a bit of baby oil can turn a habitually mild-mannered guitarist into a thrashing animal.

The right style of make-up can help this transformation to take place quite easily because the talent has usually already developed that image. You're working with what they've got. If not, it's a much more difficult task. Image management and visual credibility is a job for a band or a stylist, not for the director.

What hot and sweaty shouldn't be is spotty and ugly. The point of any make-up is to create the perfect representation of *that person*. Perfection covers the skin, too: blemish-free and attractive within the scope of their video-based personality. Like any shoot or any edit, it's a form of controlled chaos.

For this reason, a musician or singer will usually wear clothes that say they are a musician or a singer. A hip-hop artist may wear a baseball cap, an XL T-shirt on the outside of a long-sleeved shirt, baggies, and Converse. It says that he is a hip-hop artist, particularly if he is also holding a microphone. It's not even a deception as that is what he actually wears.

To *be* recognized as a 'career somebody', most people dress to be perceived as that person. Insurance brokers do it, bank managers do it, the postman and the police officer do it – and musicians do it. They really do tend to look like musicians... *all the time*.

A stylist will create a look based on that individual's personality, which is probably an

STITCHING UP: **WARDROBE**

Your wardrobe is not an extension of make-up; it's an extension of production design. Make-up can be adjusted quickly; wardrobe has to be ready on a hanger, it must be suitable, and it must fit the talent. It takes a lot more preparation.

***ABOVE LEFT:** Chromakey is the obvious wardrobe/background clash. Make sure both you and the talent know whether you are shooting bluescreen or greenscreen and tailor your colour choices to suit.*

***ABOVE RIGHT:** Wardrobe isn't only about image and confidence, it's often about movement. Don't let physical restriction play a part in your talent's performance if you want them to move.*

The reason that wardrobe is coupled with production design is that whatever the musicians are wearing has to complement their personalities, work with the themes, and interact with the set or location.

Personality

Some people are just born coat hangers: everything they wear just drops off them as if it were tailor-made. Others are clothes' horses, consistently displaying a lottery of combinations. And then there's the rag bag.

Clothes make the (wo)man – especially in a dialogue-free visual promo. A postman's outfit makes him a postman; a police officer's outfit makes her a police officer. Of course, if they're playing an instrument or singing, it is hardly the perfect deception.

exaggeration of what they would ordinarily attire themselves with. It is likely that your musicians won't have a stylist and that you will leave them in charge of dressing themselves. If you have storyboarded and you are directing, don't let them.

This doesn't mean to say that you have to buy a new wardrobe for all of your musicians, and that they cannot be themselves and become the personality extension that you wish for the video. It means that you give them parameters within which to work, based on their existing wardrobe. If you want to show their dark side, tell them to wear black. If you want them to be flamboyant, tell them to bring in their best party frock. If you want sophistication, tell them to bring a cocktail dress or DJ.

Whatever you ask them to bring, make sure that everyone else concerned knows. There is nothing worse than a band that nearly all show up in the same thing – and one who brings in 'kind of' the same thing.

Don't leave it up to them: they are not mind-readers. While they may have some idea of what your video is about, they won't even touch your own ideas, impulse, and instinct.

Themes

The parameters change when you don't want the musicians to be themselves. This is usually when the video describes the musicians doing something else or being somebody else. It's a thematic or set-up decision, and it doesn't necessarily mean that your lead singer is dressed up as the Easter Bunny, but that they are supposed to be themselves in 30 years' time or are playing a lame gig at a dreary holiday camp. It's a question of working their personality into a different scenario.

If the theme still contains some element of their real selves, go through their wardrobes and find the missing link. If it's entirely different from their everyday look, it's likely that you'll be going out shopping. If this is the case, they will need to feel comfortable with what they are wearing. Familiarization and understanding is the key to getting the best performance out of them on the day, no matter what you want them to wear.

Set-ups

The reason that wardrobe is so integral to production design is due to the interaction between set or location and a musician dominating the frame in a frock. You are deciding whether or not that frock or frockcoat is complementing the background, is clashing with the background – or is not going to be seen at all.

Some wardrobe simply dominates the frame, obscuring even the talent and the location. Don't let this happen. Some sets can be dirty or – in a worst case scenario – dangerous. If you are aiming to put your talent in some damaging locations – even if it's just lying on the floor, let them know in case it's a problem with that sentimental or historical garb that they'll no doubt be wearing.

Busy patterns, thin stripes, or color wheel opposites with movement can cause problems with digital images. Test this before the shoot to make sure. There's never any harm in having a dress rehearsal, especially if the wardrobe is unfamiliar or potentially ill-fitting.

***ABOVE LEFT:** Wardrobe is better where the theme is flavoured by the music. Irony, contrast, or complement can all be shown visually through attire. This shoot relies on the contrast between the reality of a bar stripper and carefree glitz and kitsch. Emphasizing this is not just the talent's job or a grading task: it can all be down to wardrobe.*

***ABOVE CENTRE & ABOVE:** If your shoot is spread over more than one day, take the time to take full-length stills of any wardrobe, make-up, and hair that needs to be replicated. While continuity isn't what a music video is all about, it can be if you're editing one shot up against another.*

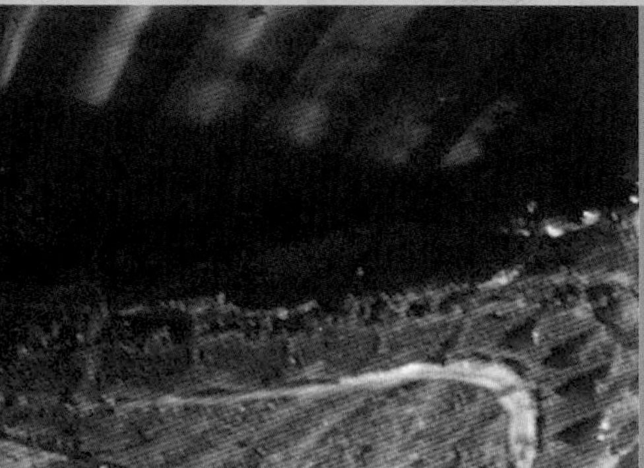

DRESSING UP: **PROPS**

Props are the third arm of the support for your production design. Along with make-up and wardrobe, they hold your set up as the believable unbelievable. Props aren't just arbitrary objects that litter the set or stop your lead from fiddling. They are the glue that holds a set – no matter how creaky or empty – together.

Your use of props for set-dressing depends on the world that you have created or the world that exists already. If you are relying on props, gathering them can be time-consuming. Always consider just how much they are going to be on display. Your musicians will always be favoured by the camera, if not filling the frame, and any prop that won't be seen, is too distracting, is too small, or that doesn't respond to any kind of interaction is probably not worth your while.

Set-dressing for the music video is not often like that of the conventional narrative, unless your music video *is* a narrative. The video focuses on belief in the musicians, not in a storyline. To shift this emphasis, sets are often sparse to let the concept shine through. If you have a good idea that centres on a shoot or edit technique, don't go in search of props that clutter or distract from the idea.

***ABOVE** Giving talent something to hold if they aren't a natural performer in front of a lens often works and sometimes doesn't. You'll always be limited by what they are prepared to do, so try to suss them out before you start throwing carcasses at them. It is your job as director to reassure them that what you are asking them to do is not going to look ridiculous.*

Locations often throw up their own incidental props. If you've been scouting and see things you need for the shoot, let somebody know to put them aside. If you're using a theatre, props come and go and may well not be there when you turn up for the shoot.

The question is always whether or not you are trying to recreate a recognized environment out of a shell. This will determine how far you'll have to go to construct the believable. If it seems too daunting, always go back to the storyboard and change it, or think laterally. Metaphoric sets are often far more interesting than the literal, and the same goes for props.

The set is predominantly about the musicians – not about the décor or what they are holding. This is why wardrobe and make-up are so important. If your concept is the as-live or sync that inspires the belief that the musicians are playing, it's likely that your lead will be holding a microphone, and the musicians their instruments. It doesn't stop there. To suspend this belief, audiences often require a little bit more – and this is where prop use gets a bit more complicated.

It's not just terminology, it's practicality and organization. The musicians need to bring everything that they would usually use for a live version of the set-up that you have in mind. This means cables, amps, speakers – anything that can be used to dress the set and exist as an authentic prop. Because these items aren't necessarily going to be used as they would in a live set, emphasize the need that they subscribe to the aesthetic or the theme. This might be bigger, shinier, historic, trashier, or trashable. Whatever works to create the visual interest.

An extension of this is the deconstructed set. This is where the props in the music video are often practical – or practicals. On a deconstructed set where the musicians are seen to be playing on a stage, or in a revealed set, you may well be purposefully showing the edge of the set in frame, the monitors, cameras, and crew. This is not warts-and-all video: it is still an artifice. In this case, the entire set, kit, lights, and crew are just as much props as they are functional, and it is important that everyone and everything is as directed and positioned as the talent.

ABOVE RIGHT: Getting the right location to shoot in can be half the battle for props. Bars serve beer by definition, which is both great for props and performances... in moderation.

RIGHT: Don't let props be a disguise for your talent unless it's part of the video. Props aren't to hide behind, they're there to help the performance, realism, or artifice of the set-up.

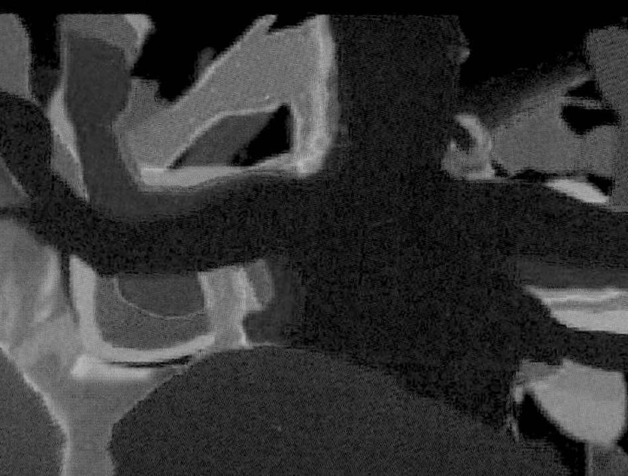

STICKING UP: **TRIPODS AND CAMERA SET-UPS**

If you are following a sensible shooting schedule, it's probably the master shot that you'll be tackling first on the shoot. If you've got a number of set-ups during the day, it'll be the first of a few. Each master shot will incorporate all the elements of the set-up that you will subsequently break down or fragment. Any shot that is going to provide this kind of guide is best undertaken with a tripod.

If you are going to do this, frame the shot to the edge of the set. This is the parameter within which the talent will be working. Static shots with tripods work a lot better with dynamic performers. Allowing the talent to strut their stuff energetically within a fixed frame allows a viewer to concentrate on the performance. In this case, the master shot can become a useful shot.

Static shots are dull unless things happen. A movie composed solely of tripod shots can maintain the interest level because it has plot and dialogue. While cinematography has progressed beyond theatre-on-film, there are plenty of instances where it is exactly that and still entertains.

A music video audience has a very low tolerance threshold for nothing happening – even if they *like* the musicians. There isn't often a plot to be found – just a series of irrelevant set-ups. Therefore, to use a static frame and keep it interesting is a challenge. While it may be down to your direction and performers to keep the frame going, you may have other ideas....

If a static shot isn't quite static, it becomes either an apparent error, or just unnerving. Cameras directly on the floor and cameras tilted from a ledge are both susceptible to movement and vibration. The spread, sticks, and head of a tripod mitigate a lot of this movement to give a stable, static shot.

Static shots with wide-angle lenses are now firmly embraced by the rap industry. A wide-angle close to a fisheye, mounted just above floor level creates 'that' look, should you wish to embrace it.

If you choose to use a static with a wide-angle, it's the set that should be your concern. It will peel off quickly to reveal the studio or surrounding area if you aren't tight or close enough.

Extreme close-ups can just look nasty if a tripod isn't used. An eye, a mouth, a plectrum – all of these things move. Adding the magnified shake of the operator and a few defocusing problems equals a rough shot at best. Locking off a camera on a tripod and engineering the action in front of it makes the shot usable for longer periods within the video.

Mise-en-scène

The Golden Section has been around a long time in the art world. In film or video it is a variation on what it once was. It has a few holidays in Hollywood and short breaks in the music video. The golden rule is that the screen is divided into nine equal parts, which are used to create a pleasurable aesthetic. This might be symmetry or non-symmetry, but it always guides the viewer to look at various part of the frame by design.

The most used aspect of the rule is the Rule Of Thirds. Staple to text on images, it can also be used with the images themselves. This rule states that things happen one-third of the way to the right, left, top, or bottom of the screen. A static camera enables the accomplishment of this a lot easier than a moving camera, and framing shots where the subject is guided by this aesthetic avoids the obvious: the tedium of centre-frame.

BELOW: Technical composition is a huge part of planning your aesthetic edit. If you know what is going where and how each part of the image interacts with the other parts, composite imaging and transitions can transform a music video from the efficient to the spectacular.

LEFT: If you are shooting to speed up in the edit, any slight repetition of camera movement (hand-held shake) will make it laughable. If you are shooting for slowmo in the edit, even one adjustment will become an entire move. Unless either of these are designed, lock-off the camera on a tripod. This will allow for whatever is happening in the frame to be a deliberate victim of speed without frame movement appearing as a comical or ill-judged mistake.

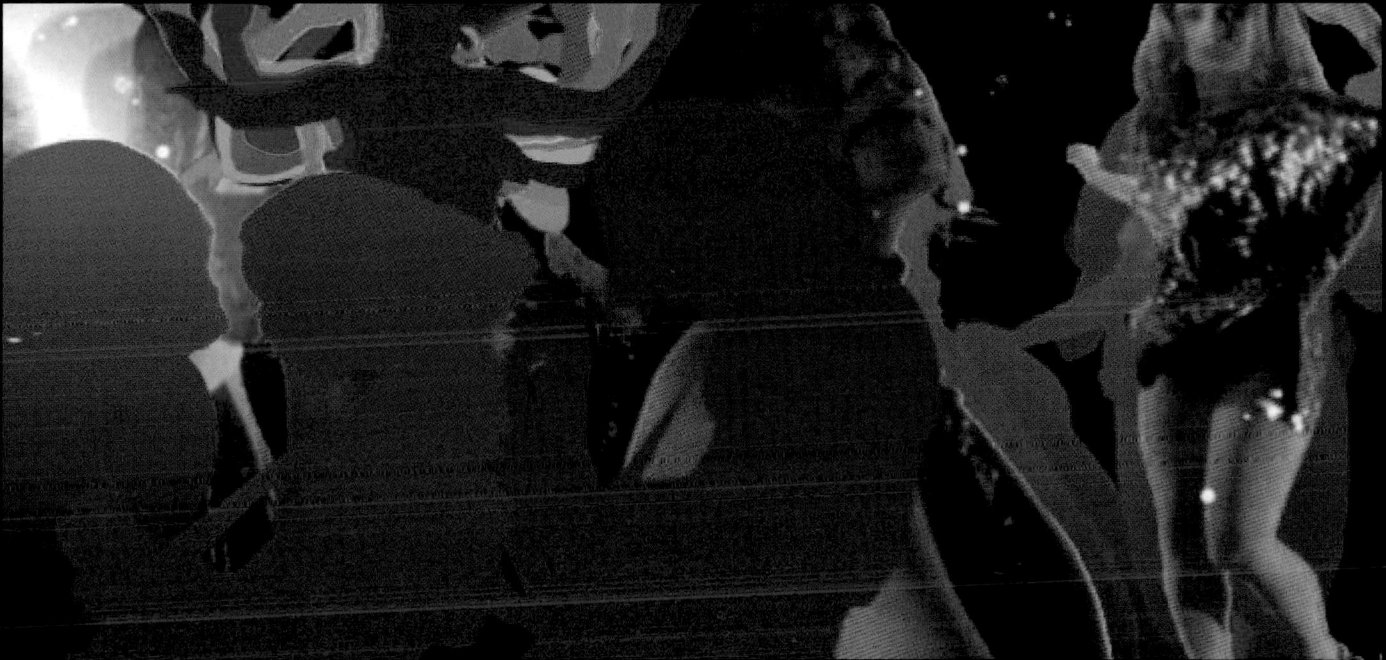

SHOOTING UP: **CAMERA ANGLES**

Before the camera even starts to move, it's got to frame exactly what you want. And if it does move, it'll re-frame constantly. To get exactly what you want, it's important to consider how a viewer responds to different framing and angles.

A viewer's response to camera angle is as it would be when watching a traditional movie, but the time spent with each shot is less. Each shot is a puzzle piece in a whole jigsaw. Unlike a full-length feature film, though, this completed jigsaw puzzle doesn't necessarily form a comprehensive picture – and it doesn't have to. It just has to be nice-looking.

In a movie you have more freedom but the music video is often concentrated around the waistline. Often this is to incorporate instruments (guitars, drums, keyboards), and equally often it is because the video fetishizes and sells sex. This is why framing is so important in music video.

The Establisher

This is the shot that establishes from the start of the video (or sometimes at the end) what is going on and where. It sets the scene.

An establisher is often a top-shot; an omniscient eye that observes the entire set-up. If the video relies on this as its main idea, it will usually put this at the end. Indeed, a lot of establishers are used as play-in and pay-off to the music video as an intro/outro sandwich: we arrive and we leave. In this respect, the establisher becomes any shot that establishes the prologue and epilogue of the story.

The Wide

A wide is usually your master shot. It is wide enough to see the musicians in their location. Viewers like to be reassured that they are seeing the complete picture. Because it includes the entirety of their body (feet to hair), it is a good way to display wardrobe if the clothes define the performer.

LEFT: An establishing shot doesn't always have to be a top-shot. It can be anything that is used to set the initial mood and scene of the video.

ABOVE LEFT: The wide shot gives the viewer the chance to see the whole setting, whether it be a concert hall or the local bar, and makes them feel like a part of the audience.

ABOVE RIGHT: A point of view shot doesn't necessarily mean that it's seen through the eyes of the subject, as this over-the-shoulder shot shows.

The Medium Shot

Medium shots operate from roughly the waist up, finishing just over the top of the head. In the music video, they may well clip the top of the head in order to reach slightly below the waist. This puts any waistline instrument or gratuitous belly or hip shots in frame.

Medium shots, of course, contain a lot more detail than wides. The detail that you want is that of the face, of the clothes, and of the action. For very physical performers, medium shots come into their own. They allow for facial expression as well as healthy space on the horizontal (specifically in 16:9) for the performer to move without leaving the camera behind.

The Extreme Close-up

Make-up at the ready: it's the XCU. There aren't many reasons to use an extreme close-up of anything unattractive in the glossy world of the music video. XCUs reveal things that perhaps an audience don't usually see or don't *want* to see.

The good and bad, therefore, is to make sure that what you are isolating (again, fetishizing) is precisely what you want to show. Eyes can be lovely in XCU, but clogging mascara or bloodshot corneas are only useful for concepts that call for the flawed or ugly. It's easy to create the unattractive in XCU. Creating the attractive is purely down to attention to detail. Mouths look better in slowmo, hands look better when you use a hand model...

The Close-up

These are mainly for sync purposes. They show the face of the singer singing or the fingers of the guitarist playing. They are particular shots that show something for a reason. The reason that you are making a music video (as far as the audience would like to think) is so that the musicians can showcase their talent. Close-ups enable viewers to believe the unbelievable: the musicians are actually singing and playing.

Because they are more likely to concentrate on faces, they are there to capture the mood of the video. Your lead might be smiling, winking, screaming, sulking – and any emotion that the performer has dictates the mood of the video for the viewer.

Close-ups make for essential cutaways. This might be a hand moving over to grasp the mic, a musician smiling, or a foot on a drum pedal. They are not only great for getting out of sync, but for pacing the music video.

The POV

The point-of-view in music video is not used at all like it is in the traditional Hollywood movie. In the movies, it is used predominantly to disguise an individual or to allude to audience incrimination. In music video, you are not hiding your musician.

A POV in music video is generally used as a cutaway from an as-live. It will aim to the audience, it will be wide and maybe have some stage-light flare. If it isn't officially a POV, it's an over-the-shoulder or reverse angle. This removes implication and replaces with intimacy.

You shouldn't use *all* of these shots, but there should be variant shots, and these have to progress. Conventional progression goes from description (establisher, wide) to emotion (close-up, extreme close-up), and each is cut against medium shots to get there over time. In the music video where anything goes, it can become a framing free-for-all. Don't let it; have some kind of control.

***ABOVE LEFT:** The medium shot is a good choice for showing the lead as the focus, but also including the other band members.*

***ABOVE CENTRE:** The close-up is there to highlight the band's talents. It's also a great shot for short links between longer sequences.*

***ABOVE RIGHT:** The extreme close-up, rather perversely, often makes the viewer feel more detached from the performance. It lends a slightly surreal edge to the video.*

In-camera

In-camera moves are the zoom or push, and the pull-out or pull. Without any other movement involved, this can be a static shot that moves from a wider frame to a tighter frame, and vice versa, with the centre as focus. These types of shots are not popular in the music video. They can look like home video because that tempting little button is exactly what tentative home video users tend to play with.

Crash zooms are used a lot more in the music video. These are sudden – and sometimes subject-hunting – propulsions from the wide to the tight, or indeed a tight to a wide to reveal the 'bigger picture'. They are dynamic shots – and, if used with slowmo – can be dramatic to boot.

MOVING UP: **CAMERA MOVES AND RIGS**

Tripods can be the death of a music video that doesn't have the strength to support itself as four minutes of entertainment. If you've got a lame idea, not enough shots, or uninteresting musicians, just keep the camera moving.

Hopefully, you won't be moving the camera around just to detract from a dull concept, but you'll be working with the shot. When you get into the edit, it's going to rely on pace and progression – and while this is down to progression of themes and pace of editing, it is most visibly demonstrated in the camera move.

This means that you are shooting to edit: there is no other way to do it properly. If you know how your camera will move through the shots, it will make more sense in the edit. Your camera is the transitioning thread throughout the course of the video – and it's the first chance that you have to get the video going.

Camera moves can be undertaken in many ways, and in many combinations. The most immediate is from the body or a tripod, and it goes all the way to dollies, arms, cranes, and gyros. There are essentially three ways that a shot moves:

***TOP:** Anything Available. The AA for camera ops is one that means bunging a note to the resident of a flat for a top shot, to a cherry picker operator in a warehouse – or to the driver of a tuk tuk... Everyone has a price; don't be shy to ask.*

***ABOVE RIGHT:** Camera rigs don't have to be expensive. If you've got a crew member (or bouncer) with broad shoulders, get yourself a ride; it won't be a smooth one, but you'll get a shot...*

Pivot

Pivot moves are where the camera remains on the spot and moves in a direction while pivoting from the centre of the camera body. A vertical move is a *tilt*, and a horizontal move is a *pan*.

For the music video, tilts are best used with the camera away from eye level. From the floor, it can tilt up to show the musician above; from the brow, it can tilt down to the instrument or mic. Pans, on the other hand, are (like zooms) a little too *World's Funniest Home Videos*. *Whip-pans* are the x-axis version of the z-axis crash zoom. They are fast, furious, dynamic, and usually work as a transition from one shot cut invisibly to the next.

Physical

Physical moves take the camera from one place to another to form the shot. The easiest way is with a hand-held shot that takes the shot from one position within reach to another. This sounds basic, but it's a

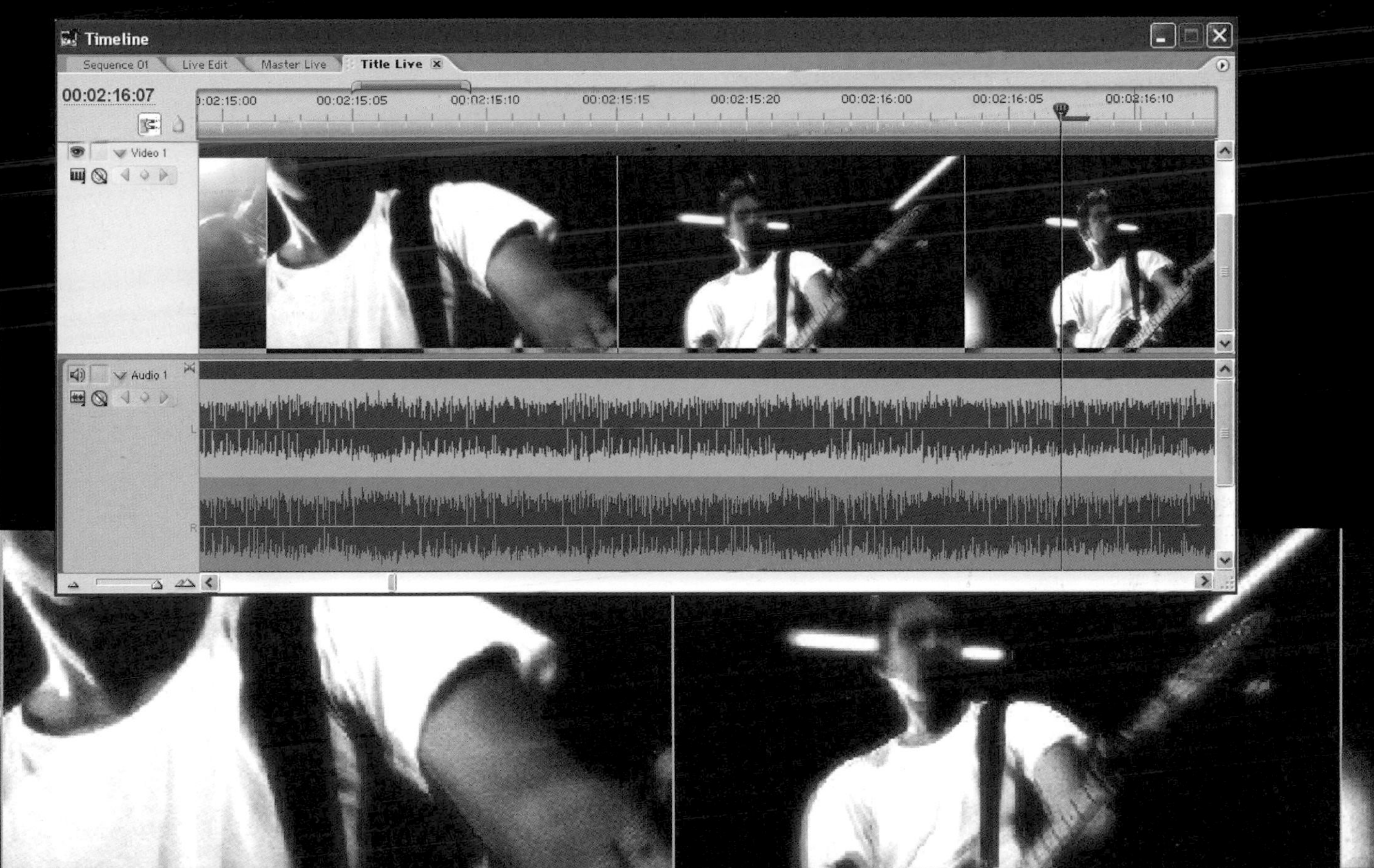

***ABOVE:* For dynamism, pull-outs work. They only work, though, if they are short, sharp, and not pregnant at the beginning and end – unless the pull-out accompanies a music phrase or sound in the middle. If you're going to use them, a visual echo is often a good way around it to make the shot have some pretension to the professional.**

classic sexy move in the music video – a gentle glide across the lead during sync. It's hardly noticeable, but it creates *that* moment.

Using perambulation, the hand-held can become a make-shift Steadicam. It's not perfect, which is why short bursts in the video are enough. Emphasizing this kind of body movement can be achieved by fastmo or turning off any anti-shake feature. Steadicam re-defined the camera move, although it still hasn't been invested in with the music video as it has with the movie. This eliminates all sharp body movement with gyros by compensating. The reason that it's easy to get away with *not* renting expensive gear and using it, is that it works so much better with long shots – something that the music video isn't so keen on.

Instead, the dolly is far more utilized. Again, expensive to rent, but with cool results when taking the camera on an impossibly smooth journey along either x-axis or z-axis. A dolly is a weighted tripod on tracks that offers these options. If you want to emulate this effect, skateboards or wheeled spreads on a tripod running on underlay can do it… to an extent.

Cranes and jibs are best left until you've got insurance. It's likely that you won't be with your kit when it disappears up into the rafters. If you are, you've got a cherry-picker – something that works for omniscience of the set-up, but is slow, and often jerky enough to preclude a smooth fastmo.

This doesn't even touch the combination of moves: a tilt down to compensate a crane up with a slight push and a pull-focus, anyone? They're all there to make sure that whatever you create is unique. There are plenty of average music videos out there but there really is no excuse with all of these options. Watch any music video, and look out for all these moves one after the other to discover how it creates the pace. If you've storyboarded well enough, it will eventually pay off in the edit.

LOCKING UP: **LOCK-OFFS**

Whether you're shooting in the studio or shooting live, you'll always be grateful that you kept a camera locked off – that is, set sturdy on a tripod with a fixed frame and settings, with your tape rolling away until it finishes. In the studio the tripod can be reset and reshot – something that cannot always be done at a live gig or event. For that reason, the lock-off for a live gig becomes an essential tool.

It's all very well getting excited about shooting your music video: that excitement can be over very quickly when it comes to the edit, if you don't have the tools to cut what you want.

A lock-off gives you your master shot – a resource to cut back to, whether synching sound or live. It's your master cutaway, in effect. With a gig, the master shot should be wide enough to incorporate all band members and locate them on stage with an extent of audience. Those are the three factors that need to be within the shot. The master shot in such a set-up is all the more useful for being lip indistinct. Lip-sync is the most tell-tale sign of a bad edit, but there's no risk of that in this case.

Within a studio or controlled set, the lock-off as master shot shows its other value: as a reference. A wide, here, is as much as you can keep contained in the shot without making the shot redundant. The shot will become void as soon as the edge of set, lighting, crew, and reflections show themselves within the ratio image. While this can be used within the edit itself, it makes the perfect guide track to edit everything else by.

LEFT: Servo intrusion is anything that causes the camera to stop functioning physically. It also stops if it's stolen. This lock-off shot was a problem all of its own due to the amount of people squeezed into the bar. An hour's gig: an hour's tape. The tape had to be started as soon as the band started – but both camera ops had to be located elsewhere at this time. Allocating a bouncer to one of the camera ops and getting him through the crowd at the last moment to put the camera up and roll it required nothing but brute force.

ABOVE LEFT & RIGHT: Not wishing to lose any of the gig, the bouncer gives the camera op a piggyback ride to his position on stage. The camera op shoots it as a roaming top shot that made it into the video (not from the master shot…).

The basic plus of a lock-off is that it gives you an extra shot without an extra camera op. By proxy, the practical side of a lock-off is avoidance of interruption while it does its own thing. Interruption fundamentally consists of three types of intrusion: audio, visual, and servo.

Audio intrusion is the placement of the camera near to interrupting audio sources. If you're shooting sync to a pre-recorded track, this is of no concern. If you're shooting live, any parts of audio are going to be of use – *really*, they'll be useful. A waste of a camera's audio track in this case is a waste of a third of your potential, and can be highly regrettable during the edit. Set the camera on the tripod as high as you can take it. This doesn't mean extend the legs as far as they can go, but rather find an opportune place (or get one built) where the camera can record audio away from immediate sources.

A lively audience is a great thing to record: it's one of the reasons why a live lock-off audio track is a huge benefit to an editor. The worst thing that an audio track can have is the loutish screaming of one individual – and yes, they're usually at the back. Setting the audio high not only balances *that* individual with their surrounding audience, but relieves the audio track of excessive bass that is noticeable from lower proximities. If a higher-set camera is the wrong framing for your master shot, take an external mic and secure it from an elevation, ensuring that the camera is recording it solely on both channels.

Audiences (or crew) aside, kit interference can ruin your audio. Look to place the camera away from amps and speakers. While feedback is highly noticeable through the speakers, any hum or hiss on your tape won't be discovered until it's too late.

Setting the camera in a lofty position helps avoid visual intrusion as well. Again, while some semblance of an audience is a good thing to have in shot, an audience that obscures the band themselves is not – certainly not as a master shot. What you also need to look out for is lighting. While a flare in the lens can be mightily effective, again, if it's repetitive within a master shot (and if the lights are computer-operated, then they may constantly repeat the move), leaving you with far less useful coverage for the edit.

Visual intrusion, though, isn't just in front of the lens. Vibration from bass can completely void the entire shot. Adjacent speakers are often to blame, but even an audience on a floating floor can do the damage.

ABOVE TOP: *The master lock-off can make for the perfect cutaway. Keep the master track running along one so you can cut back to it whenever you're missing a shot. Acting as a guide, it will always be there as a video and – sometimes more importantly – an audio reference.*

ABOVE LEFT: *Remember: even if your master lock-off is shot from one position with a fixed frame, it can change in the edit. Just by adding video effects and motion within the clip, every cut to the lock-off can take on the appearance of a different shot. This version has been subject to a monochrome gaussian blur on the vertical…*

ABOVE RIGHT: *…while a combination of techniques (greenscreen keying a superimposed night vision shot, with a blue and green tint to the whites and blacks of the zoomed monochrome master…) turns the inoffensive lock-off into something effectively ghastly.*

REHEARSING

With any lock-off, rehearse with cans on before locking off. Set the correct ratio, shutter, and aperture settings with all crew, lighting, and band members operational to ensure that you're getting the right shot. Listen to the audio, checking and adjusting volume with the loudest track that the band will play. If the shot's not right, think about using an external mic and make the shot and audio work for you. Always remember that it's your shoot: it's not the band's rehearsal. On a shoot day, without you, they're nothing…

Servo intrusion can be due to combinations of any of the above – or worse still, just down to the fact that you didn't put enough tape in, or didn't charge the battery fully. Editing is too fraught a process without hating yourself into the bargain. Always have a battery fully charged and always put a new tape in, no matter if the track is three minutes long. Shooting from rehearsal to audience/crew arrival to takes to restarts isn't going to do any harm. And speeding the entire process up as a lock-off may even be the effect that you want.

RIGHT: Never be afraid to show what you're shooting. If you're editing bold, you don't want to be shooting coy. Huge exposure can be terrific with mid-range temperature lighting.

BELOW: Some lighting moods cannot be better than those that you have. These stage lights are hot, the sweat is hotter and the beer is scorching. The combination of all three and a camera setting with a small aperture captures the set-up immaculately.

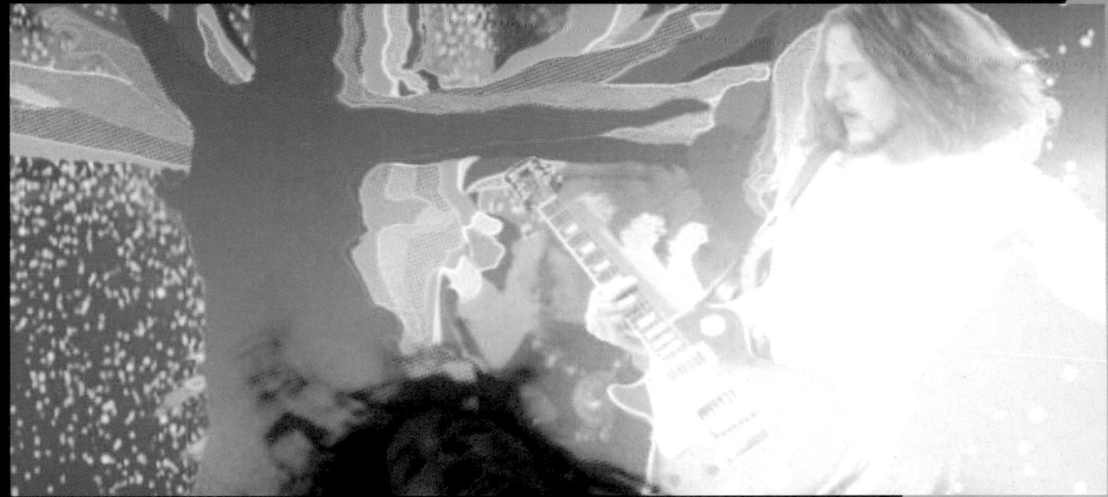

BRIGHTENING UP: **LIGHTING THE SET**

Your video-editing tools can add colour and limited lighting-based effects to your clips after the shoot is over. However, without careful manipulation of your light sources during the shoot, your editing app won't be able to save what will be a series of lacklustre images.

When lighting your set, revisit what you've established: without light you won't have an image. Light has direction, quantity, quality, and colour. Without changing these values, you won't have mood.

THREE-POINT LIGHTING

To recreate a real world, a studio shoot conventionally starts from darkness and works up.

> Components of three-point lighting: a backlight that floods the background
> A key light that illuminates the subject
> A fill to compensate for the shadow cast by the key

backlight
subject
key
fill
camera

Real life is full of different light sources. It needs to be so that we can see. The real world has lamps, candles, spotlights, headlights. When these are inserted into the set, they're called *practicals*. These are any additional light sources that are there to add to the reality, but not specifically to light the set.

If you are using practicals like this, you will often find that they don't offer the direction, quantity, quality, or colour that create the mood. Hiding your more powerful lights on set, or by using deflectors or foils on those off-set *recreates* the realism of these practicals.

The other kind of practical to light up everyday lives, are those things that enable and warn. On a darkened set, these are often emulated. They might be a computer monitor, a television screen, a fire, paramedic flashing light, or even just light thrown in from a window or doorway. These effect lights are something that music video doesn't just emulate, but exaggerates and builds on.

The reason for this is that the music video *doesn't* often work within the real world, and more often than not, it chooses to distort it or blow it up completely. It's not a complete farewell to three point lighting, though. Concealing (shadow), insinuating or threatening (low-light), or screaming (high exposure) are all part of exaggerated mood, and these can all be delivered by three-point.

When you are working with lights, keep your zebras on the camera and study the frame or the move. If you are moving the camera, turn off any automatic neutral density filter. This has a habit of kicking in and completely changing the look of your image with any camera move from dark to light or light to dark. If you do have a move that requires a

different exposure in the same shot, don't rely on an automatic exposure to change it smoothly. It will often overshoot and adjust itself back into check. It looks amateur, at best.

If you have this issue, think about an invisible edit during a whip-pan, or shooting it slow, adjusting the exposure as you go, and speeding the shot up in the edit. When you have lights at your disposal, there shouldn't be any need to up your *gain*. If you do get tempted, remember that it adds noise to the entire image.

Lights on set can be harsh, and high contrast can often betray the flatness of video. Bouncing light with *scrims* which might be black-painted foil or simply a white board, throws a more balanced light around the set. Alternatively, using diffusers on direct lights softens the reflections of the light and causes less contrast. The more lights that you can do this with, the more form you can create, and your set will benefit from depth, if that is what you want.

Party gels can also add to the design of your lighting. Primary, secondary, and every colour in between can be used to control the colour saturation of any light in shot. Work *with* the colour temperature of the lights. If you want to correct the colour from lights, use colour-correction gels or camera filters – but make sure that you white balance first.

Party gels, because of the nature of the plastic – can also be hand-operated to ripple in front of a light to create movement of colour on subjects or objects. Sweeping hands in front of blue gels create the illusion of an off-set television, and doing this with deep orange gels alludes to fire.

Romantic watery reflections on ballad-singing subjects in the music video are the product of refracted light from broken mirrors in shallow water. Manipulating unpainted foil as a reflector can effect a subtle movement of light on faces, also.

So, if your performers aren't animated enough, don't just move the camera – move the lights, too...

***ABOVE:** The same strong effect works vibrantly with natural light. Blues from UV can be brought out to prove that in terms of lighting, there is really nothing new under the sun that is better than the sun.*

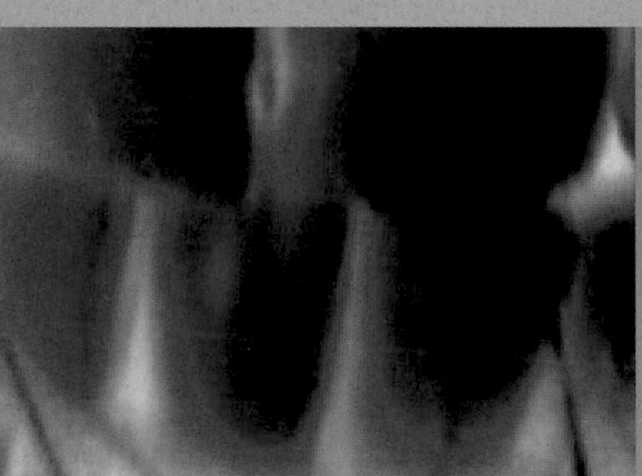

SYNCHING UP: **LIP AND INSTRUMENT MIME, SLOWMO, AND FASTMO**

Synching on set is one of those things that is incredibly easy in concept but incredibly complicated in practice. You are trying to create the believable: your artist is singing and the musicians are playing. Your vocalist should be well-rehearsed in miming, and should know the song inside out. It's another matter completely, however, when they are working for slowmo and fastmo.

In order to achieve speed and slowmo in the edit, you have to work against it on set. The benefit of shooting sync as slowmo is that the performer is given a slightly sexier image. Physical movement, hair, clothes, and sync are all given a dreamy makeover. The more exaggerated you want this, the more speed the performer will have to mime to.

Slowmo in the edit at half speed is 200% speed on set; slowmo in the edit at an eighth speed is 800%. It is unlikely that your performer will be able to mime at much more than 400% speed on set without you losing conviction of performance in the edit.

Miming at speed requires only the mouth to move, and while your vocalist may wish to sing to keep themself in rhythm, it becomes impossible to eject sound at the same time with higher speeds. Worse still are breathing patterns, which change completely, and often give the game away in the edit.

***TOP:** Miming to a slowmo track is equally hard to hear at drastically reduced percentages. Again, maintaining pitch helps, but the bonus is that there are no physical delivery issues. For musicians, like this drummer, any mistakes are likely to be timing-related – and this is something to be fixed in the edit when shooting slowmo for speed. Tailoring your speed to the music is the fix-it option.*

***ABOVE LEFT:** For vocals, the things that you will want to watch out for is that the performer matches body movement with the speed of their mouth moving – i.e. at 25% speed, you are asking the performer to take four times the amount of time it would normally take to move their head or hand. Breathing patterns too, give the game away in the edit – and this control is hard for the performer. Shooting tighter, using wardrobe or planning a masking effect in the edit will help disguise the throat, where the tell-tale signs show.*

Unless you're using a long shot and the performer's mouth has to be exaggerated, then the easiest way to mime to speed is to keep the teeth slightly parted so that you can see the tongue move behind, move the throat, and form the words with the lips over the top. Keeping this medium point of movement as a neutral allows for the least amount of time taken for all silent syllable and vowel pronunciations. In this way, the artist can keep in time either by singing through their teeth or by humming through their nose. On set, this sounds a little like a didjeridoo, but it works in the edit.

For miming at greater speeds, it is usually the intro for which the performers will require the most guidance. This is because music at higher speeds – especially with compression involved – sounds very different. Try to play the music at speed without losing pitch to keep the octaves familiar. A lot of editors and sequencers have a facility for pitch-friendly tempo increases.

ABOVE LEFT: This sequence was mimed in reverse as the performer walked backwards. It's 100% speed to mitigate complete disaster, but still required the artist to learn her chorus played in reverse. It's hard to perform and requires practice – but is nevertheless possible.

ABOVE CENTRE: Many takes and cutaways are handy with this kind of set-up, so make sure you get them. It's not often practical to use playback in reverse on location to ensure that you've got exactly what you want. Cutaways and alternate versions will cover any flaws in the mime.

ABOVE RIGHT: Mime and action on a hot set or busy location can be distracting for an artist – and, again, the cracks may show in the edit. If your performer is having difficulties, try to eliminate any action that they have to undertake at the same time, and either use an out of frame operator, or give the action to someone who isn't miming.

The playing of the music itself is much harder to mime to at speed. For instruments that use dextrous skills, it can be simply impossible. Signal response and physicality are the two factors that will impress their own time limits on speed. This is the reason that most music videos only ever use slowmo on the lead singer.

Miming slowmo on set for speed in the edit usually only happens in videos that market to a harder audience. Speeding up slowmo to 100% emphasizes jagged mouth movement and jerky body movement, and is sometimes used for increasing speed in the action around the vocalist while they appear to sing at normal speed. This is usually only undertaken where it is impossible to detach the vocalist from the background for a key. With this set-up it is a lot easier to negotiate vocalist and background speeds by shooting one for slowmo and one for fastmo. The composite creates the medium that emphasizes the difference.

ABOVE: For sync, keep the music source as close to the talent as possible. The human ear concentrates on the nearest or loudest sound available and this will help your artist keep that concentration going throughout the most ludicrous of direction…

ABOVE & RIGHT: Decide how you want to play the sync. There are always at least two options: to the viewer or not. Breaking the fourth wall depends very much on the lyrical content. If the sync lyric is contemplative, it makes sense that they are looking to themselves. If it is confrontational, then delivering it to the lens or insinuating an audience is absolutely right. Breaking walls is breaking rules, of course – something that the music video does very well. Incorporating both perspectives won't harm your video at all.

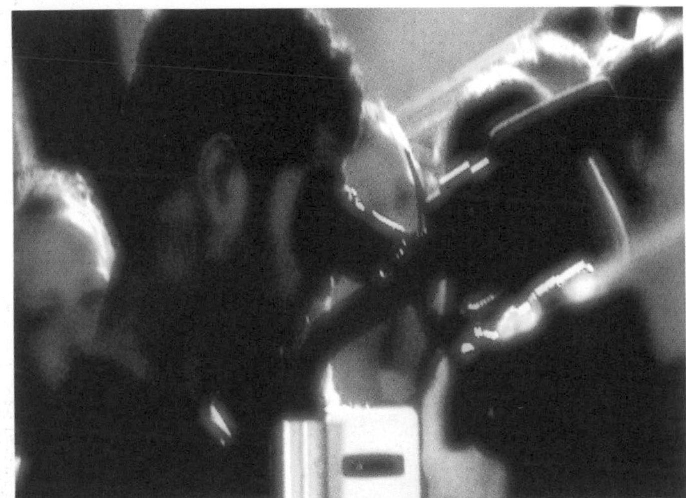

LIVENING UP: **SHOOTING LIVE**

When sound is recorded, broadcast, or played through a PA system, the dynamic range must be restricted at some point due to the peak signal limitations of the electronic system, artistic goals, surrounding environmental requirements, or a combination of all of these.

Typically, dynamic range must be compressed because, for artistic reasons, the singer's voice will have a higher average loudness, and compression allows vocalizations such as melismatic phrasing and glottal stops to be heard better when the vocal track is mixed within a dense pop record track. With recording, the dynamic range may be too large to be processed by succeeding recording equipment and recording media. Even with the arrival of 90dB-plus dynamic range of digital recording, huge and unexpected swings of level from synthesizers and heavily processed musical instruments can overwhelm analogue-to-digital converters, distorting the recording.

Shooting live can be a dangerous game. Any shoot offers a certain amount of unpredictability, but a live shoot serves up an entire smorgasbord of confliction. The plus side is that once you've planned and organized, you can only hand yourself over to the music gods of fate and serendipity. It's a short, sharp shoot.

A live shoot is where the instruments and any vocals are performed without mime and the performed track used in the edit as the master audio. Both video and audio in a live shoot have their own challenges.

To tackle them separately, the main issue with video is getting enough coverage. A live performance happens once. Even if it performed again, it won't be exactly the same as the first performance – and this is the advantage for both a live audience and a live band. It's fresh, unpredictable, and interactive.

The live performance is often undertaken as part of another agenda – and it's usually a gig. Aside from the political and financial implications of commanding authority with a set-up that is merely tolerated, if not obtrusive, there are the practical challenges of the shoot. How do you get from one

***ABOVE LEFT:** It is your right to do the best job you can, and your privilege to always put a camera op at the front of the stage. Make sure that they set a tripod there to maintain the space if there isn't sole access. Don't accept any compromises, just as the musicians won't accept any video imitations…*

***ABOVE RIGHT:** Make sure that security know you and you have the right passes to access all areas. Backstage soundbites and cutaways can make your live music video come to life.*

side of the stage to another? Are you in the way of the audience? Do you require different lighting? Do you have the right to choreograph the performance? Are you responsible for distributing release forms to a 400-strong audience? The questions are endless, and the only way of realistically tackling a shoot of a performance in front of a live audience is to have as much information at your fingertips as possible in order that you can anticipate on the day.

None of these variables helps the video shoot of a live performance where control of every aspect – including the performance (over which a director cannot expect to have control) – is the essence and key to success. This is why it's a question of silk purses rather than shooting to edit.

output of the mixer. Jacks, though, won't give you the most amazing quality, purely because of bandwidth. They also tend to pop out easily. The alternative is XLRs – and high-end cameras will offer this. If you're tempted to use an XLR adaptor to your mini-jack, it's even more likely to disconnect or crackle.

All of these can quickly become cabling nightmares, especially with an audience and a master shot that is taken from behind them. Secure everything with gaffer tape, and try to get as close to the mixing desk as possible. The mixer has to output digitally with a peak of 0Db – anything over will distort horribly. It's better if this is a sub-mixer from the master that is specifically tailored for input to that camera.

The best thing that you can hope for with a live shoot is enough coverage to get you through the edit. A live shoot is not an excuse for a dull one-shot video. The best deployment of crew is to lock-off a master shot and have two hand-held cameras as shot/reverse shot. This will give you the angles that you need to cut together.

While music videos can break space and time rules, they won't if you are shooting live. If you do, it breaks the believable truth – and thereby makes the object of the shoot redundant.

Audio challenges are huge for live performances. They are hard enough for engineers, let alone the fact that that one performance's audio has to be perfect from start to end for you to cut to. What you will want is not a DAT recording of the performance, but a direct feed to the locked-off master shot. Some cameras are not equipped to deal with this properly. Your audio input is likely to be a stereo mini-jack that will need adapting from the jack

The audio and video together from a live performance throws up one important issue: sync. The reason that you don't want to work from DAT is that – just like DV – it is tape. Tape stretches, heads clog, and dropout occurs—another hearty vote for coverage on your video. With one audio track, of one performance, it has to be perfect. Nothing is perfect. It is highly unlikely that the DAT, run from beginning to end, will end up in the same position as the master shot running from beginning to end. This might just be a noticeable frame or two in the middle, but by the end, slippage becomes unacceptable. Likewise, this starts as a niggle in the edit, but just gets more agitated (as you will) as the timeline progresses. If there is any slippage, it's a lot easier if the visuals slip with it…

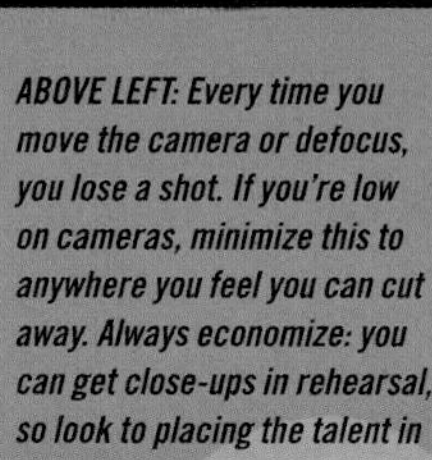

***ABOVE LEFT:** Every time you move the camera or defocus, you lose a shot. If you're low on cameras, minimize this to anywhere you feel you can cut away. Always economize: you can get close-ups in rehearsal, so look to placing the talent in their environment.*

***ABOVE RIGHT:** Above all, if it's live, try to capture the spirit of the event and any energy in the location. This is, of course, very difficult – but it is the lifeblood of the live performance.*

FILLING UP: **THE 8 BAR**

Uh-oh, here it comes: that annoying little dancey 8 bar halfway through the track that you can't cover with anything. The singer looks ridiculous not singing and you've done all your close-ups of the rest of the band. What are you going to do to stop viewers from switching off?

ABOVE LEFT: *8 bars, as conventional music interludes, provide a moment for the visuals to breathe. This might be to emphasize the rhythm…*

ABOVE RIGHT: *…or to progress the storyline using any dialogue that you might have to add.*

Well, you would have known about this moment for quite some time and have probably storyboarded it. That's fine. If you haven't, it might well be an edit job.

Shoot ratio is the amount that you shoot versus the amount that you cut together in the edit. The more experienced you are, the more likely that your ratio will be smaller. Filling an 8 bar can be a whole lot easier sometimes if you *are* inexperienced.

The reason for this is that your large ratio will leave you a whole load of shots and angles that you aren't using. These are what you can use to fill an eight bar. It's a question of balance. If the shots aren't that good, then it's up to you to make an audience believe that they have intentionally made it into the cut. Audio is going to help you here.

Cutting poor shots brilliantly to audio will disguise the fact that they're so lame. Don't worry: effects will do the rest.

8 bars exist to relieve the singer of duty and to showcase the musicians and their talent. Because it is a relief from the hook and the lyric, it's a chance to do something completely different with the music video – and get away with it. Because there is no space and timeline in the videoscape, you can go anywhere in these 8 bars.

If you've got rehearsals, take the time to go back in time. Giving them a completely different look also helps to consolidate the fact that the shots are entirely different from the rest of the video.

There's still hope even if you don't have these offcuts to play with: go out and shoot something else. If you haven't the time, look around your immediate vicinity. Some graces are saved simply by having the camera you're using for capture at hand. If your surroundings are ordinary, there are

plenty of ways to make them interesting. It takes an artist's eye to see the other side of life, but the camera's not so bad at it either, given a wide-angle, telephoto, or macro lens.

Remember that you are not alone in having to kill time. The lead singer is doing it, too. There are a lot of fantastic music videos that ignore the sync of the musicians playing and concentrate instead on the idling lead. If you're on the shoot, it doesn't even mean that you have to encourage them to perform during this time. An idling or genuinely bored singer can be just as interesting to watch as one who is acting up.

When you're on the shoot, look for those moments that give musicians a chance to be natural. Arrival on set, in the make-up chair, waiting for the set to be rigged, having lunch – all of these will be an insight into the *real* personalities of the talent. Smothered with a reality cam effect it becomes an utterly convincing wallpaper.

Whatever it is that you fill the gap with, it cannot be a turn-off. It either has to be interesting or have an aesthetic. 8 bars are not long but they give you a chance for intricate cutting, knowing that there is a definite end to your trials. This given time is also not long enough for an audience to reach irritation point. This makes it perfect for any repeated effect that you've hit upon that would ordinarily grate. Better still, it excuses – if not welcomes – the fact that it *is* repetitive.

An 8 bar is the perfect time to win over an audience because it *is* different. With as-live videos, the tendency is to keep the lead's sync going no matter what. However you've shot it, it can become very one-flavoured and the 8 bar provides an opportunity to break from the standard visuals and add a bit of spice to the mix.

ABOVE LEFT: Traditionally for as-lives, 8 bars provide a moment for demonstrating believable skills, avoiding the trap of smug glances between musicians...

ABOVE: ...or for a spot of dancing...

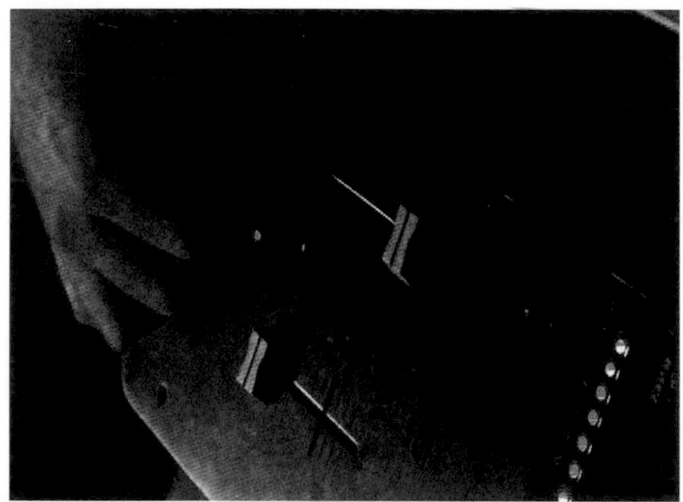

COVERING UP: **CUTAWAYS AND COVERAGE**

Cutaways aren't just filler for your tum-de-dum 8 bar. A cutaway is any shot that takes you away from the master shot or your set-up to break up the scene.

Cutaways are used for many different reasons in many different genres. The most important thing about them is that they are *practical*. A cutaway in the Hollywood movie allows room for dialogue. A cutaway in broadcast television allows seamless cuts to be made as the news item is shortened throughout the course of daily bulletins.

Both of these genres use the cutaway to make sense of a sequence. The language of cinema and television is such that the viewer can make sense of a story if it is told with visual logic. Visual logic is the transition from establisher to wide to medium to close-up; it is the 180° rule (only shoot dialogue sequences from one side of the two-hander); it is the reassuring use of cuts to let the viewer watch and understand without distraction, jump-cuts, or any change that will break their concentration and understanding.

The music video operates without logic, breaking rules, logic, narrative, and operating in a timeless, spaceless videoscape. Cutaways become something entirely different...

...almost. Shooting sync doesn't always go to plan – especially with talent miming for speed or slowmo. Cutaways become nigh on essential for live or as-lives. The last bastion of the cutaway is to wallpaper over cracks. And this is perfect for sync.

When you're shooting, *always* shoot cutaways. It doesn't have to be composed or contrived; it can be a wobbly, badly focused, accidental shot of your talent's nose and it'll still get you out of a hole.

Cutaways don't last very long on screen. A second – maybe three in a music video – but not long. If the shot that you have to cover bad sync is even shorter than that, there's always slowmo. Slowmo cutaways, though, are very 'eighties' video, and a nose shot is meaningless – but this is the worst case scenario.

***LEFT:** The cymbal hit: a great 18-frame sting for visual rhythm.*

***ABOVE LEFT:** The mixer: a visual slide to anticipate a transition.*

***ABOVE RIGHT:** The scratch disk: anticipate a reverse shot, or perhaps use slowmo or speed.*

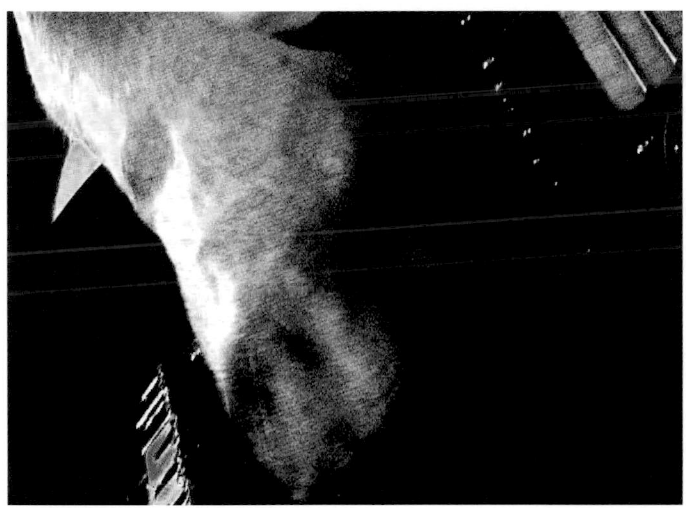

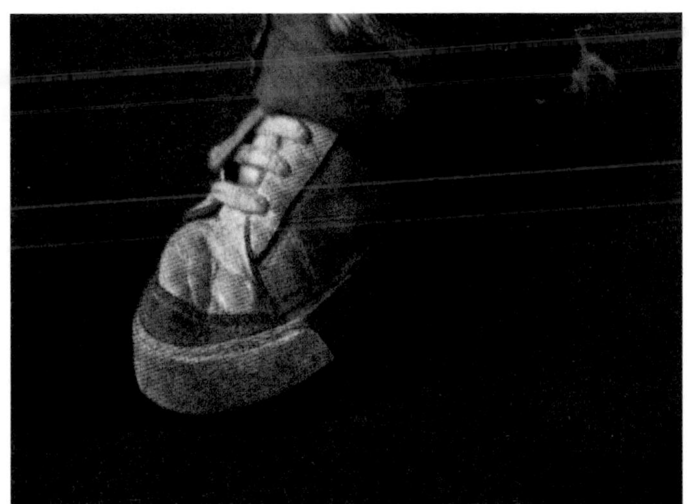

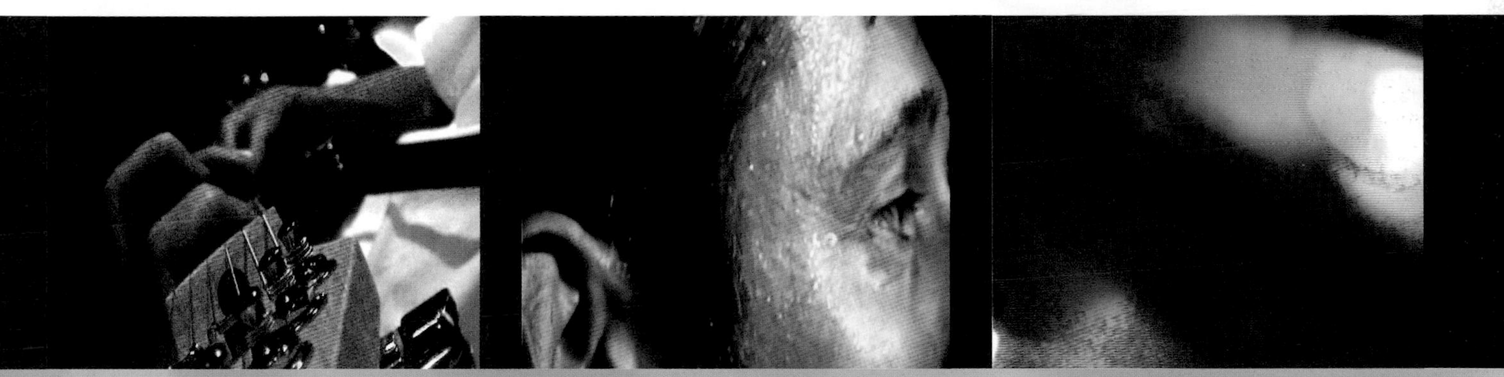

Cutaways in the music video, aren't just for sync papering. They can pace the video, anticipate transitions and evoke belief in the unbelievable by showing detail. Practical? Useful? Aesthetic, even? Bring 'em on...

TOP LEFT: The dextrous hand or pickfinger: an insight into technical artistry.

TOP RIGHT: A tapping foot: a bit grandad, but emphasizes rhythm (and provides an opportunity for a lucrative deal with Nike).

ABOVE LEFT: The guitar POV: cliché, obligatory, but classy with a focus pull and wide-angle.

ABOVE CENTRE: The eyes: a device to make sense of a change in perspective.

ABOVE RIGHT: The lights: breaking stage lights with foreground action creates rhythm and anticipates wipes.

RIGHT: The meaningless blur: best as a whip pan, this can describe sound and aid transitions.

RIGHT BOTTOM: The audience: without them, both you and the musicians are nothing...

WHAT YOU SHOULD END UP WITH

Everything that you need is:

- **> Every shot on your storyboard**
- **> Your master shot**
- **> An establisher – even if it's not storyboarded**
- **> A Martini shot as an alternative ending**
- **> Cutaways of every talent performing physically in make-up, wardrobe and on location**
- **> Cutaways of the set, and the set or location reverse shot**
- **> Get two minutes of atmosphere whether you need it or not**
- **> Head and shoulder portraits and full-length stills of every talent in make-up and wardrobe (but not necessarily on location)**

WRAPPING UP: **FINISHING THE SHOOT AND TROUBLESHOOTING**

When you call wrap, mean it. Only call it when you've got everything that you want from your day. Nobody wants to restart once you've said it, and if you forget anything, you won't want to start organizing re-shoots.

Calling wrap is usually the start of a psychotic rush to get to the nearest beer. In this rush, no piece of equipment ever fits the container it came in, and if it does, it won't be there when you get home. It is also the time that wardrobe is damaged and the general housekeeping and care that you came in through the door with goes out of the window. It may sound obvious, but a bit of organization here can help to ensure that everything has been done properly.

Director

Importantly, you are responsible for everything that you have shot. Get the tapes – including that one that is still in the camera – safety tab them, and make sure that they are all written up on the tape and the box. Those little tapes, after all, are the point of the day.

Your second priority is the talent. You must debrief them, thank them, congratulate them on their performances, and give them detailed instructions with regards to what you want them to do next, and how, where, and when this must occur.

Producer

While the crew is striking, the director will want to make sure that any necessary release forms have been signed and filed. The producer, in his or her most ferociously efficient way, will be organizing this. It's really handy to have a producer on set – and not least when the time comes to strike.

All paperwork for crew and talent can be handled by the producer at the end of the day. Shooting schedules, timesheets – and most importantly, the retrieval of all receipts from each and every crew member and musician who was involved in that day's shoot.

FAR LEFT & LEFT: Three little words can turn tension to party time – and this is precisely why you have to say it only when you mean it.

BELOW: Wrapping is not just when you are happy, it is when your crew and talent are happy, too. If they feel that they could have done better, then take or make the time to make your music video better.

Crew

Striking set needs to be undertaken as methodically as the rigging was. Lead the talent off set first and then strike. Make sure that cables don't just get thrown in a bag; lenses don't just get squeezed into the camera case. Do it badly and further shoots will take forever to set up. The last thing that you're likely to do when you get home is reorganize everything – and if you don't do it *then*, you won't do it until the next shoot – until you're cursing your crew for being so slow and not having everything at their fingertips: yes, *that* next shoot…

If you're renting gear, concern yourself more with not giving your own stuff away when returning the rented gear than returning the gear itself.

Art Department

A lot of this is probably your property, or your responsibility. Make sure that you walk away from the shoot with everything that you brought and that is yours. This includes make-up, wardrobe, and props to add to your growing collection.

Comb out wigs before they start to knot, and make sure any prosthetics are removed without tearing for future use. Don't forget to take your storyboard or anything marked up specifically. Oh, and if you didn't bring your laptop, the CD is probably still in the player…

POST-PRODUCTION: RAPPIN' IT UP

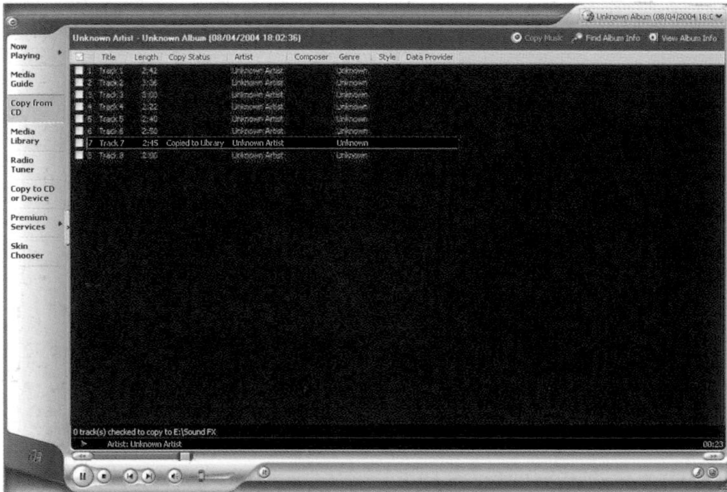

>1<

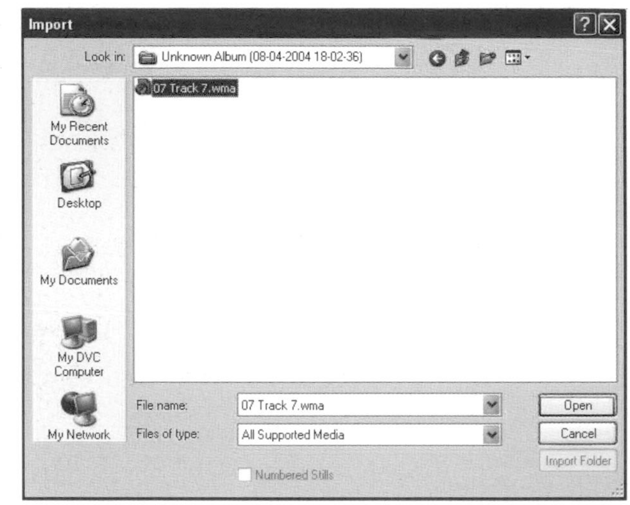

>2<

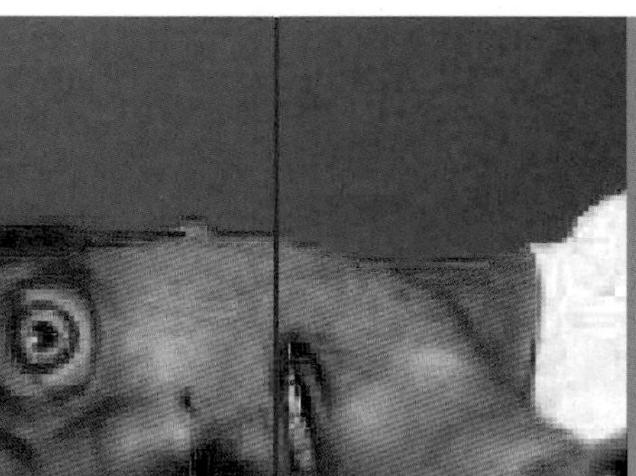

STARTING UP: **OPENING THE VIDEO**

When you're starting in your non-linear editor (NLE), you'll be falling over yourself to see the images because you can lay claim to them. Unfortunately, the most important thing in the music video edit is the track itself. This is the track that you've heard many times, and the track that you're going to hear just a few more times (in your dreams…).

Before the fat lady sings, though, get your settings right from the start. As soon as you open the application, set your ratio (4:3 or 16:9) and your standard (PAL or NTSC).

Any *Preferences* or *Options* should be addressed thus:

- **Unless the musicians have recorded the master audio in 5.1 surround sound, make sure that you're working with 48KHz, 16-bit CD quality stereo**
- **Make sure you can hear audio while you scrub – you'll need it to find those tiny sounds that inform a cut**
- **Use your video card's device control for capture**
- **Set your scratch disks to capture and preview on different drives if at all possible; ideally, use the higher performance, larger capacity drive for capture, away from the drive that holds the edit application**

The track that you're going to edit against needs to be the best quality version available. You don't want to work with an inferior compressed version (MP3's 'click') or you might have to replace it at a cost to a slight change in duration, which will put all your careful images out of sync. The version that you have must be the version that will be marketed.

Be methodical in everything that you do and treat the entire edit as a work in progress until you reach a point where your video feels like it's being overworked. There's certainly no point in attempting to reach anything like spit and polish time if you haven't had an okay from the client. If you've agreed to show them a rough cut, don't get so involved that you can't pull it apart again without problems or time issues.

Exactly for this purpose, it's worth saving your project as a different file twice a day so that you can easily retrieve old edits, or access elements from previous versions.

>1< The ideal formats are CDAs (PCs) or AIFFs (Macs). While AIFFs can be used directly on a Mac using Final Cut Pro, CDAs often need to be reformatted for use on a PC's NLE. Windows Media Player likes to get hold of CDA files and reformat them to WMA files.

>2< Once it has done this, it's possible to import them into your edit application.

>3< Once the audio track is dragged to your NLE's primary audio track, lock it in place. This baby ain't goin' nowhere…

>4< Capturing is a logical process, and should be undertaken logically. Whatever your order of shooting, cut your master shot first. This is the one that is going to form the basis of your timeline.

>5< The whole process is one of logic, organization, and – specifically – good housekeeping. Creating new bins for each scene and naming them is certainly one way that you can help yourself. Anything that saves you time can only be a good thing.

>6< From here, creating separate sequences for each scene and nesting them is an easier way of dealing with complicated sequences when it comes to render time. Remember, if you can't create such separate sequences, think about cutting set-ups and exporting them as AVIs individually.

>7< Sometimes your timeline with nested sequences, keying, effects, and transitions becomes too much like hard work for a computer. This is where you need to export the entire file and start cutting into what you've created. Editing is very much a process of elimination. Clearing up the mess you've left behind is good for the mind and good for the processor.

>8< This kind of sequence, where the same clip is used time and time again, is simply a case of copy and paste. When it comes to changing each clip slightly – in this case every other one has a reverse speed applied – it soon becomes unmanageable, let alone tiresome. Always do what you can to save time, and then export and progress the sequence as a separate AVI to save more time in teeth-pulling and rendering.

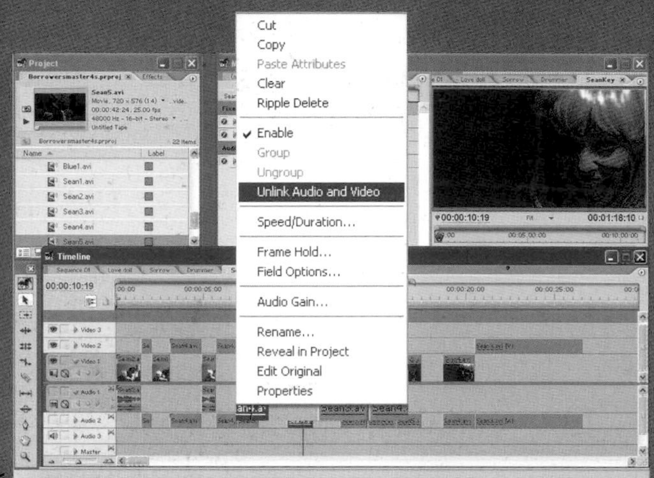

>1<

>2<

CUTTING DOWN: THE EDIT AND THE MASTER SHOT

When editing your music video, be brutal. Unlike any other genre of video-making, this is time critical – both to the track, and to the rhythm or beat.

The one thing in a music video's favour is that it doesn't rely on all the regimented language that the motion picture tries occasionally to break out of. Boundaries of space and time are relaxed, if not on vacation completely. First up: tips on how to get the best out of your edit.

>3<

>4<

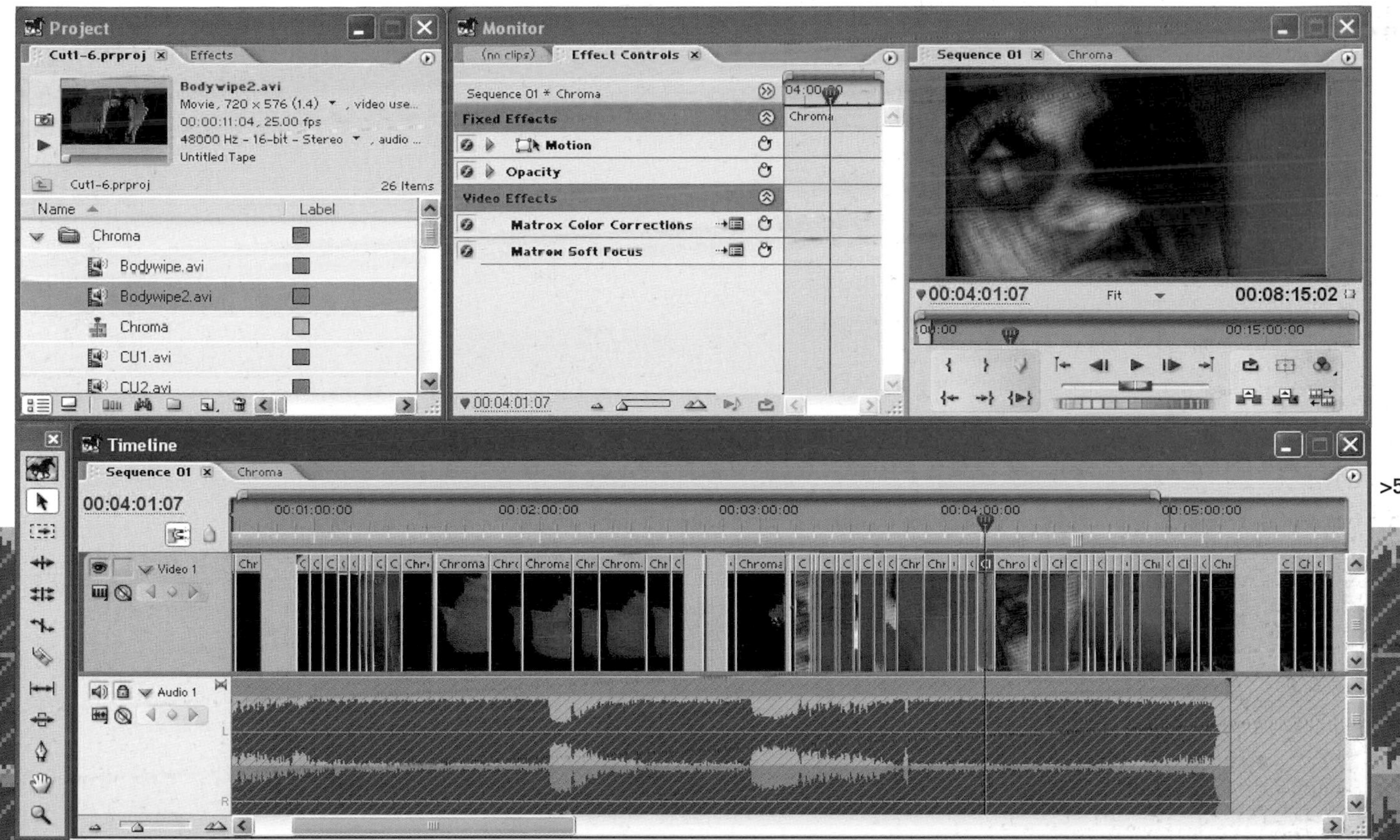

>5<

>1< You are highly unlikely to be using the audio on your clips. If you don't need them at all, opt out of capturing the audio. If you need them for sync reference, use the audio for all it is worth and then unlink it from the pictures as soon as you can. This will give you the versatility to cut and paste, drag, and razor your pictures wherever you want, whenever you want.

>2< With free-shooting – and this is highly usual with an as-live – every clip has good and bad parts. Keep dragging the same clip to the timeline and keep dragging the in and out points until you've got a whole bunch of clips from the same capture that are useful.

Always remember that you are eliminating the bad performances, mistakes, and poor camerawork, and isolating each separate camera shot, camera move, or good performance.

>3< With this free dance sequence, the performer changes her moves as well as the camera. It is the change in dance moves and not the change from one to another that dictates a further set of isolated clips from the same capture.

Work out which bit of the shot that you want. Do you want the camera move? Do you want the framing when it settles? Do you want the performance? Do you want the change in performance? Do you want the cutaway? Do you want to use the transition from one shot to another?

>4< The other thing that determines usage and usability here is the greenscreen clipping. While some can be cropped and rectified, other shots will be hard-pushed not to lose resolution.

Selecting as many shots as are usable is just the first step. Refining them to your first cut is dependent on your music and your storyboard. However much of a free rein you have, though, your job is always to keep things interesting.

A music video defies time and space, but the time and space of your music video needs to be defined. If you're breaking conventional edit rules (i.e. *this* won't cut against this without this cut between them, then work out your rules. Define your parameters before you start cutting.

The particular language of the music video (as opposed to traditional Hollywood cutting) is that beats and rhythm allow for transition. A beat is where the standard rules of space and time can be bent, snapped, and reassembled.

For the moment, though, in order to create usability and versatility, cut, cut, and cut again. This is the reason why fast cut movies (those with less than three-second shots) are often sneered at as being mere pop videos. Forget the snobbery, remember that you're not telling a conventional narrative (even if you're telling a narrative) and start paring your shots and entertaining your audience.

>5< This edit sequence, made up of 21 different shots cut into three or four clips apiece is now cut again, stripping six minutes of usable shots into something a lot shorter with greater effect.

When you're putting your shots together, try to stay kinetic. Paring clips means losing pregnancy and maintaining momentum through movement. A music video is short; there's not much time to get your pictures across, so use the time wisely. Stay with the pace by not letting any frame be bare or stagnant. If your talent is clearly losing interest, cut 'em before your audience does. If a shot feels like it's long to you, then it will feel *really* long to everyone else. And plastering an effect over the top won't make it much better.

>1<

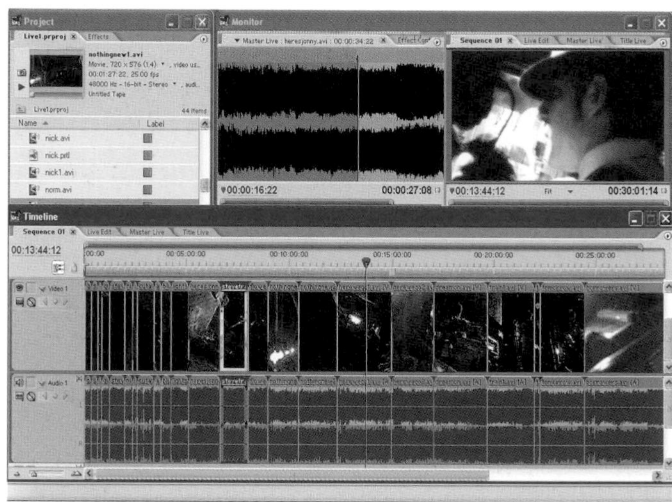

>2<

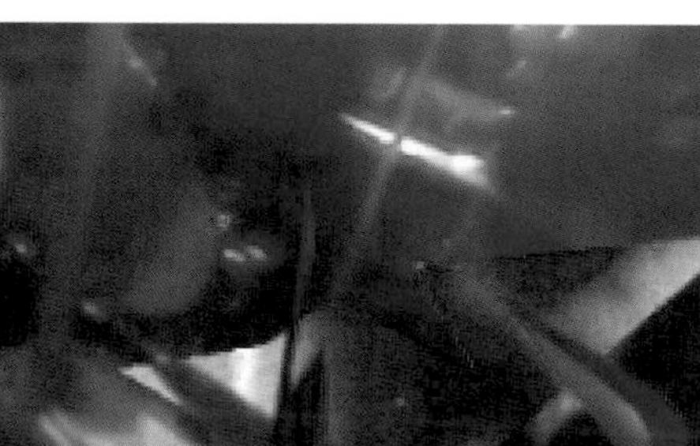

TRACKING DOWN: **USING AUDIO TRACKS**

Your audio is as important as the visuals. It may not feel that way to you if you are not responsible for the audio, but then you wouldn't be making your music video if it weren't for the music. You owe that audio track…

The track is the one thing that you should be happy about when you start editing. It's there, and there's nothing else you can do about it. In a perfect scenario, you import your mastered track, drag it to the master audio track, lock it and load it with visuals. That's it. In an ideal world.

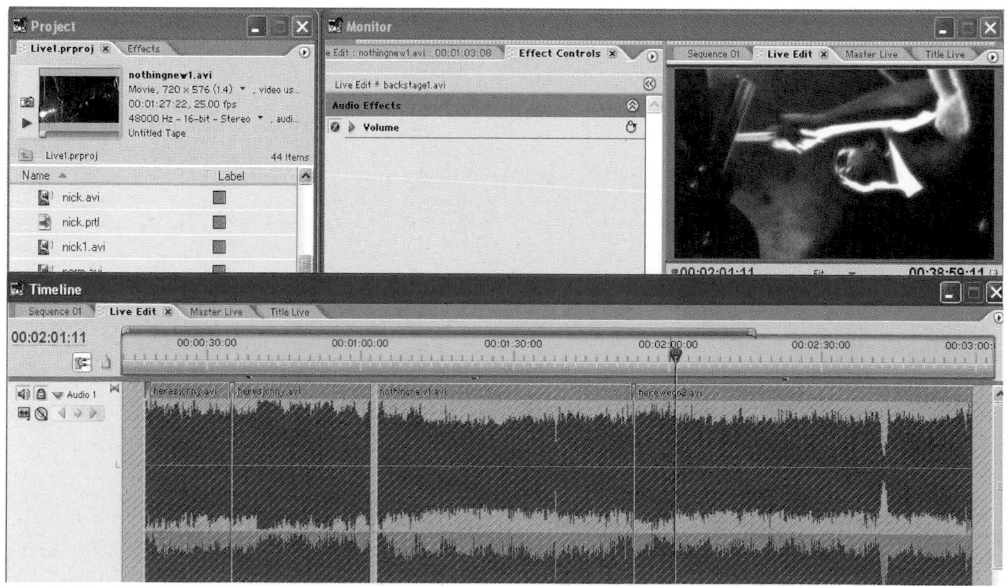

>3<

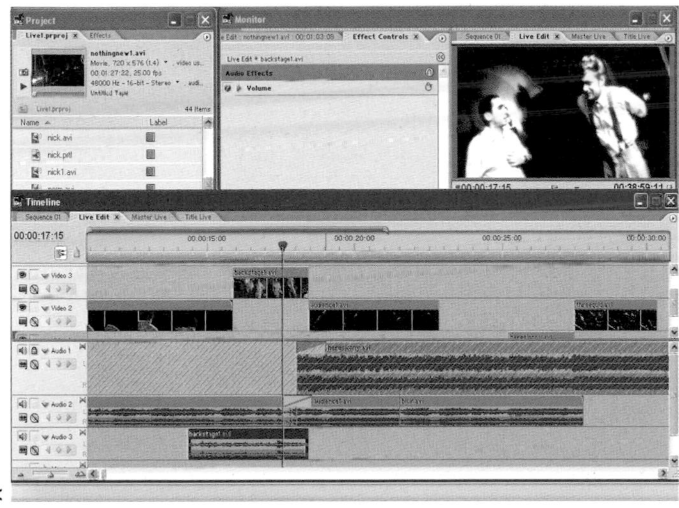

>4<

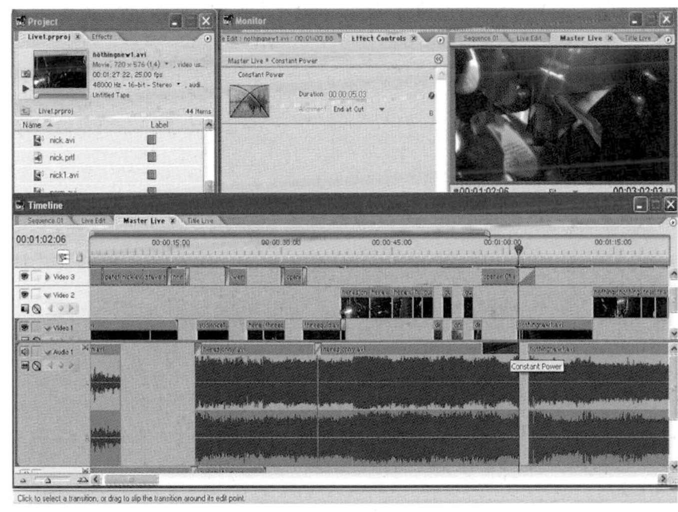

>5<

>1< Unless you lock a track or purposefully put your video clips on tracks that don't interfere with your audio master, then you'll get interference from any video clip with a linked audio track. Lock and unlink as you go.

Any other problems that you might have with audio tracks usually only transpire if you are cobbling together an unconventional music video – that is to say, when you don't have a mastered music track that you are editing the visuals to.

This is an edit of a live gig. From a performance of eight songs, the concept is that three are abridged and edited to form the showcase edit. That kind of ratio – from one hand-held camera shooting constantly – is doable.

The challenge will always be the audio. Keeping the shots cutting in sync without cutting the audio is at least a headache, if not a reason to retire to bed.

>2< Again, it is the formation of the audio bed that provides the key to the visuals. Selecting three tracks to use from a set of eight is governed by two main factors: the need for a variety of different tracks (showcase) and the need for those that already have a body of vocal sync working for them (coverage).

This choice is made only by watching and listening to the visuals and audio available. It's a migraine management and mitigation decision.

>3< This is the time to make sure that the audio chosen is as finished on the timeline as you imagine it to be in the master edit. This might be that it has to fit within a certain time threshold or that you speculate that you might only have a certain amount of shots available. Things will change, but getting it right at this stage means that it will only be a question of tweaking and not remaking. Once you've got it, lock it.

>4< Selecting those audio tracks means that the linked video can then be razored up where it *isn't* a useful shot and replaced it with visuals from the remaining five tracks that *are*. Every bit of video will, by default, drag in its own audio. Unlink it from there to increase the versatility of your wallpaper and audio mix. This audio may or may not be useful, and as long as your master audio is locked, it's always best to keep it there until you officially don't need it.

>5< Keep papering the audio with video across the timeline, making audio the priority. All audio transitions, reverb, leaving pregnant, pulling up, and volume control should be controlled as you go, creating the track's pace to which the visuals contribute.

Time to backtrack: to get that audio track ready to work with is a very particular process. It needs to be as easy on the ear as your visuals are on the eye. Light may travel faster than sound, but the ear is a lot more sensitive when it gets the audio, and it has to be treated with a little TLC...

heresjonny.avi
audience1.av

>1<

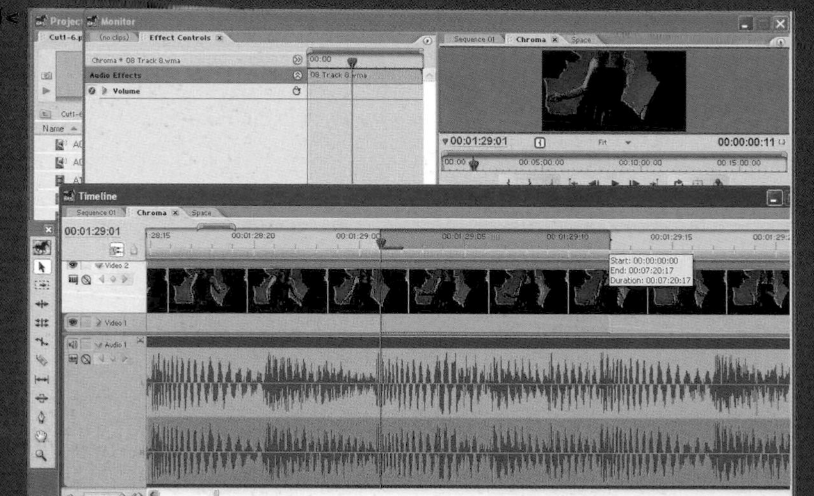

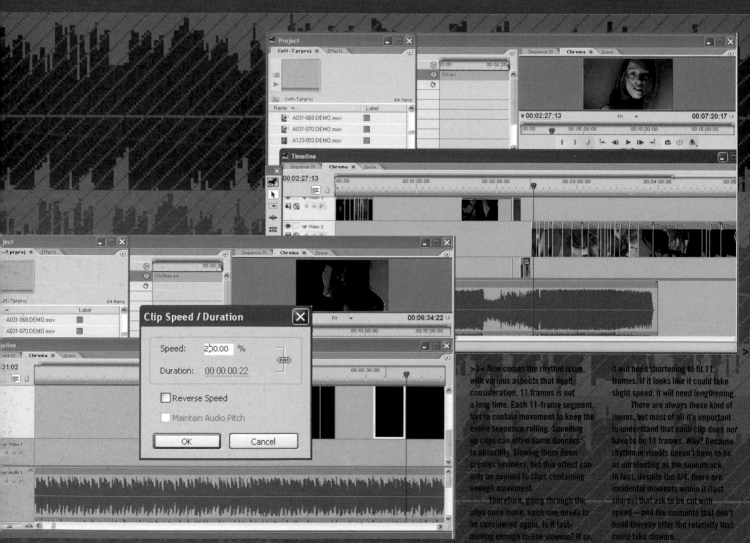

>1< This edit has a distinct 4/4 beat. To cut the clips to the beat is a question of cutting one and locating the exact amount of frames that it covers. It's 11 frames.

>2< To find the right 11 frames from each chosen clip requires good organization. In a sequence, it's often better to start off by going through all of the clips, putting the ones that you need on a lower track and the ones you don't on a higher track. Don't delete them: you might find that you need them.

Going through the clips provides a good opportunity to reorder them slightly. Each clip will be a lot shorter (at 11 frames or multiple) and therefore an allowance is made to drop clips beyond the limit of the guide audio track.

This will leave you with a sequentially re-ordered timeline with clips of different lengths, and a track of discarded items . . . for the moment . . .

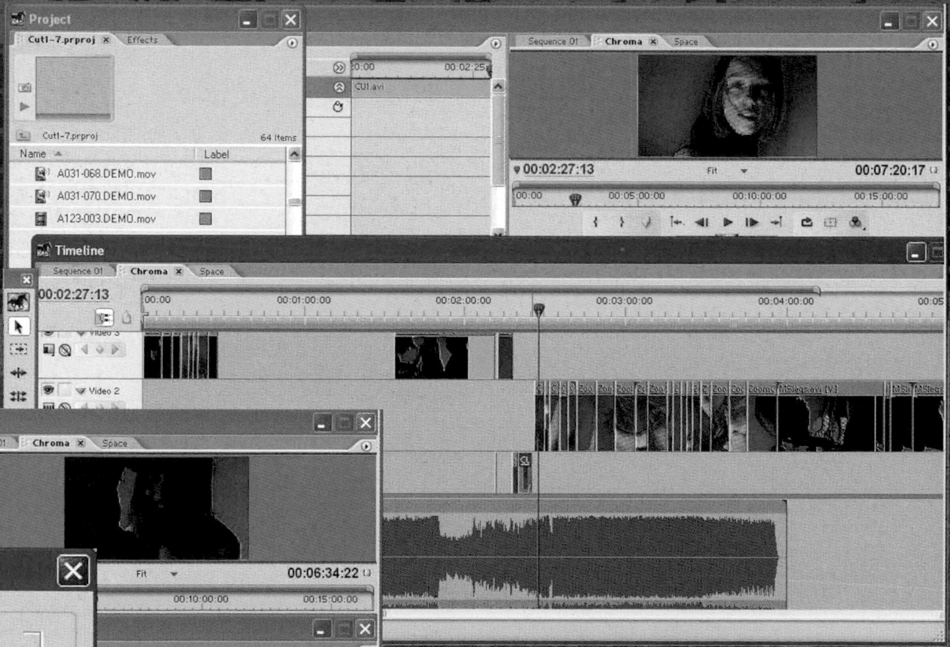

>2<

>3<

>3< Now comes the rhythm issue, with various aspects that need consideration. 11 frames is not a long time. Each 11-frame segment has to contain movement to keep the entire sequence rolling. Speeding up clips can often damn dancers to absurdity. Slowing them down creates sexiness, but this effect can only be applied to clips containing enough movement.

Therefore, going through the clips once more, each one needs to be considered again. Is it fast-moving enough to use slowmo? If so, it will need shortening to fit 11 frames. If it looks like it could take slight speed, it will need lengthening.

There are always these kind of issues, but most of all it's important to understand that each clip does *not* have to be 11 frames. Why? Because rhythm in visuals doesn't have to be as unrelenting as the soundtrack. In fact, despite the 4/4, there are incidental moments within it (fast snares) that ask to be cut with speed—and the moments that don't build thereby offer the relativity that could take slowmo.

>4<

>4< If it's not 11 frames, it is 22 frames or – in PAL – 01:08 frames. Multiplication becomes very handy with rhythm. Twenty-two frames at 200% gets the clip back to its timeslot. To get 50% slowmo for the 11 frames, though, it becomes 5 frames and one field: hardly convenient. A beat, though, will always allow for an *occasional* frame-drop, and sticking to 5 frames with half speed requires immediate compensation on the following clip. It's a case of human algorithms this time, unfortunately, and the more complicated you make your sums, the more tiresome the edit will become.

Using a combination of all of these techniques, guided by the project timeline, and altering the order of clips again while progressing, eventually yields results. This is not a job for the faint of heart or the clumsy of finger. For nearly four minutes at 22 frames? Take a day out of your life…

Cutting to rhythm always requires the image to change perceptibly. The human brain responds to changes in light much more than it does to changes in color. Lens flares to a beat – especially a fast one – work; changes from saturated color to black and white don't. Remember that there is no room for frame inaccuracy. If visuals *look* like they're *supposed* to be cut on the beat, but miss by a fraction, it just looks shoddy.

>5< It doesn't stop there. Changes in harmony or notes are perfect places to change the theme or feeling of a music video – and it creates pace. On the timeline, this dance track has such a change, but because the dancer is cutting every 22 frames, any change is meaningless. Because of this, it's the keyed background that will change.

You cannot underestimate the value of scrubbing audio to the timeline and hearing every change in pitch at every frame. Cutting *has* to be that precise: frame-accurate.

Exchanging the entire first harmony with a test card-like colour bar background changes the whole video: it makes it look as though you're *going somewhere*.

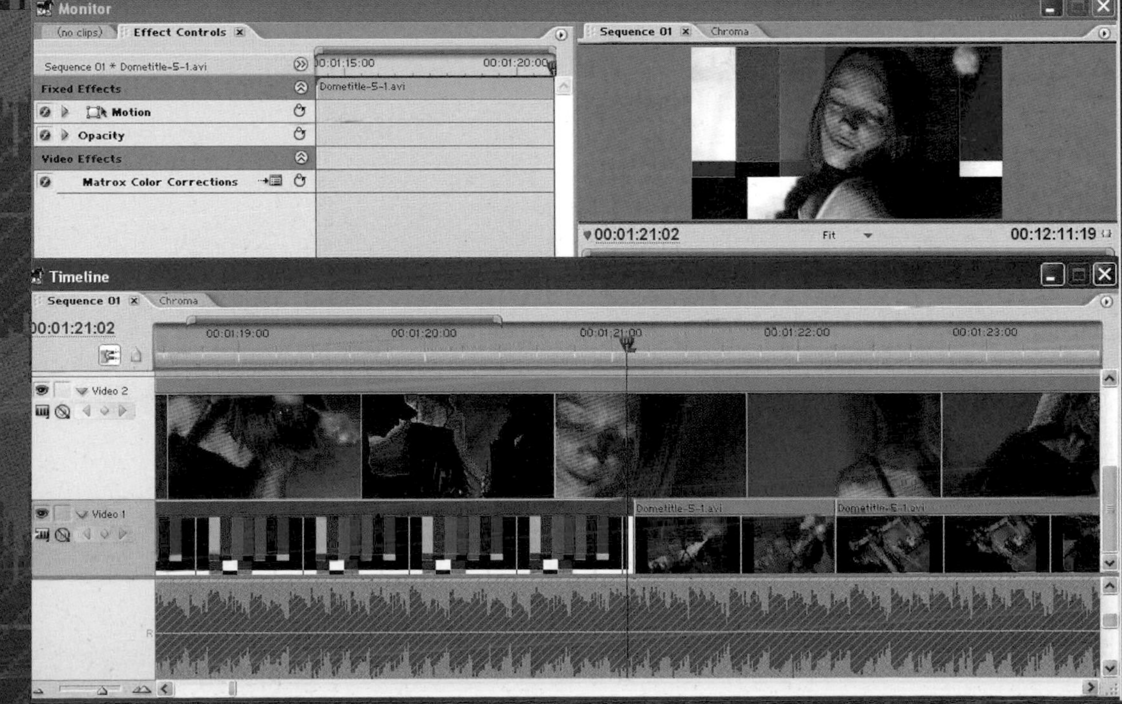

>5<

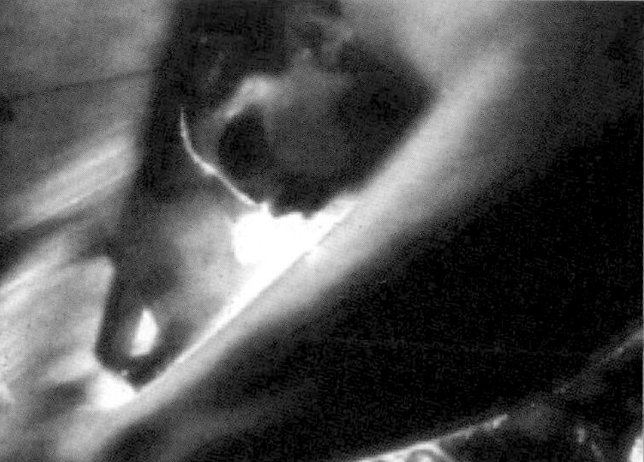

SYNC UP: WORKING WITH SYNC

Creating the believable (the vocalist is singing, the musicians are playing) is all down to your sync. If the sync doesn't fit, you've lost the core of the video.

If you've shot it right, there shouldn't be too much of a problem. Shooting it right is the avoidance of a third variable (DAT) to work against your shots on DV tape and your track on CD. Shooting it right also means the track is played on set and – if at all possible – the artist is vocalizing or playing their instrument in time.

If this is the case, just drag the linked video and audio to the timeline and match up the audio itself. The easiest way to match up the sync to the imported CD track is through the waveform on the timeline at a point where there is a change in dynamic range. Expanding them should show matching waveforms that simply need to be frame-matched on top of each other.

If your vocalist or musicians weren't performing to the CD track on set, the music is probably still there as a small waveform in the background. Either expand this, or add a whole load of gain or volume for the purposes of viewing it in order that you can match them.

If you've done this with your master shot, it is all the other sync shots (mediums, close-ups) that need to cut into it. Doing this means that you are layering both audio and video. You will be concentrating on putting the video in the right place, but do make sure that your audio isn't chopping into itself in case you do need to move or remove shots from the timeline.

There are many situations, however, where sync doesn't appear to be frame-accurate. This might surprise or frustrate, but there is always something that can be done to rectify it.

First off, look for the obvious. The obvious is as simple as the clip merely being a few frames out. The tiniest difference can make you feel as though you've got the wrong clip altogether. The second most common problem is block displacement.

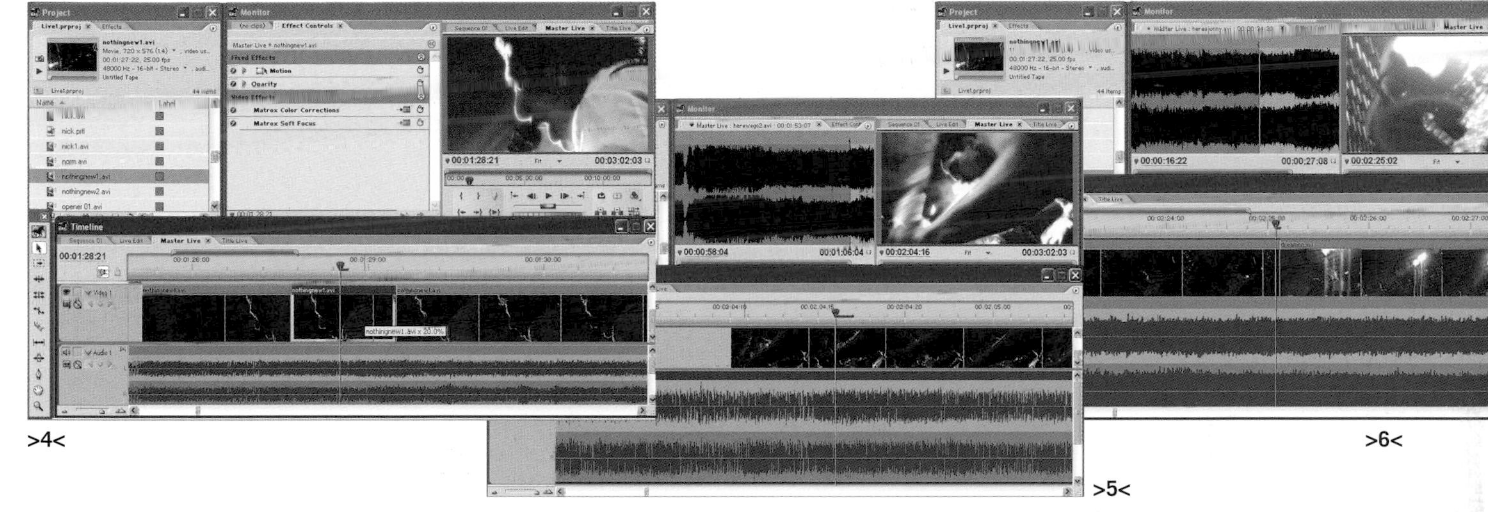

A chorus is usually sung somewhat differently every time; there may even be a slight lyrical change. Make sure that you have got the right chorus in the right place on the timeline.

If the performers aren't actually vocalizing or playing on the soundtrack of the clip, then you need to look for 'moments'. This can be a mouth open at the apex of an *O* or the tongue hitting the back of the teeth for a *T* or an *S*. These moments will get you frame accuracy.

If you are getting slippage of sync as time progresses, it will either be that you have captured each element (clip and track) at different frame rates or that the track is from DAT or an analogue source.

Frame rate is easy to fix; slippage from DAT or analogue is not. This is where the real challenge of sync begins.

>1–2< This is the start of the best performance from the vocalist, but his intro sucks. Recorded at speed for slowmo, it was a fumbling start despite the cue. Introducing the lead musician over him to reveal the moment where the sync starts works in the video's favour to tease an audience. Find a reason that will hold up three months down the line for wallpaper decisions.

Live music videos have terrible sync issues. Either the audio is good, or the video is good—but it is rare that both are perfect.

>3< This edit is a showcase for live performance and consists of three abridged tracks. The useful audio doesn't come with the useful pictures. Using chorus audio from later in the set-up against a shot from earlier in the set-up, the lead delivers the line with a completely different emphasis.

>4< This might ordinarily be a write-off, but razoring the clip during one of the middle held notes and using slowmo, puts the singer back in sync. This technique can be used a lot more effectively with musicians. Of course, you can't fool all of the people all of the time – other musicians, for example – but sync for some instruments can be a bit more relaxed.

>5< Drums *have* to be timed right to the beat...

>6< Guitars – especially noisescape guitars – are a little more general...

There are plenty of other weapons that you have to cover your tracks so that you can put together different audio and video clips as if they were in sync.

>7< Shorter shots or music punctuation shots marry well...

>8< Use an instrument (or two) that's out of frame...

>9< A reverse or obscured angle...

>10< Or simply a cutaway to get your sync back *in* sync...

>1<

>2<

>3<

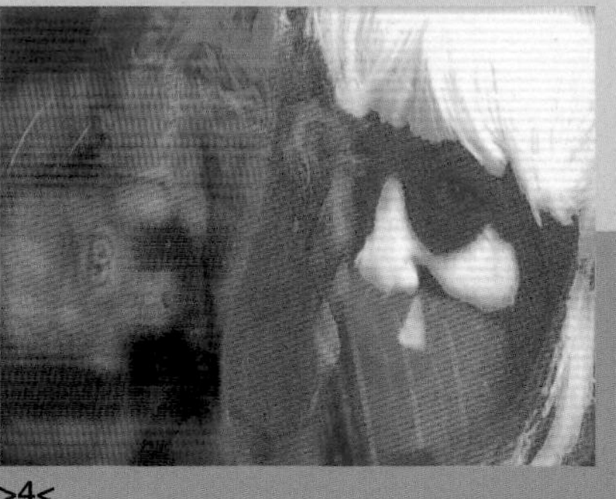

>4<

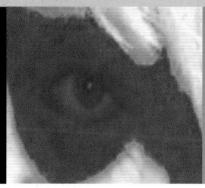

DOWNTIME: TRANSITIONS ON THE TIMELINE

Because you are working in the world of the nonsensical, logic- and language-free music video, transitions take on a different meaning than in conventional narrative: they don't mean anything.

Unless your music video describes a conventional narrative, a cut isn't significant to the shot preceding it and a dissolve doesn't necessarily mean that time has passed. Because there are no rules, your video is in danger of becoming a zippy-zappy blam-fest of transitions, effects, and...*nothingness*.

To keep your music video solid, use transitions and effects wisely, if at all. If you choose anything fancy, it will just look like a preset transition or effect that you have arbitrarily dragged in from your software app – which is, of course, exactly what you have done.

Instead, consider music video's use of transitions as visual onomatopoeia. The anomaly is that the transition used is in direct relation to the bar, note, sound effect, instrument, or beat that is present on the soundtrack.

>1< Changes in pitch, use of flange – anything that transforms the master mix of the audio as a smooth audio transition begs for a dissolve for the duration of that sound. Here, a cross dissolve is added to take the artist out of frame during his last fading guitar twang.

>2–4< Reverb carries dissolves until they fade – and if it's the end of a track, it's a fade to black.

>5< The other way of working with dissolves, of course, is to let the visuals alone justify the action. This sequence was inserted to match the music break, but getting it back into the master sequence simply worked better *visually* as a cross dissolve.

>6–8< Anything other than a standard cut or dissolve becomes a transitional effect. The only real way of judging the right transition is to choose the one that works with the music and your edit: could you justify its use at the Pearly Gates of Pop?

If the idea is that your music video is a consolidated whole that zips along with the music, transitions are the place to energize, dynamize, and harmonize the visuals with the music. *Listen* to what is going on in the track. Looking back on an edit, it is often a cut or a transition in the wrong place that will haunt you. If it doesn't sit well with the track, a transition can be jarring. Work it with a dissolve.

The Dissolve

This is the seamless way of moving from one image to another without agitating the eye. The length of the dissolve assigned depends on the accompanying note or style of music.

Lush strings may well be married to long dissolves from 18 frames to three seconds in order to create a calm transition.

Transitions work inside clips, too. While sticking with a video clip, you might want to stay with it while providing a transition to another *part* of it.

>5<

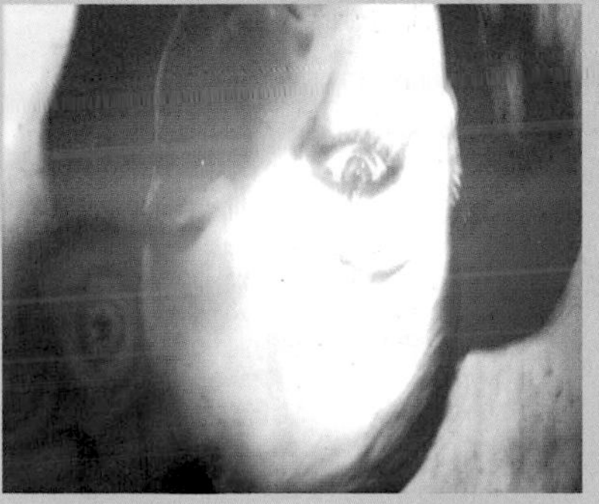

>6<

>7<

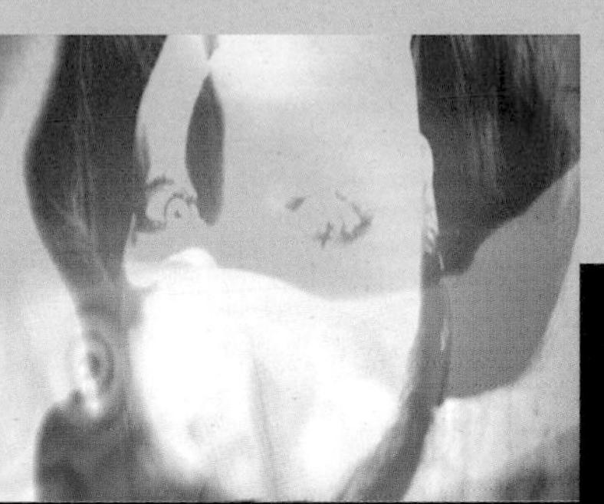

>8<

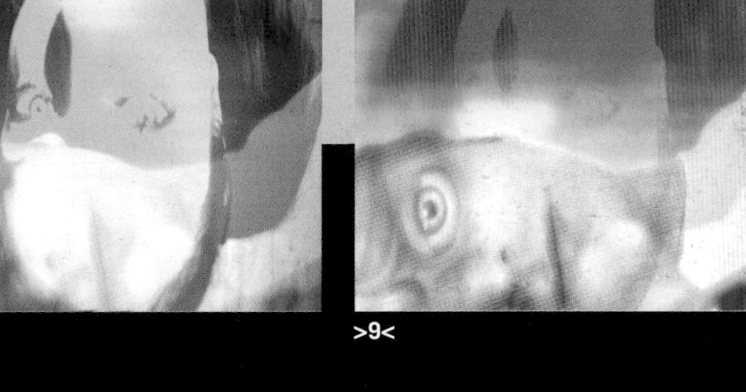

>9<

>10–11< Applying a gentle push to a key allows for the subject to gradually move stage left or right to make way for the action.

>12–16< Adding a 'ker-ay-zee' transition like this might appear to be a terrible mistake, but works as a way of taking the viewer from a geometrically symmetrical image (bands merging with the push to the image) to the horizontal lines of the television image behind the key.

>10<

>11<

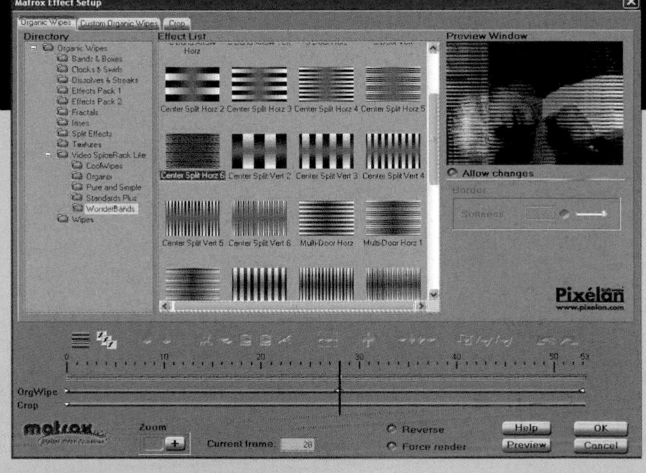

>12<

>13<

>14<

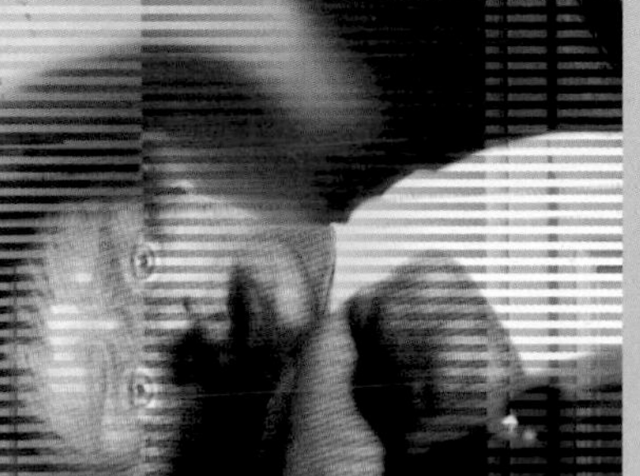

>15<

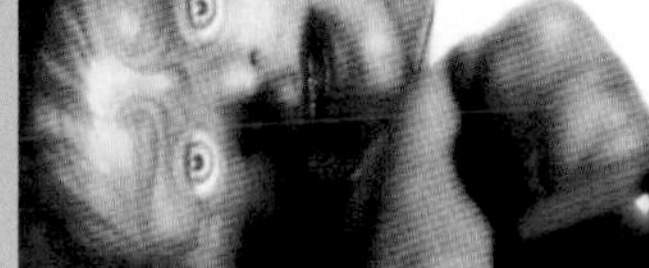

>16<

>3<

>4<

>2<

>1<

PARING DOWN:
AUDIO EDITING AND LOOPING

Your musician will have given you the right master of the right track in the right format. Right?

There are plenty of reasons why you might have to indulge in a bit of audio editing as you edit the visuals. If you are altering the length of a track to suit, extending the intro, reducing the music break – anything that messes with the track itself, always ask the musicians first. If you're adding your own audio to the track, it's slightly less contentious…but legally advisable.

>1< This edit was undertaken without the benefit of the scratch track from the DJ. The visuals were completed with the capability to move the talent around from his slots within the video. On playback, though, it was the new audio that felt a little uncomfortable in the context of the existing track and video. A decision had to be made, and the only way of widening the options was to discuss the situation with the band.

This kind of discussion has diplomatic, contractual, and artistic consequences, and it's up to the director to negotiate tactfully.

>2< Before you begin any audio edit, always make sure that your audio sample rate is between 44 and 48KHz, and that the format is 16-bit stereo. The new audio is the isolation of the scratch for the duration of the track at the level that the musicians require it in the video. It isn't, however, distinct enough for the edit. Lowering the volume level of the existing track makes the entire edit clearer.

>3< One of the issues with the scratch track is that it arrives on the soundtrack at the beginning of the video. This interferes with the illusion that the musician on-screen is playing the lap steel, inferring that he might be scratching discs. Any meaning is lost.

>4< Indeed, the second and third time the scratch manifests, it sounds intrusive while an audience begins to get used to both the song and the visuals. Getting rid of these clips may seem harsh, but it is not as harsh as leaving them in.

>5< The DJ doesn't appear in the visuals until almost two minutes into the track. This could be the start of the scratch, but that would be a little obvious. Introducing him earlier creates audience recognition of what the blurred man kneeling on the floor with a wig in his hand is doing. Audiences *like* getting things, and warm to videos this way.

>6< Therefore, any entry point for his scratch before that event needs the video to introduce it. The most suitable place here is at the first chorus, where the video and audio noise levels are amplified.
The crux of any audio edit is the seamless transition from one source to another. In this case, it's the seamless *addition* of one source to another – and that still requires a transition. The ear is an incredibly sensitive part of the anatomy, and most importantly, it's sensitive to change. A transition is a change and this has got to be gradual to go unnoticed.

>5<

>7<

>6<

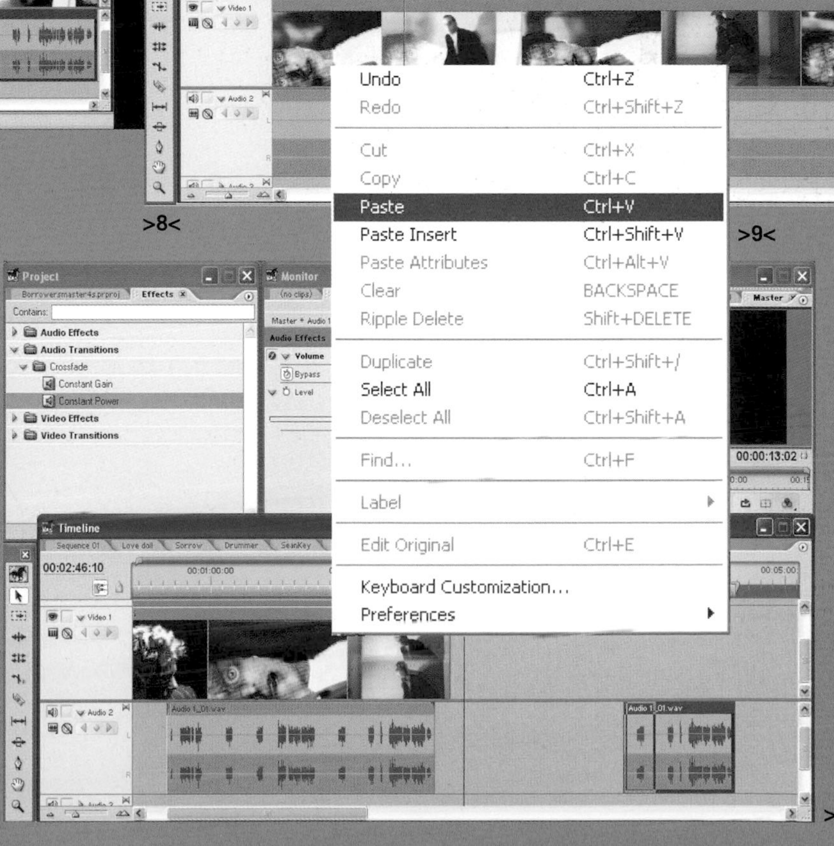

>8<

>9<

>10<

This is the essence of audio editing, whether achieved by using sliders, rubber bands, or transitions to take audio from one track to another *at the same level*.

The difference between *Gain* and *Power* at a constant is that Gain is the mathematical digital procedure that keeps the levels the same during a transition. While this might *sound* as though it makes sense, the ear's sensitivity doesn't necessarily hold true to strict maths. *Constant Power* is a preset that imitates the perception of the human ear, and your success in choice is based on audio playback of options.

Whenever you introduce audio or cross fade between two tracks, always encourage some sort of transition. If the new audio has been recorded live, there'll be a difference to some extent in background noise – a difference in hiss/hum frequency. If it's computer-generated, it becomes good practice rather than essential.

>7< Even in this new track, there is an audio signal apparent on the mixer during the *Constant Power* transition applied. But the main audio track is loud enough to nullify this.

>8< The other issues that this director has with the new scratch audio is timing with the visuals. The introduction of the DJ has no scratching as an audio intro to him. Again, this is not an editor's responsibility, but nevertheless allows for this editor to get ideas above his station...

>9< Making a copy of the new audio track...

>10< ...isolating the requisite scratch to introduce the DJ...

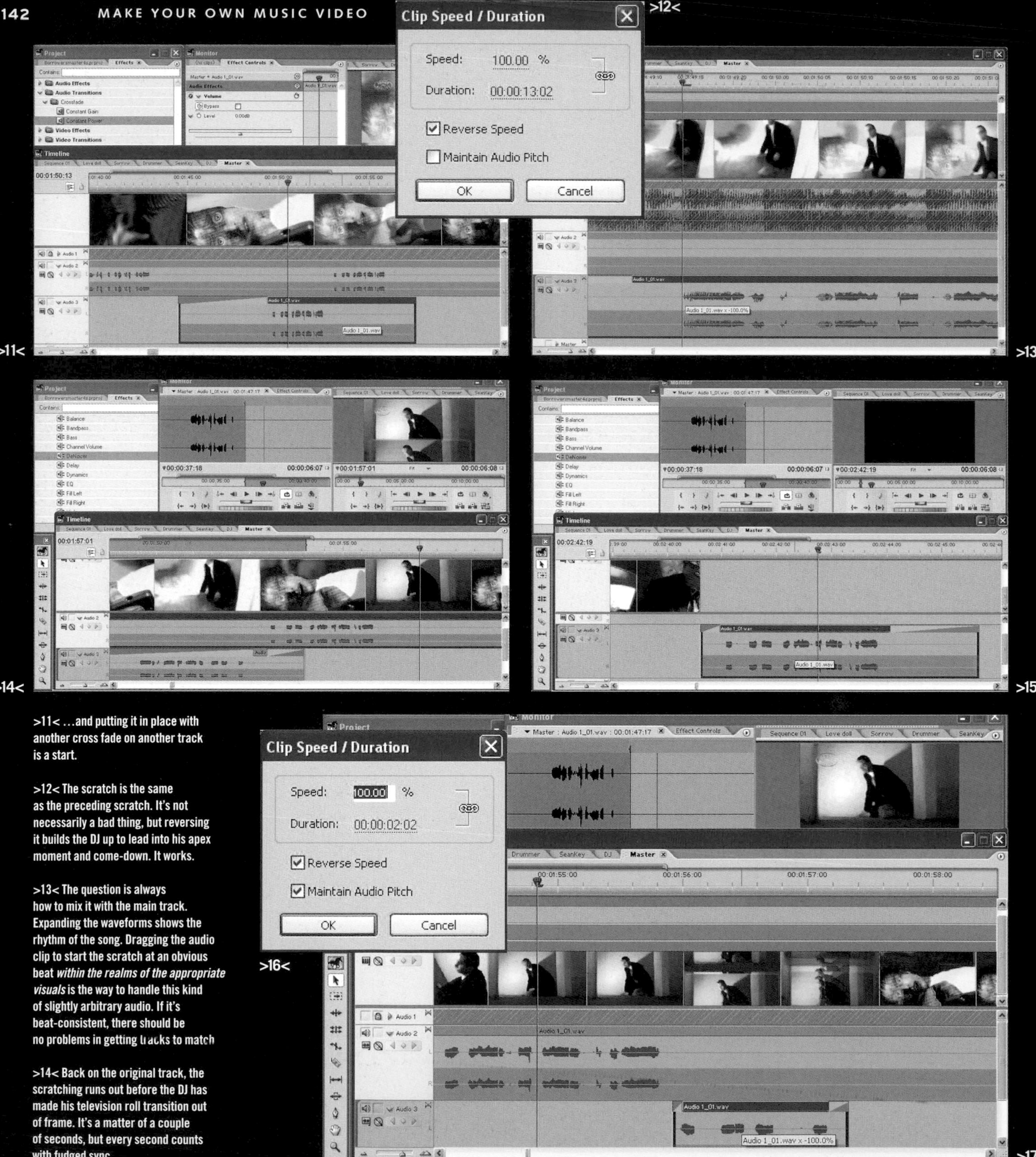

>11< ...and putting it in place with another cross fade on another track is a start.

>12< The scratch is the same as the preceding scratch. It's not necessarily a bad thing, but reversing it builds the DJ up to lead into his apex moment and come-down. It works.

>13< The question is always how to mix it with the main track. Expanding the waveforms shows the rhythm of the song. Dragging the audio clip to start the scratch at an obvious beat *within the realms of the appropriate visuals* is the way to handle this kind of slightly arbitrary audio. If it's beat-consistent, there should be no problems in getting tracks to match

>14< Back on the original track, the scratching runs out before the DJ has made his television roll transition out of frame. It's a matter of a couple of seconds, but every second counts with fudged sync.

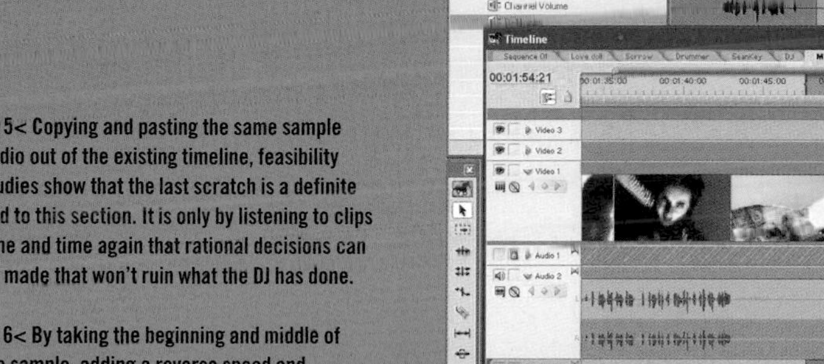

>15< Copying and pasting the same sample audio out of the existing timeline, feasibility studies show that the last scratch is a definite end to this section. It is only by listening to clips time and time again that rational decisions can be made that won't ruin what the DJ has done.

>16< By taking the beginning and middle of the sample, adding a reverse speed and maintaining the audio pitch to match the original, the clip becomes usable and non-repetitive.

>17< Matching up the audio section with the original and the pictures allows for any necessary trimming for length.

>18< Like images, audio can be cut up, and a quick razor in the middle of the problem original splits it in two. Pulling the two audio clips apart and inserting the new copy between them lengthens the audio to suit.

>19< Finding the added clip's duration allows for exactly *that much* to be trimmed after the end of the original audio sequence.

>18<

>20<

>20< Pulling the rest of the audio back into place brings it back into sync with the music track.

>21–22< Finishing off, cross fades need to be added for finesse. Turn the volume back up on the main track and it's playback time.

And now ditch your burgeoning career as a music video-maker and go join a band…

>19<

Cut
Copy
Paste Attributes
Clear
Ripple Delete
✔ Enable
Group
Ungroup
Speed/Duration…
Audio Gain…
Rename…
Reveal in Project
Edit Original
Properties

>21<

>22<

SOUPING UP: **EFFECTS**

Effects, like transitions, only have effect if there's a reason for them. The best and most common reason for an effect is an aesthetic one. Where anything goes, effects can be applied simply because they make the shot look better.

An effect alters your pixels, whether this is changing your chrominance, luminance, and saturation values or re-ordering their appearance on screen. If you have a lower-end effects application with your video card, the algorithms that are used in the software are less sophisticated, and the changes made are less precise. This will degenerate the picture through mathematical compromise and by rounding off figures.

A higher-end application will work the sums out better. The values will be more precise and the effect won't degrade your image *as much*. The fact is that any change to the pixel values will always degrade to some extent.

If you do have a cheaper effects app, you may well be stuck with the presets that are offered. Presets are the algorithms themselves, and low-end apps won't have the capacity to recalculate any more specific effects, nor to fine-tune how they manifest themselves on screen. If this is the case, use them sparingly. Cheap effects always look like cheap effects and unless you are trying to emulate the early days of the music video and want to throw in some low resolution to boot, it's best to leave them alone.

ABOVE LEFT: This sequence has had an effect without adding an effect. The same clip has been copied and pasted, and every other clip has been reversed. It's untouched by any effect, purely because it is so tedious copying and pasting effects to every clip.

ABOVE RIGHT: Exporting the clip repeatedly to render up complicated equations like this median noise application will save time, guaranteed, and allow you to create your individual effect through scale, motion, transition, and further tweaked presets.

Of course, the good thing about *not* using effects is that the music video becomes very much your own creation – and you will be forced to be creative in order to maintain the entertainment level throughout. This is not bad practice.

The way to look at your array of effects is as a tool and not a toy. They are there to help you get the best out of your images and to inject personality into the product.

Preset effects used in conjunction with others – or that you keyframe to your own edit requirements – can be utterly fantastic in their place. If a preset doesn't do the job for you, always think logically. A lot of work can be done quickly if a clip is exported with an effect, then re-imported and chopped around again.

The layering and combination of different effects increases the amount of mathematical gymnastics. This is thrown right back at you in terms of rendering time. While presets may be pre-rendered, your own keyframing and combinations of effects aren't. This is where some kind of realtime capacity – as well as a super-fast machine – will act as your best friend.

TOP: If this is the introduction to the first noisy chorus (Soft Focus, Colour Correction, Zoom Blur)...

ABOVE LEFT: ...then this is the quiet acoustic guitar intro (no effect)...

ABOVE RIGHT: And while the screaming 8 bar is shot and cut to be dynamic and needs only Colour Correction and Soft Focus...

LEFT: ...the layered climax to the track has all the elements used throughout in composite: Colour Correction, TV Roll, Soft Focus, transitional horizontal bar wipes, dissolves, and keying.

>1<

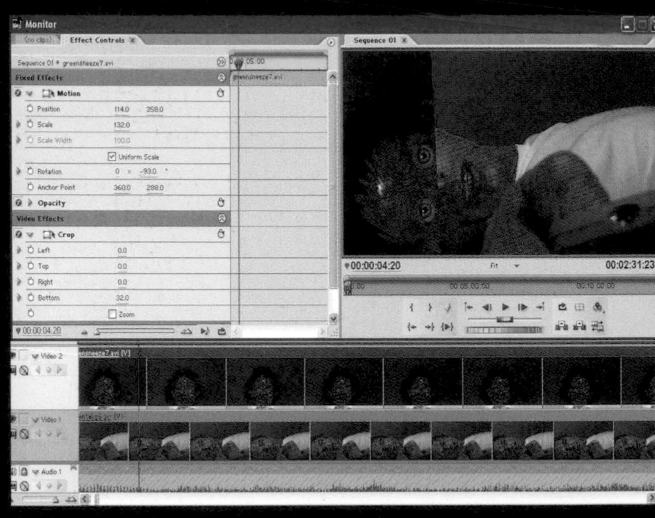

>2<

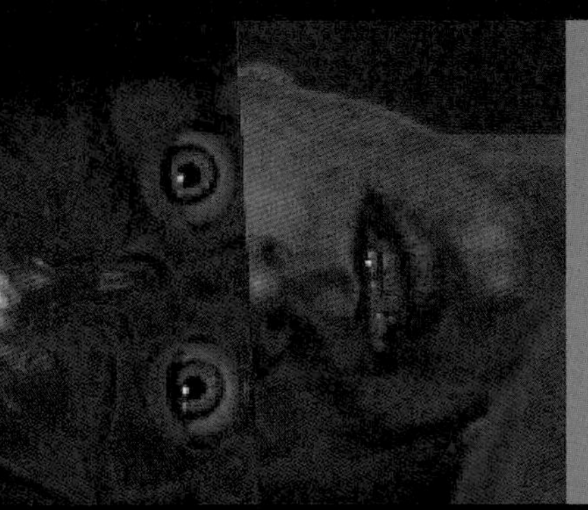

BLUE DOWN: **KEYING IN THE EDIT**

If you've been shooting for keying in the edit, you probably know what to do when you get there. Because chromakey can be effective, it's sometimes nicer to push it a bit – especially in these barmy weathergirl days where moving backgrounds are two-a-penny.

>1< This greenscreen master shot has two elements: the puppet and the lead. The idea is that the puppet forms the top half of the lead's head while a background behind changes. The puppet has been shot vertically to incorporate all parts of its head; the lead is lying down. It's pretty much asking for problems…

>2< The first thing to sort out is getting the puppet to line up to the singer. Using motion controls (x, y, z, and rotation) and cropping the image, it sits on the lead's face in the right position.

>3< Cropping and fading the puppet through to the lead is done using the video card effects software…

>4< …before making all the colour correction changes that will match one shot to the other – most importantly, a uniform green background.

>5< Once these are happy enough together, take them into a second sequence and apply

>6< For this sequence to work with the lead's remote control, the chromakey applied is effected with a pre-rendered rolling television flicker.

>7< Got one in the can? Easy. How dull the master shot is, though, unless you demonstrate that you're not just covering up to fill a gap. Here, a different take of the master with a different take of the puppet is a different frame altogether. Like movies, music videos can progress by getting more intimate with closer shots.

>8< The challenge is that the shot of the lead begins with a pull-out and a push-in from the greenscreen. For the puppet to look as though it moves with him, key-framing motion (scaling and position) with the lead's move is the only way to pull it off.

>9< And it works. Creating a new chroma sequence and then putting the original master shot over the top then allows for the cutting

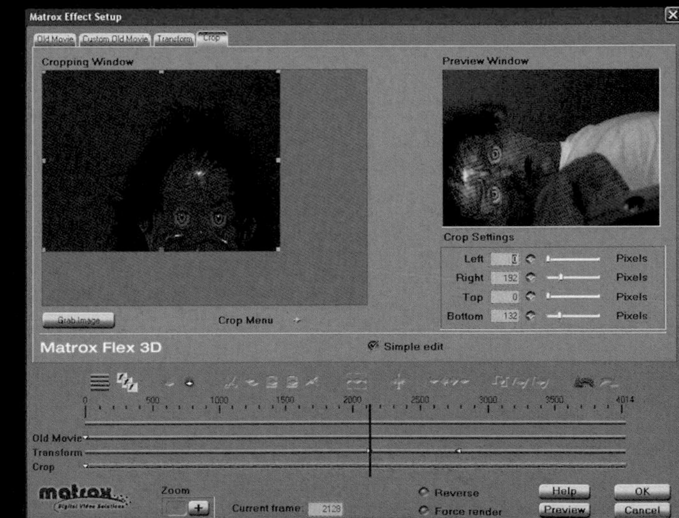

>3<

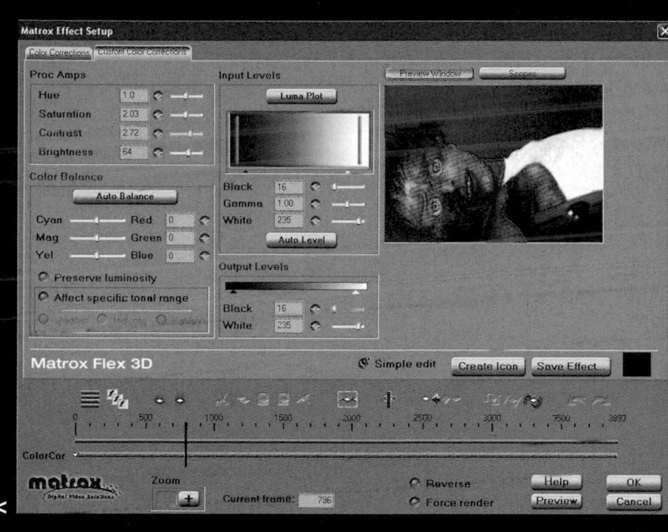
Matrox Effect Setup
Proc Amps
Hue
Saturation
Contrast
Brightness
Input Levels
Luma Plot
Color Balance
Auto Balance
Cyan
Red
Mag
Green
Yel
Blue
Preserve luminosity
Affect specific tonal range
Black
Gamma
White
Auto Level
Output Levels
Matrox Flex 3D
Simple edit
Create Icon
Save Effect
ColorCor
Zoom
Current frame:
Reverse
Force render
Help
Preview
OK
Cancel

>4<

Project
Monitor
Effect Controls
Chroma
Fixed Effects
Motion
Opacity
Video Effects
Matrox Chroma Keys
Timeline
00:01:08:12
00:02:45:20

>5<

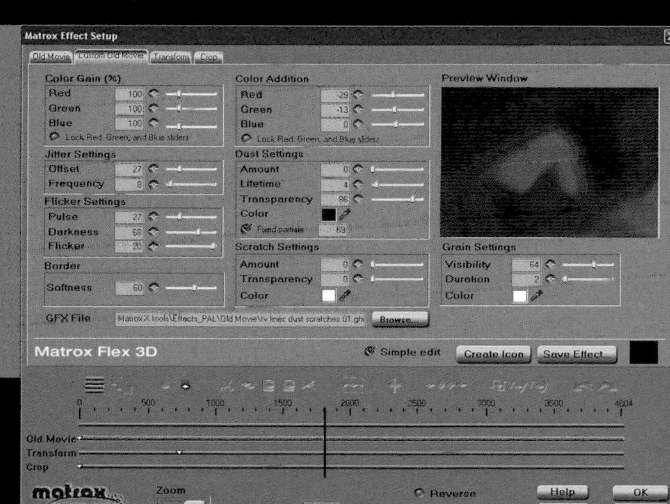
Matrox Effect Setup
Color Gain (%)
Red
Green
Blue
Color Addition
Preview Window
Jitter Settings
Offset
Frequency
Dust Settings
Amount
Lifetime
Transparency
Color
Flicker Settings
Pulse
Darkness
Flicker
Border
Softness
Scratch Settings
Grain Settings
Visibility
Duration
GFX File
Browse
Matrox Flex 3D
Simple edit
Create Icon
Save Effect
Old Movie
Transform
Crop
Zoom
Current frame:
Reverse
Force render
Help
Preview
OK
Cancel

>6<

Project
Effects
Monitor
Effect Controls
Sequence 2
Fixed Effects
Motion
Opacity
Video Effects
Timeline
00:00:49:21
00:02:59:15

>7<

Monitor
Effect Controls
Sequence 2
Motion
Opacity
Video Effects
Matrox Old Movie
Timeline
00:00:28:00
00:02:59:15

>8<

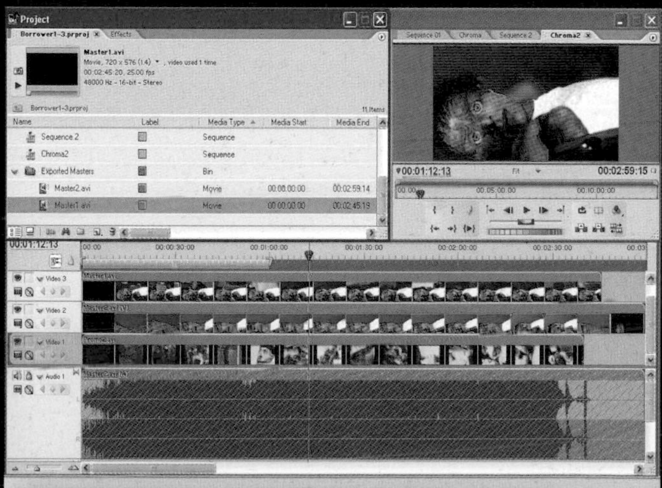
Project
Master1.avi
Sequence 2
Chroma2
Exported Masters
Master2.avi
Master1.avi
00:01:12:13
00:02:59:15

>9<

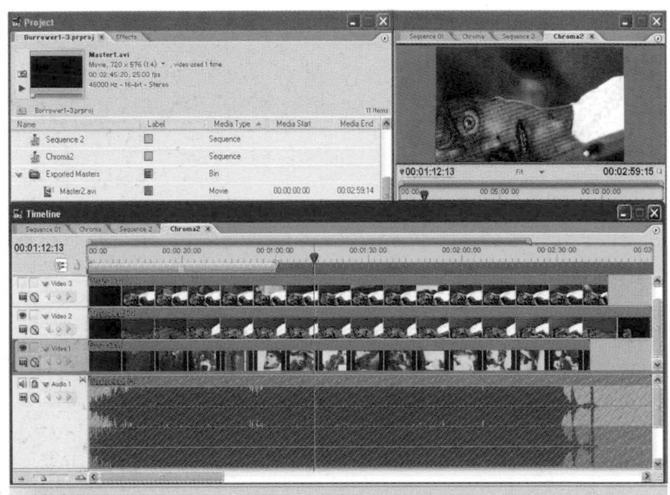

>10<

>13<

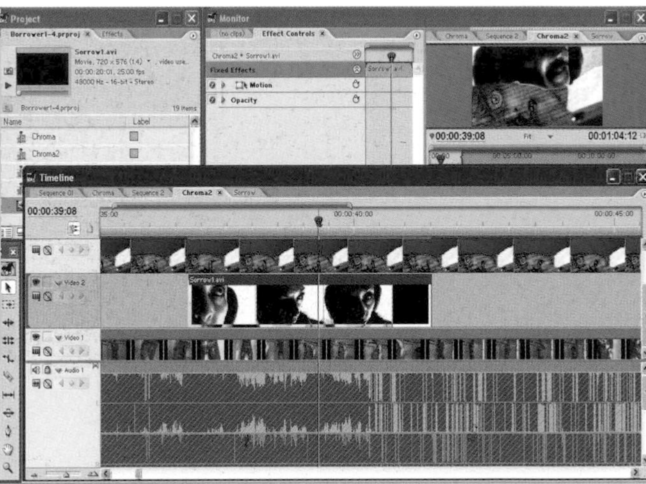

>11<

>10< …and the other. Better still, it's all in sync.

A contentious issue with chromakey cutting between two master shots arises if you're looking for the chromakey itself to form the transitions. This would mean that the keyed background is to develop into your screen shot. So, you've got to work within the NLE at a stage where you can still do something about it.

>11< This exported clip will be the start of a new overlay to the whole image. For the first shot, it just appears as a keyed background.

>12< To correspond to the existing background, the same television effect is applied with an increase in the blue channel and the same soft focus. This can then match cut to the existing background.

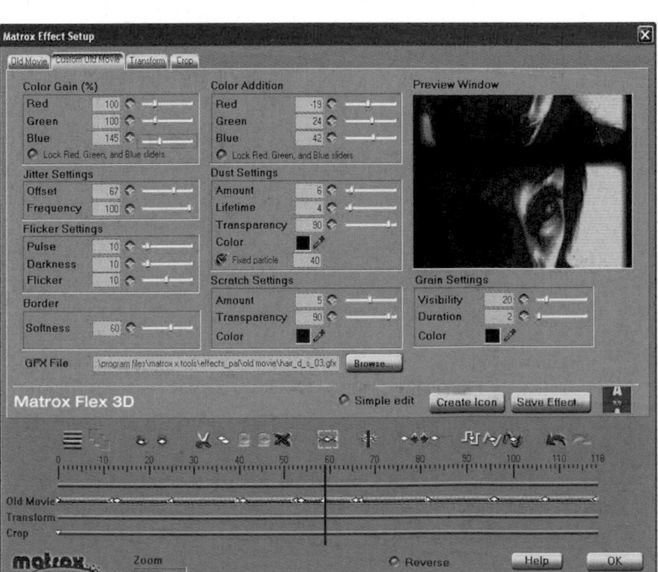

>12<

>14<

>15<

>16<

>13–14< The cut then, can be made in the background with verisimilitude – and no seam…

In the world of the music video, though, where no world is a real world, keying can be used to 'key' keys.

>15< In this part of the edit, the exported key master becomes the background to the new key, created in exactly the same way in another exported sequence. It's the final frisson of the music video and requires something a little special.

>16< Razoring up the new key clip means that another layer can be placed on top of the two existing keys and the image becomes a composite of three keys.

This is a very useful way of creating interesting images – particularly if there is some contrivance involved. In this case, used with the television effect, it becomes a question of who is watching whom…

***BELOW LEFT & RIGHT:* Don't forget Luma Keys. Allowing images through on the alpha, they create a few transitions of which standard cross dissolves are simply not capable.**

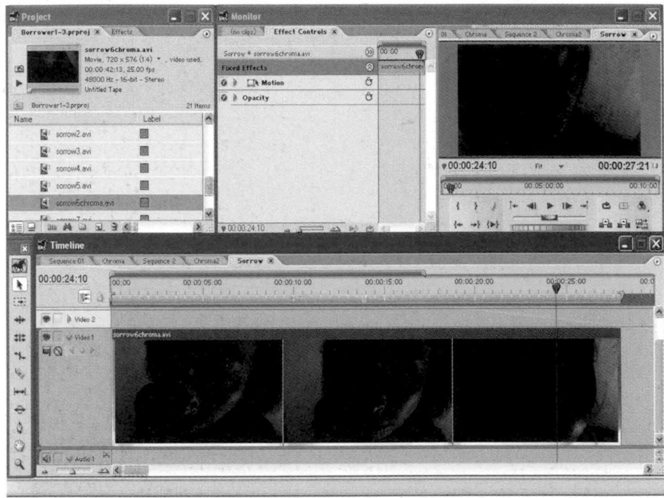

>2<

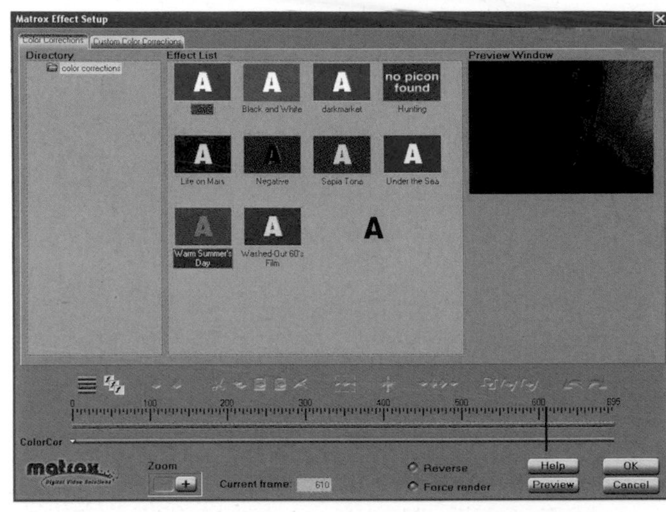

>3<

BLACK UP: COLOUR CORRECTION IN THE EDIT

Because you can get away with murder in the edit, creating worlds that don't exist, colour correction can become your biggest ally. The music video doesn't live in a normal universe: it's monochrome; it's highly saturated; it's a freak of nature.

>1<

Some of the time colour correction is exactly what it says it is: you are trying to save shots from being completely redundant.

>1< It's not a good look when the exposure used on the shoot doesn't quite make the grade. In effect, the image is indiscernible to the point that it is difficult to edit.

>2< On the timeline, there's a whole load of clips lined up and waiting for the edit, but unless the first shot is corrected, there won't be any progress.

>4<

>5<

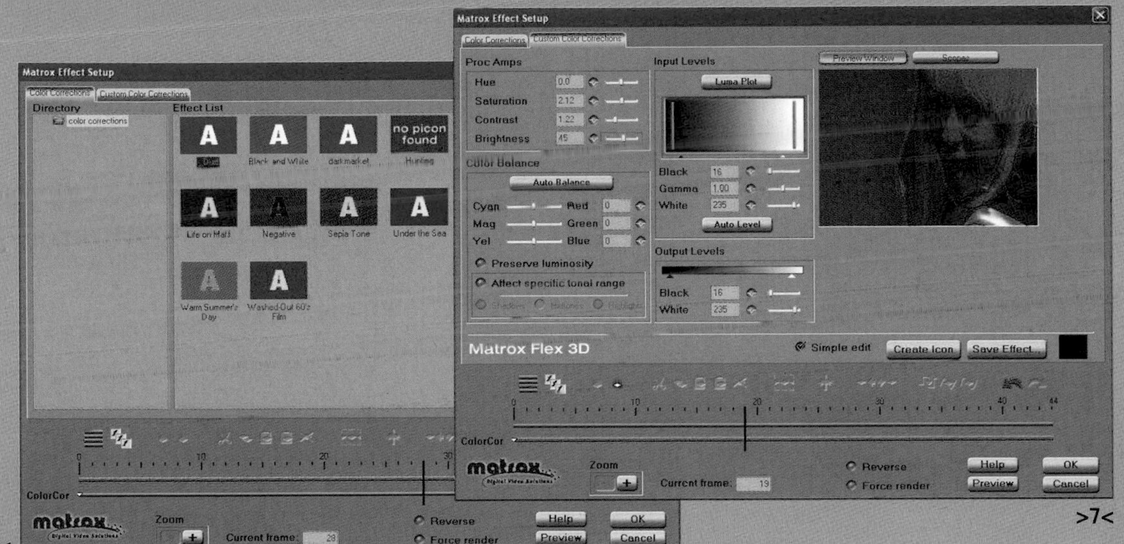

>3< Colour correction applications come in all shapes and sizes. Most have presets like this and allow for quick alterations to be applied to your pixels.

>4< For this kind of shot, the brightness and contrast are the most important levels to juggle. These are the black, white, and gamma levels, where gamma is the output for mid-range tones. The shot needs to be stark.

>5< Applying different levels to the output of black and white gives you a lot more freedom than just brightness and contrast value adjustment. What's more, it makes a previously unusable shot a music video-friendly shot.

***FAR LEFT:** The term 'correction' isn't strictly accurate. Most of the time colour creativity is more applicable.*

This can apply to just a shot…

…or to an entire movie…

***LEFT:** Sometimes, colour correction is necessary for the whole edit to progress.*

>6< This greenscreen shot is neither balanced enough nor good enough to key properly.

>7< Increasing saturation and luminance brings out the green to allow for the key to take place. The values, though, have affected the rest of the picture to the point of over-saturation.

>8< Taking a *Color Pass* effect, thereby sampling the green on top of the clip, keeps the green in place and allows for a value to be input that eliminates the excess of yellow.

>9< Applying these values to all the other clips from the same set-up keeps the shot consistently usable for keying, but the important thing to consider is whether the master shot and other shots from the set-up need their own colour correction to remain consistent. This is where the rulebook states that there are no rules. Rejoice, it's a choice…

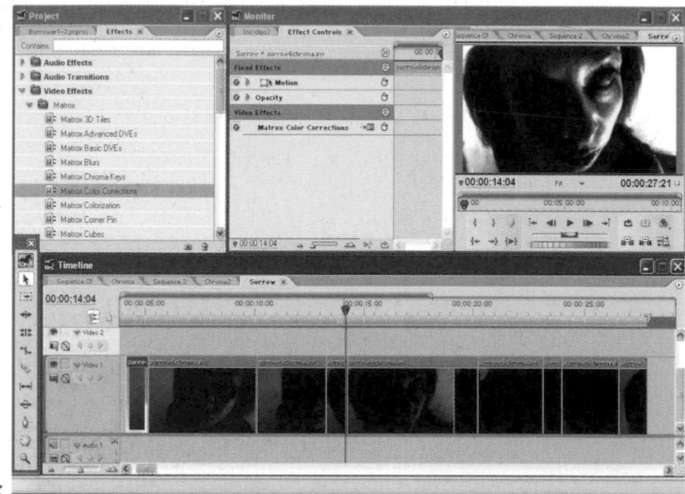

>1<

>2<

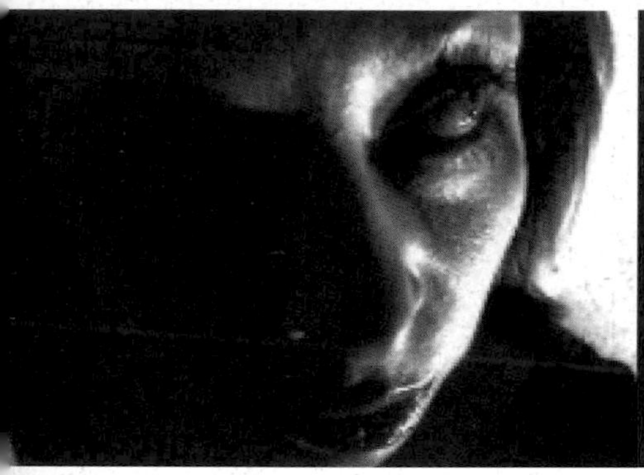

SPEED UP, SLOW DOWN: CLIP SPEED IN THE EDIT

There are various schools of thought with regard to using different speeds for shots in the music video. Purists would probably say that slow-mo is fetishistic and speed-up is adrenalizing. Both are right and neither is wrong.

>3<

>4<

>1< In attempting to create an automaton-like movement to this talent, the clips have been razored at every point that the camera or the talent makes a significant movement – that is, every blink, every head turn, head tilt, camera pan, and camera tilt.

>2< When you are working with different speeds within a single clip, make sure that you split each razored part of the clip on to different tracks. This will give you enough breathing space when you are slowing down elements and extending their length on the timeline.

>3< Depending on whether you are working to duration or whether it is the speed of the clip that matters, altering each value changes its duration on the timeline. In this case, the entire shot will be exported and changed again to sit at the right place in the master sequence.

>4< Drag all the clips back together again and the shot will have a sense of the unreal.

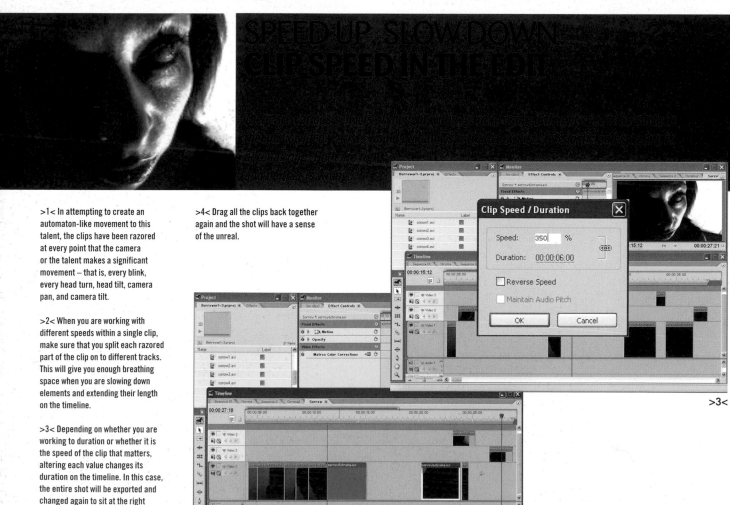

>5< To further the effect, the entire clip is exported, put into the master sequence, and reversed, adding a new speed to fit its 'slot'.

>6< Sometimes it's not just speed that creates the desired effect, it's speed with a designed reverse shot. This actor was asked to walk backwards away from the camera in order to get the desired awkward walk.

[illegible]

[illegible] Applying faster speeds [illegible] exporting and importing the clip, it [illegible] possible to slow the clip down for effect [illegible]

>7<

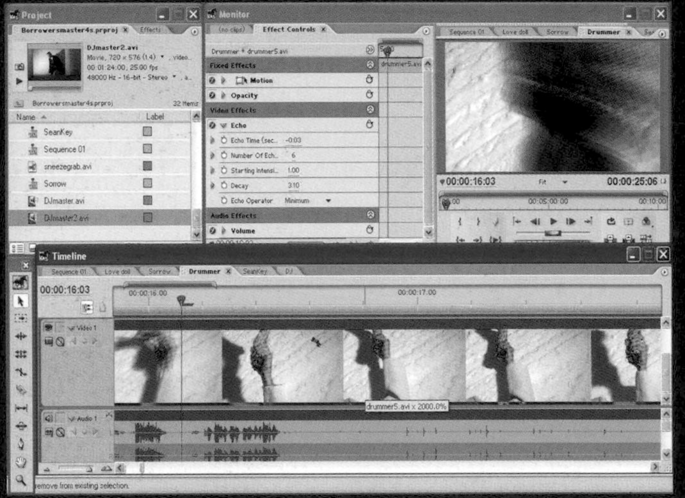

Project
Monitor
Effect Controls
Drummer
Fixed Effects
Motion
Opacity
Video Effects
Echo
Audio Effects
Volume
SeanKey
Sequence 01
sneezegrab.avi
Sorrow
DJmaster.avi
DJmaster2.avi
00:00:16:03
00:00:25:06
Timeline
drummer5.avi x 2000.0%

Project
Monitor
Effect Controls
Drummer
Fixed Effects
Motion
Opacity
Video Effects
Echo
Audio Effects
Volume
SeanKey
Sequence 01
sneezegrab.avi
Sorrow
DJmaster.avi
DJmaster2.avi
00:00:07:20
00:00:25:06
Timeline

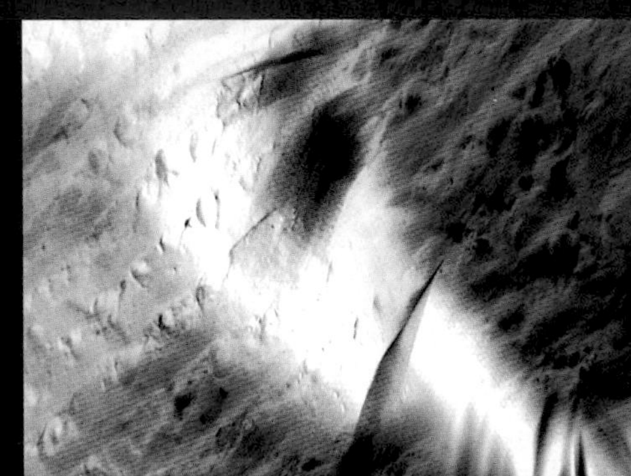

>14<

>15<

>14–21< Thinking about how you are going to use speed, reverse speed, and duration in the edit when you're on the shoot is essential to success. The talent walking backwards is reversed to get the bizarre approach to the camera here. Chopping out sections, adding a soft focus, using colour correction, and reversing at different speeds turns an amusing shoot around into a sequence that befits the screaming 8 bar.

>16< >17< >18<

>19<

>20<

>21<

DOWN AND DIRRRTY: **DISTRESSING PICTURES**

There's something about a grubby image that music video loves. It's all to do with marketing a style of music – the dirtier the music, the dirtier the video. Video can be horribly pristine at times, which is why music video-makers often use film effect. Film has that dirty quality: as an analogue format, it is inherently noisy, flared, and flashy; as a tangible medium, it can be scratched, dusty, jittery, and downright dirrrty.

Like applying effects, soiling your images has to be undertaken wisely, with consideration for the music and the style of the video. In the typical dirty music video, the music is loud and the shots are handheld, unestablished and unresolved.

Dirtying can work in two ways: it can apply itself to one particular shot that you return to, or it can be applied to the entire video. Whatever its application, it must be consistent and not arbitrary.

When it comes to the values that are introduced in distressing images, think of it as you would do jeans. If you rip the knee of your jeans, would you chuck them, sew them or add another few rips to match? Music video directors don't chuck, they sew or patch-up (*see Hiding Mis-Takes, pages 160-163*) or they make a feature out it. They make it look *deliberate*.

Continuing with this ludicrous analogy, consider why today's market believes that designer distressed is more appealing. Why buy an expensive, distressed pair of Levi's when you can chop up a cheaper 'straight' pair and create an expensive pair? This is what good jeans designers, music video directors, and editors do. The secret is knowing exactly the point where a tear becomes a designer rip.

The answer ranks alongside the meaning of life. It's how you see it, how your client or musicians see it, and how the audience will interpret it. It's before an audience gets bored, annoyed, or frustrated simply because they can't see the image that they want to see. Anticipating this is hard, and bear in mind that the viewer's tolerance threshold is always a considerable percentage lower than your own.

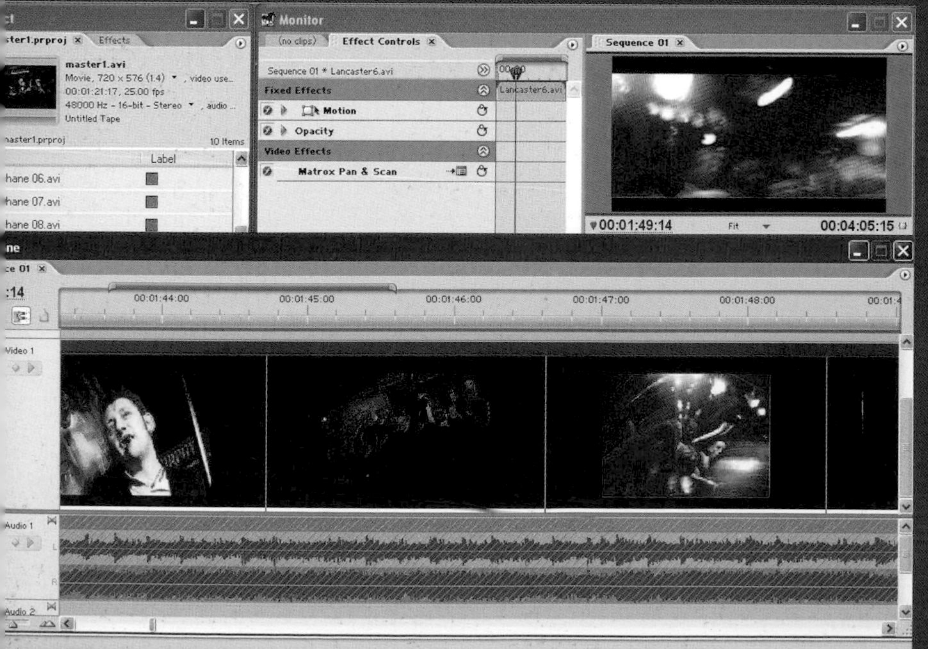

>1<

>1< This video absolutely shouts out for a bit of grime. It's a sweaty gig for musicians and crew: the audience are pushy and drunk, the cameras hand-held, the band free-wheeling within the parameters of miming to the CD.

But in a way it would be just a little too *obvious* to mess around with these images. The track and music video run over six minutes and visual distress can often outstay its welcome or become invisible to viewers once saturation point is reached.

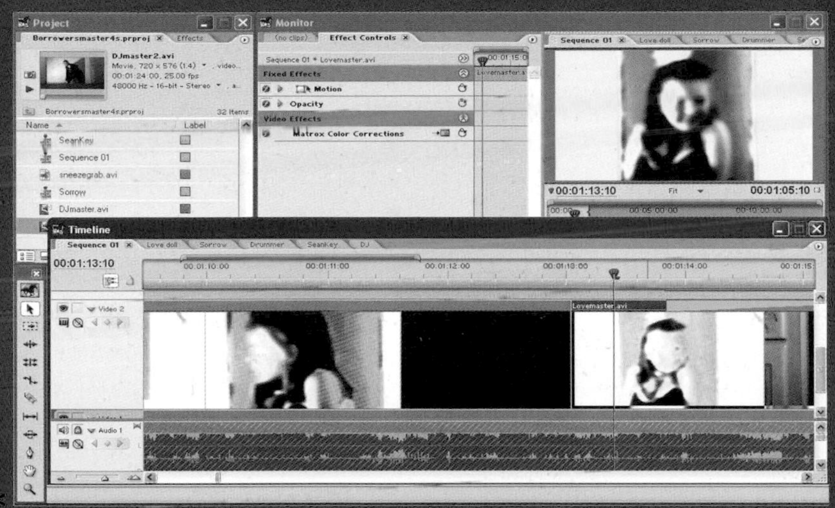

>2<

>2< This music video is set in a memory state wherever the shot doesn't rest on the singer. The lyric describes the loss of emotion from childhood as borrowed toys. To represent this in the video, distressing the image informs of an alternate reality somewhere between metaphor and history. Distressing an image by defocusing and burn-out recalls photographs which hold their own truth and time.

Indeed, the contrast between sharp video and a distressed picture that smacks of history often smacks of truth. History is truth, not myth. History is analogue, from the vaults, scratched, dirty, and usually within a messy, unresolved shot.

>3< It still needs that one thing – and the answer is in the one and only lock-off master shot. This shot is revisited for those few times when the mime or the shot doesn't work. It's not a clever master shot; it's just a good reference and a good wallpaper tool. Monochrome has already been applied to give the shot its own identity.

>4< What a noise value gives is *not* Personality Plus to the shot, but an *overall* feel to the entire music video. It's an element that contributes to the mood of the whole video *because* it's only present in one shot.

>3<

>4<

>5–6< Adding median noise to an image simplifies pixel data on screen (while in reality, it's a rendering nightmare). This type of noise creates anonymity – and in that respect, hides the truth. In this case, a hidden truth is made sinister.

DREAMS, HISTORY, TIMELESSNESS

> A change in time or state of mind can be represented visually with noise and distress. Humans are programmed to believe that in the future, things are cleaner, clearer, sharper, and shinier. In effect, the future is as simple and clean-cut as 0 and 1: the future is digital.

> Clean pictures will always represent this contemporaneousness, no matter what designers would like the current fad to be. Distressed pictures – the by-products of an analogue era – will always represent the past when used next to sharp digital images. It's a question of relativity.

>5<

>6<

>1< Consolidating the look in this video is all to do with the as-live motion. The cameras move a lot in this video and it needs a bit of a smoothing. This kind of counteraction keeps the slightly amateurish hand-held feel in check, which – coupled with the noise values attributed – might be otherwise construed as cheap and cheerless.

>1<

>2< Adding a key to an ellipse and feathering a roll blur around the image applies itself to the entire music video. The effect is then very much one of control within chaos.

Cleaning your pictures up is one of the essential parts of producing a quality music video. While you have probably been altering the 'look' of your shots throughout the course of the edit, cleaning it seals a 'look' that consolidates all the clips into one hermetically-sealed music video.

SCRUBBING DOWN: **CLEANING PICTURES…**

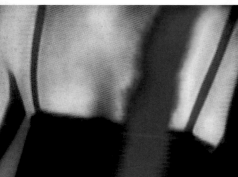

If it's not a mistake that bugs you when watching your music video back, it may well be that the video is just not cool enough. Trends come and go, but that X-factor of style is unmistakeable. It's also very hard to pinpoint.

Understanding style is easier than creating it. Style is fundamentally aesthetic. At a production level, it is framing, choice of shots, depth of field, exposure – the entire mise-en-scène. It's too late to make any changes in this respect – by the time you reach this stage. Fortunately, there is a very large school of thought that believes in the power of the edit. Style becomes colour, contrast, crushing, cuts – it becomes an aesthetic that binds the entire video.

Cleaning your pictures does two things: it alters the look and it alters the quality – and these are inextricable. Cleaners as software applications are encoders, and they offer a last-chance dash to polish the video in much the same way that effects apps work. They may be inextricable, but you might want to work that last finesse away from the encoder.

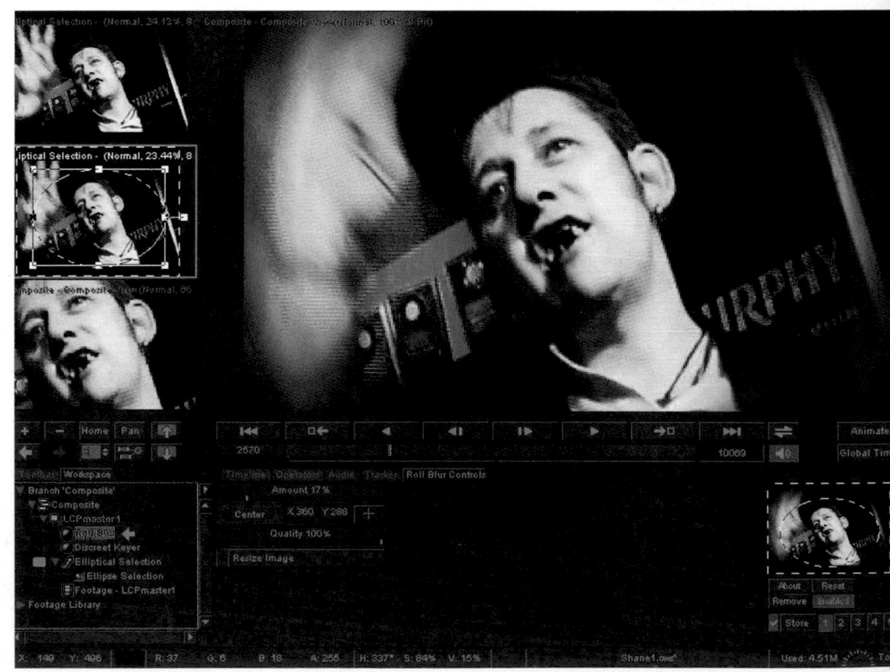

>2<

>3< There are two ways to clean pictures. The first is to export the entire time and bring it back in as a new project. This is the way if you are encoding with your edit application.

The second way is with the use of a specific cleaner application. There are plenty of these around that both clean and then encode. They may just call themselves encoders, but they will probably have a lot of presets that you can make use of.

You might have saved all of your effects until this moment. If you have, you can expect a whole load of render time to your completed video.

Cleaners have to be good to do their job. The algorithms that they use need to be complex to ensure that they're not approximating your data too much. If they do, it leads to artefacts, streaking, colour loss, and low resolution. To make sure that they do their job properly, they have to have all the information that you can give them before you even introduce your music video.

>4< This is the start of the basic preset.

>5< From there, the best way to handle any cleaning of your image is to bring up a before and after split-screen. Cleaning is basically hue, light, and saturation – just like any colour correction. The issue is that encoding AVIs in different formats always affects the image in some way, and often in a way that you will not be entirely happy with. This may be that it's not what you had in mind – and if this is the case, watch it again. Unfamiliarity has a habit of breeding an impulsive contempt and a second or third viewing is advisable.

Most of the time, transcoding results in the loss of the resolution of the image. Quality versus quantity is a perpetual juggling act – especially with streaming media. For DVD purposes, MPEG-2 can be encoded from an AVI the most faithfully. The drawbacks with MPEG, though, tend to be related to luminance issues.

>6< In the edit, this looks like a perfectly well-managed and balanced shot.

>3<

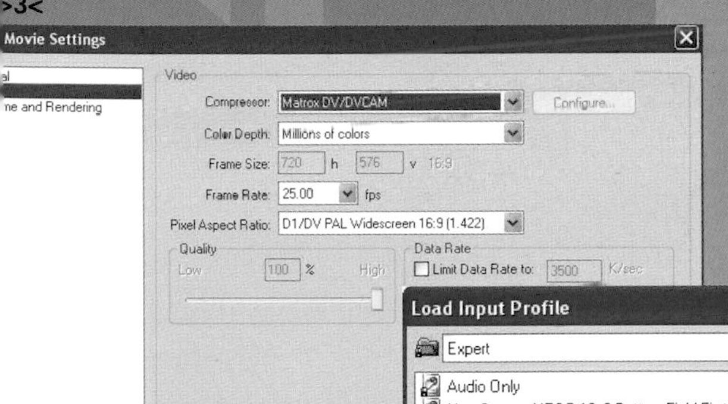

>4<

>5<

>6<

>7< Changing the gamma, black and white levels to it, reveal the ugly secret. The shot was repositioned in the edit to place the subject at the left of frame for aesthetic purposes. While the computer monitor reads heavy black levels as heavy black levels, there is a difference in signal between a dark image and a black matte. This is exactly what transcoding or recompression like to show in detail – and so do CRTs.

Cleaning your pictures is also a chance – if you need to – to convert the video's entire chrominance and luminance values to a broadcast-friendly version. This is usually done at the click of a preset.

If it's going to be streaming media, it's not just simple Web colours, it's movement, contrast, and size issues that you will have to deal with. This is far better achieved outside the cleaner and in the serious encoder.

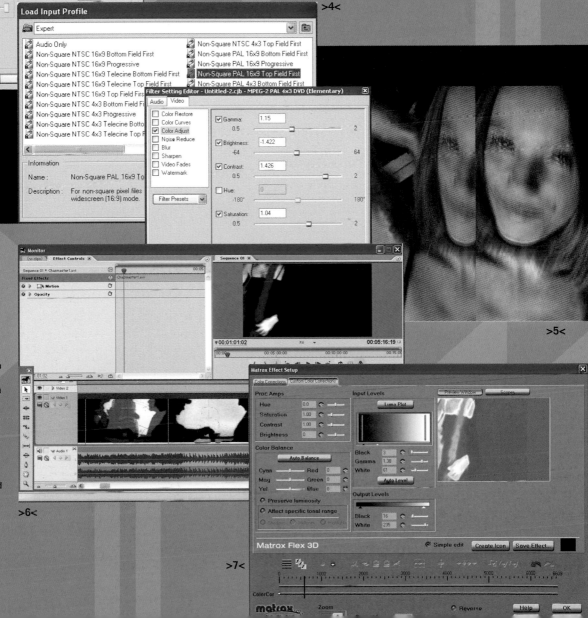

>7<

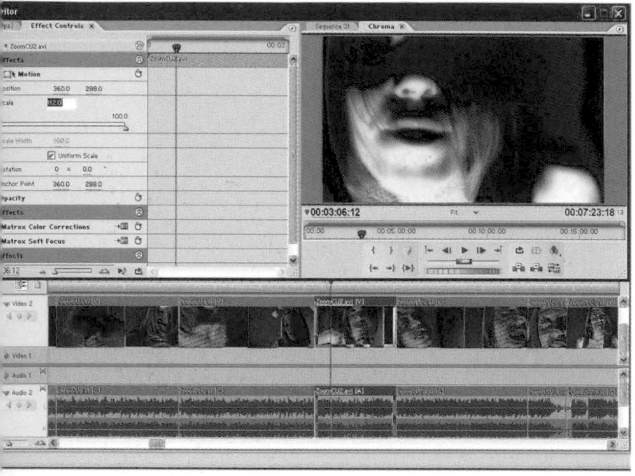

>2<

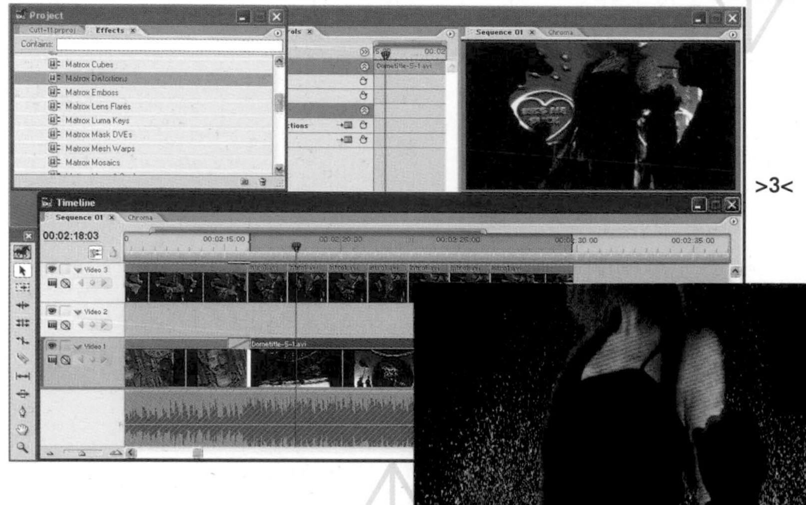

>3<

>4<

>1<

HUSH UP: **HIDING MIS-TAKES**

Mistakes are not always mistakes. They can be simply leaving the camera on while you shifted position, as the talent fluffed, when you altered focus, or after you called cut. The rubbish that you're left with is usually trimmed away at the first cut, if you've captured it at all. Sometimes, though, these mistakes can not just save your edit, but throw it a million bucks.

>1< This sequence is free-dancing, free-camera: the worst world for greenscreen. There's a shot that could well be used were it not for the clipping of the screen.

>2< Scaling up slightly on the shot doesn't just make it usable for keying, it creates a more intimate feel to the clip – something that the sequence was missing. Mistakes can also be due to historical bad workmanship – and this can be even more frustrating when it's a legacy issue. Try what you can.

>3< A few light years later in this edit, there are meteoric problems. This keyed background doesn't respond to the same colour correction. The original background edit is gamma-ed to the hilt. It also doesn't exist anymore in any form that will help it to be corrected. The solution here is to listen to the soundtrack – it's wallpapering a snare build.

>4< When colour or luma correction only creates a badly resolved image, make it obviously and deliberately badly resolved. Adding a distortion effect to the background not only treats the snare audio as a sting, but serves here to highlight the repeated forward/reverse actions of the performers.

The problems with black mattes showing as black mattes when compared with the crushed blacks of an image during compression, is as real an issue during presentation as it is with an MPEG on a CRT. With any movie that you might watch on DVD, these differences in saturation are quite apparent between 16:9 borders and any black shadow in the movie itself.

The better solution is always to revisit and resize the original in the edit. That's hardly a challenge, though, and often such issues are not so much sent to try us as to offer an opportunity to experiment.

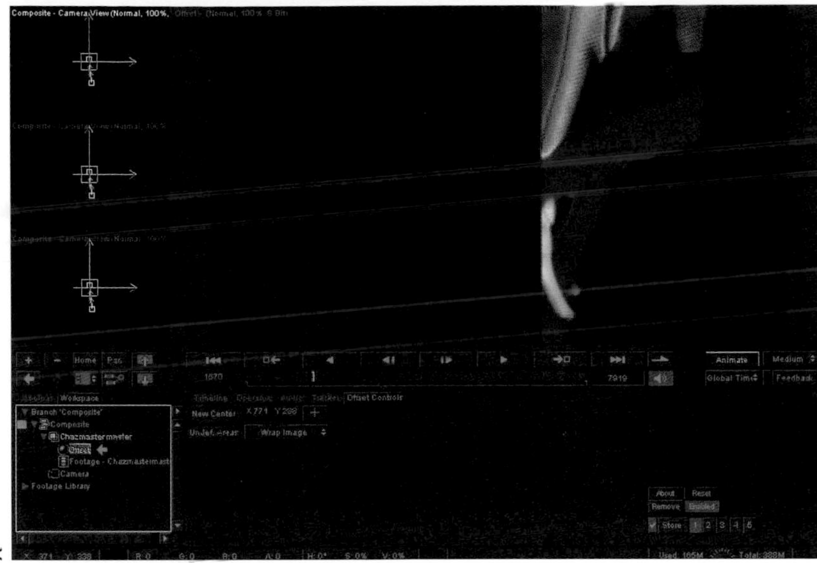

>1<

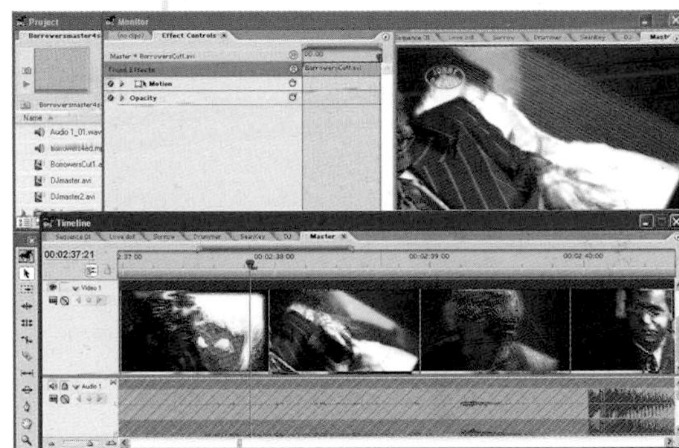

>3<

>1< In this case, taking a keyframed pan during the problematic scene to move from left to right controls the obvious revelation of the black matte. This, of course, only brings in the left edge of the frame – hardly a solution.

>2< Selecting an option to repeat the edge pixels continues the image over the black matte, and the pan not only solves the problem, but effectively also ups the ante of the video itself: even the closed frame is not sacred...

>3< Using an outtake of a musician falling off his stool, enabled the video to go somewhere. By using it as a pay-off to the musical epilog, it offers a chance to lighten the tonal play-out after a darkish video.

Sometimes, just re-watching your video at the end of all of your tweakings reveals niggles, glitches, and bugbears that just don't sit well. It may well be that no-one else will ever notice...but that's hardly the point.

Fixing clips or entire sequences and covering up mistakes is part and parcel of the product – and *including* mistakes is one of the liberties that a music video can take.

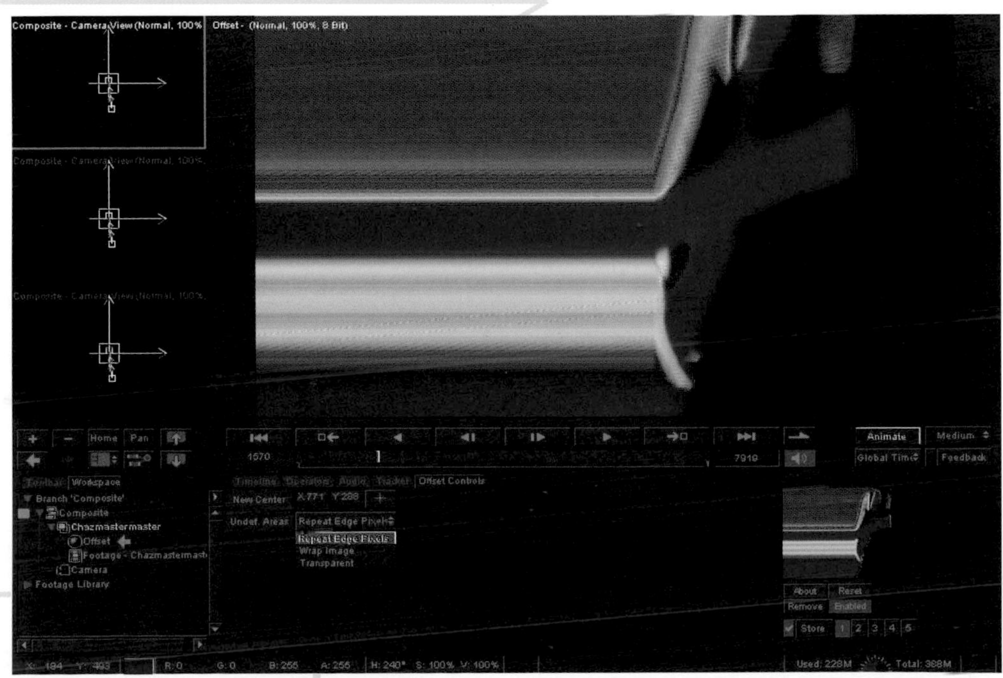

>2<

JONNY
QUALITY
>4<

JONNY
QUALITY
>5<

JONNY
QUALITY
>6<

JONNY
QUALITY
>7<

JONNY
QUALITY
>8<

JONNY
QUALITY
>9<

JONNY
QUALITY
>10<

>11<

>4–10< With broadcast, pay-offs like this encourage play to the end of the video; if not, they at least encourage a volunteer viewer to stick to the end. For the musicians themselves, it also has meaning. The lead singer has had to endure puppet eyes for the entire video, while the band's brains has only had to endure glamour. A quick role-reversal that accounts for nothing in the video becomes just desserts…

>11–12< As-lives can let you keep your mistakes in the shoot. The more obvious the mistake, the more believable the sync is. This outtake cutaway was put in because it said so much more than the mime itself – a candid shot is reality.

>13< With this shot and subsequent reverse shots, both cameras – if you care to look – are not hard to spot. It creates the essence of the video: a get-what-you-can free-for-all – and not at all like the three mimed takes that was the reality.

>12<

>13<

their own and emphasizing them can simply open them up to ridicule.

Sometimes, though, in-video captions work with the video as a standalone artform. Jake Scott's *Everybody Hurts* for REM uses them to read thoughts, StyleWar's *Main Offender* for The Hives uses them as superhero camp. They can contribute to the visuals on an auteur level.

But while titling or crediting has the amazing ability to build the video up to be knocked down, branding the frame can sometimes add an edge of marketing professionalism. It stamps an identity in the same way that television channels (born out of MTV/VH1 rivalry) and video property copyright holders do when they identify themselves.

TOP: The intro to this as-live music video is a 50-second visual documentary that leads to the venue for the gig. In this case, the track (A Town That I Love So Well) and the Irish transition to New York, has certain post-9/11 connotations. Coupled with this, that day's date helps to create the believable unbelievable: the band is performing live.

One other tricksy way of using in-video titles is in order to introduce the band. From S Club 7 to The Gorillaz, this is based on the utter conviction that the musicians *will* return… If in doubt, don't stick your neck out.

For marketing's sake, it may well be necessary to incorporate text on the product. Don't automatically run text, captions, and graphics on the video itself. Video boxes have printed sleeves, DVDs have root menus, and websites are born for text. The music video and your own attachment is not the point of the exercise – the music itself is.

Low-art or pastiche sometimes resorts to the lyrical bouncing ball. This is the lyric in captions to serve as a translation, irony, or artistic pomp. This can be laughable for all the wrong reasons. Lyrics, when spelt out, often take on a new life of

In effect, it's working in the right circles, and accomplishing this with your own music video distinguishes it as privileged viewing for non-broadcast marketing purposes. It becomes a band brand.

Branding with logos works at a psychological level. An audience reads frames just like they read a book. In the western world, this is from left to right. A viewer attempts to get every bit of information available from an image quickly and then re-scans to read change. The process is similar to variable bitrate webstreaming. Those things that don't change are stored until they do. Therefore, the best positioning for a logo is in the top left. It's the first thing that a viewer will spot, and the first to be stored away, allowing them to continue watching without distraction.

Sometimes, the changing frame defines the location of the non-changing logo. If emphasis is given to a certain part of the frame throughout the video, don't put the logo there. If the top left interferes, go for the bottom left. If it covers essential information on the top or the bottom left, put it in the top right.

Use logos discreetly. Make sure they are within screen safety and are small but legible. Try to use a degree of opacity and don't outshine your images with logo pizzazz. Using the GIF as a matte and adding a sheen takes the emphasis away from a monochrome stamp and allows for the logo to bleed into the frame without an opacity value attributed.

If you are going to use text or graphics with your music video, a few things to bear in mind are:

Always get the *current* logo. Things can move very quickly once marketing gets underway, and the last thing you want is to be instantly outdated.

If the band use a certain font as part of their brand, get the digital file from them to use with the video. You preferably want it in TrueType or OpenType format – and on screen it should always be anti-aliased, and high-res.

Graphics and text created in bitmap-based graphics applications will be created with square pixels. Sometimes your edit application won't do the resizing sums for you. In this case, the proportions on import will be wrong so make sure you address it to your screen ratio.

Keep captions to two lines maximum and never leave these captions on for more than five seconds.

Always work your title in the NLE within screen safety margins.

If you insist on crediting, keep them until the end. Anything up front puts the video at risk of switch-off.

***ABOVE RIGHT:** The logo works well positioned in the top-left corner of the screen. The GIF is used as a matte, and a light sheen has been added to it to help it blend with its surroundings.*

***TOP:** Sometimes, it makes sense to introduce the band by name titles. If the video is hitting the Net and watched by those unfamiliar with the musicians, and the site is backed by text concerning the band, it serves as a useful and memorable cross-reference.*

***ABOVE LEFT.** This location pictured is clearly not going to work bottom right, as it's covering one of the main focal points for the view. It is also far too intrusive.*

***ABOVE:** The bottom right of any frame may be the last focal point for the eye, but directors tend to use this x/y position a lot in composition. Any logo placement is likely to cause conflict...*

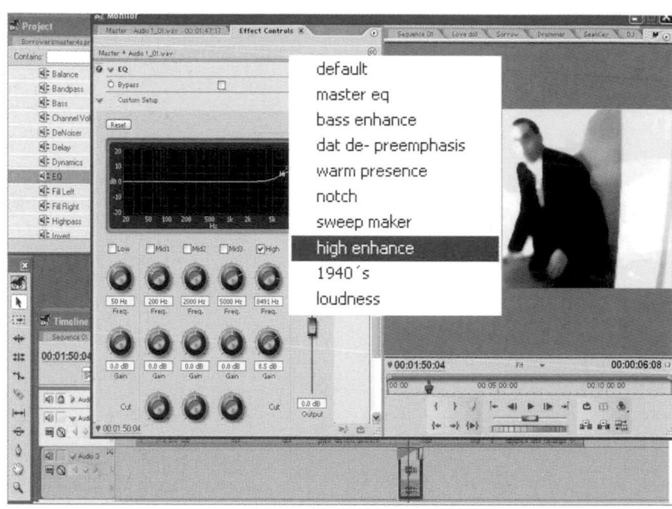

DOWN TOOLS: **AUDIO COMPRESSION AND EQ**

Audio mixing shouldn't be your concern. It should be in the lap(top) of the musicians. If you do have to fiddle with the music, however, software applications can supply a few knobs to twiddle.

First off, you need to understand how it all works. Compression sounds like a bad thing. This is because we are used to how it affects visuals. With audio, compression can help produce better quality audio than the raw studio or live recording. It keeps it within defined parameters that don't upset the human ear.

Compressors and limiters operate by controlling the dynamic range. A compressor can only define certain compression parameters before it becomes the job of the limiter. Like the human ear, they do this by focusing on the average sound in the range. To get to this average sound and to focus on it requires four fundamental processes for compressors. The following are the types of commands that will accept input values:

***ABOVE LEFT:** Default EQ is a flatline whereby all frequencies are equal.*

***ABOVE RIGHT:** Adding a* High Enhance *preset amplifies the higher frequencies of the track, which is perfect for lifting duller sound out of background audio or noise. The danger is always hiss, but presets will not let you go too far in this direction. If you still need to pull up your sound, manually controlling the higher frequencies lets you exceed or temper those presets.*

Ratio

The ratio of compression is the representation of the increase in input dB level as a proportion to the increase in output level dB. A ratio of 8:1, therefore, indicates that an 8dB increase coming into the compressor would only output as an increase of one decibel. The value of the ratio is that of the amount of change that has taken place for input and output, which makes it a constant value.

Threshold

Just as a neutral density filter kicks in when there's too much light, the threshold for audio is the defined tolerance before it has had enough. Again, as with digital video, gain helps to amplify to the point that *reduction* of gain begins to take place. This reduction of gain leads up to the point of the threshold – a defined dB value – at which compression starts to take place. While the ratio is set as a constant, gain is a variable.

ABOVE LEFT: Copying and pasting exactly the same EQ value to the original scratch track ensures that all of your sounds will sound exactly the same.

If you are using a mixer that defines the threshold as a *knee*, a hard knee is an absolute point where compression starts suddenly. The alternative – a soft knee – is where the threshold offers a slightly wider range of values that lead to compression.

Attack

The time value given for attack is the amount of time it takes for compression to occur after the threshold has been reached. Despite being measured largely in milliseconds, the attack time has a bearing on how the sound is perceived. Short attack times compress almost instantaneously – and while this means that the sound is bright and clean, it truncates the effect of short beats and instruments that develop their sound during the note or beat. A longer attack time leaves any sound over the threshold in danger of peaking. A balanced approach is thus required.

Release

The release time is the time (in anything from milliseconds to whole seconds) that It takes after compression for the sound to return to gain. This, again, is not as simple as wanting it to happen as quickly as possible. The two extremes (too fast or too slow) both lead to distortion of sound to some degree.

With quick release times, any low frequencies distort, an effect that some engineers utilize for mastering tracks, termed *pumping*. The flipside is *breathing*, longer release times that cause higher frequencies to distort as they slowly return to gain. Engineers can use this with a quick attack to create that slight backwards effect that hip-hop uses for percussion. Breathing is also apparent with the oscillation of the sound created with a high compression ratio. Because there is a greater change in the gain variable, the fluctuation of sign becomes a lot more noticeable.

Whether or not you have a chance to experiment with the sound itself depends on your job description and your relationship with the musicians. If you think that it's going to help the video on playback, though, it is questionable whether you are in charge of how it sounds as well as how it looks.

ATTENTION TO CLEANLINESS

The example used previously allows for flexibility with sound. While the existing music track stands proud and is what it is, the new scratching sound needs to shine a little more. Dull recordings are often victims of low compression, of mics with low high-frequency response, of bad room acoustics, and of degeneration from analogue sources. In this instance, the way this audio track was recorded has dulled the scratch. It needs polish.

Cleaner sound usually means higher frequencies, higher gain, and a high bandpass. All of these options can be adjusted with equalization. EQ-ing is the balancing of frequency bands by boost and reduction within a sound clip.

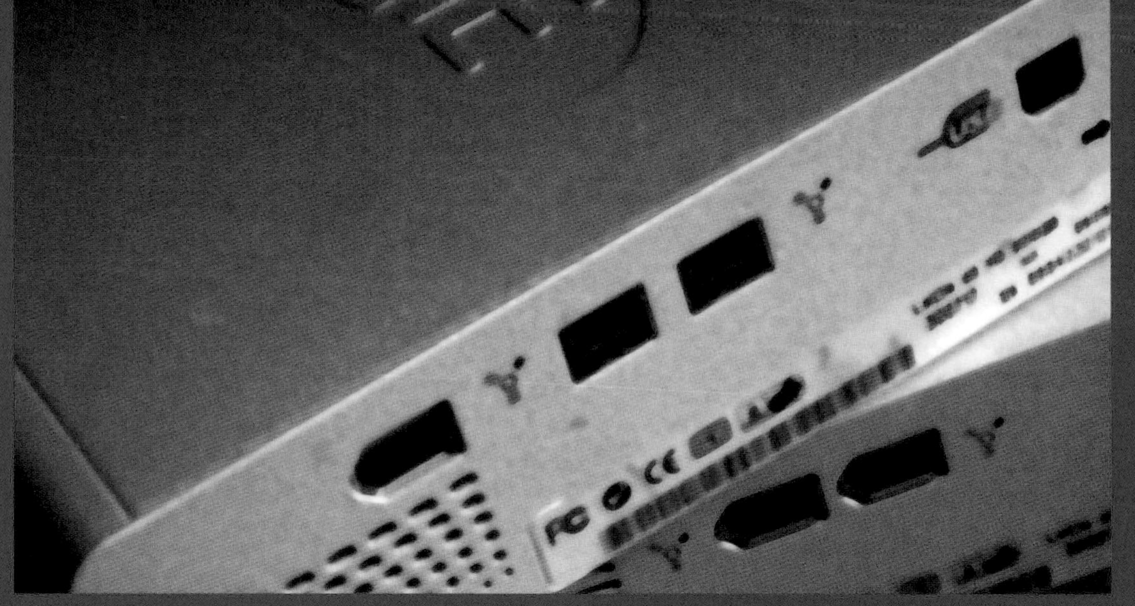

RIGHT: When files are stored on a hard disk they are split up into small chunks, which are placed on the drive wherever there's room. On a blank disk these will be placed in a nice logical order allowing the computer to breeze through them, on a disk that's had a few months heavy usage, though, they might be stored all over the place, and the disk needs to spin a lot more to find the right chunks. Defragmenting is the process of going through the disk and sorting the chunks back into order. This not only allows data to be found faster, but also means that the disk has to spin less, lowering the chances of a disk crash.

BACKING UP: **SAFETY TIPS AND STORAGE**

The music video – any video – is a time-based medium. It uses time as the fourth dimension, and it certainly takes time to get it right. Think of the time you've spent in pre-production, in production, and now in the edit. The last thing you will want to do is to go back to drawing your storyboard with nothing to show for all your hard work.

Backing up is worth your time. Video files are large; audio and project files not as large. Every 4½ minutes of uncompressed digital video will take up 1 GB of hard drive space, which makes it difficult to just burn off to CD-R. This is where an external hard drive comes in very handy. Copying your selected, captured clips off on to another hard drive and taking it with you to bed is comforting, but being able to copy entire projects over will have you sleeping peacefully.

If you don't have an external hard drive, the next best thing is to burn off an EDL. An EDL is an Edit Decision List, a list of data that informs the computer of every clip and its whereabouts on your timeline. Using an EDL is standard practice for working with off-line edits. If you have been off-lining to save render time and space on your hard drive for complex edits, use your EDL for conforming your online work.

EDLs fit easily onto CDs, and so does the data that forms the project. How the application chooses to read this – should you need it – is another thing entirely, and is dependent on the versatility of the app itself.

A hard drive after a hard edit often needs defragmenting to sequence the different clips that you've captured logically, as well as the different projects, files, and titles that you've created. Doing this at intervals throughout the edit – and before exporting and burning – eases up block space for large music video masters, and makes your computer work faster and more efficiently.

External storage systems may well be where your source footage came from. Panasonic's P2 system or even Sony's MPEG memory cards are steering the market towards non-cassette storage devices that provide a serious alternative to tapes that can be easily damaged or lost. The by-product of these methods is that they also provide a back-up –

ABOVE LEFT: With any hardware – just like any music video – it's all about connections. USB2 still hasn't set the world on fire, and FireWire now comes in FireWire 800 and FireWire DV. The differentiation between the two FireWires is measured in megabits per second (800 being double DV).

RIGHT: External storage drives come in a variety of disc sizes that will make your computer look lightweight. Lacie's range of drives exceed 200GB, which should see you through the next few music videos.

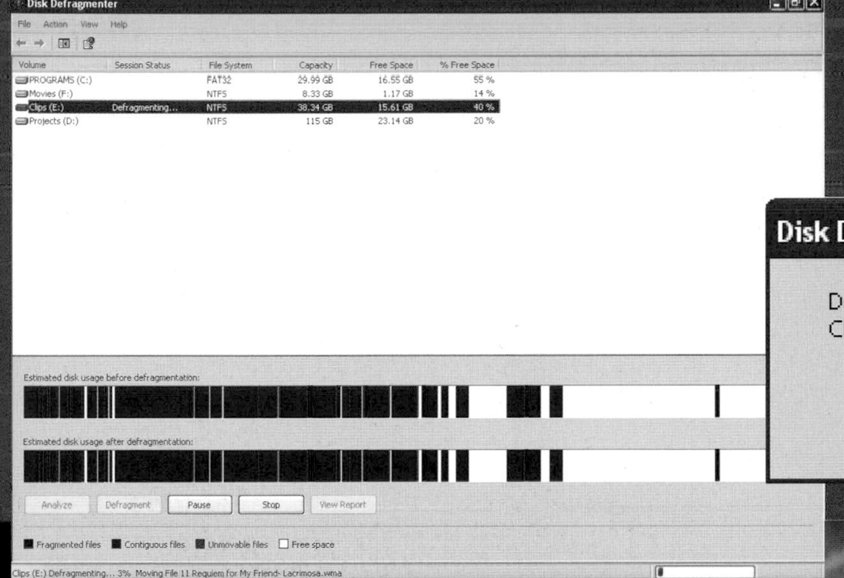

or, with transcoding from your hard drive, a viable storage means.

When you are working in your NLE, adjust your settings to make sure that projects are saved regularly. What you don't want to do is save projects so that any recent action is undo-able. The balance is a combination of saving, saving as, and creating and nesting new sequences.

Computers crash – and it's frustrating when they do. Humans aren't infallible either, and anything from not opting to remove hardware safely to simple spillage can leave you high and dry. It's a lesson that only needs to be learned once, but make sure it's not while you're working on your music video.

7
JONNY

MARKETING &
DISTRIBUTION:
BURN BABY BURN

What inevitably gives at this stage is quality. Say goodbye to it right now. In return for your DVD Devil's Pact, you can have what you want: an audible, readable, wieldable video.

Transcoding is the process of turning one type of file into another. This can be a messy operation with cheaper-end products. It's a question of rough round-offs or complex algorithms.

If you are going to transcode – and it's usually to convert an AVI into an MPEG-2 or AVI/MOV for streaming – clean your image as you encode through the same application if you can. It will be a cleaner process.

Despite the flicker (that will often appear even when the video is viewed at 100KHz), images that are displayed on a progressively scanning television or a computer monitor are a lot more stable. While television broadcast itself is only slowly moving toward progressive scanning, most movie DVDs now use it as standard. Don't think, however, that it will give your music video a movie 'look'. That is very much down to shooting with the 24p standard. If you shoot progressive, then you'll transcode as progressive; if you shoot interlaced, don't even think about trying to de-interlace it again at a later stage. What you are left with will be half the picture, and half the resolution. Again, stick with what you've shot and captured with.

>1< The most basic option is always going to be what you want to encode your project as. Your safest bet is to continue working through your video card and associated app. This is likely to result in an AVI. If you don't want an AVI, the chances are that it may have to find another compressor in your computer to carry out your request.

>2< The process of encoding involves compression. The quality of this depends on the quality of the codec. A quick look into your system will show those available. Instead of doing the work and trying out all of the codecs, your choice of file format will hopefully pick a default for that extension. If not, get on-line and search for the sophistication and spec of each one.

ZIPPING UP: **FORMATS AND ENCODING FOR DISTRIBUTION**

After all of your time spent in the NLE, you've really only got a whole load of 0s and 1s with brand new values. They can't be seen on your television, they won't be recognized by your DVD player and the file will be so large that no-one in their right mind would attempt to download it. Something's gotta give.

The point is always to avoid as many mathematical hurdles as possible. If there are presets, use them: it's likely that your encoder knows best. Here's a breakdown of the different types of presets available:

Ratio

Arcing is the practice of taking a 4:3 ratio project into a 16:9 ratio. It's kind of desperate, and leads to distortion and loss of resolution on the x-axis. When you're transcoding, adding other elements that change like this, try adopting the patience of a saintly director. Keep the ratio of the file the same and alter the size of the frame, if necessary.

Scanning

Your scanning options (progressive or interlaced) depend on how you shot and captured your video. Good cameras provide the option to shoot with progressive scanning, and if you chose to do this, then you probably know why.

Fields

No fields? Upper or lower first? These are only questions for those who are using interlaced scanning. Using the same field order as the original source material will stop any sign of jerkiness on playback after transcoding. The software should find this default depending on your region, and if you captured using the same software, there shouldn't be an issue. The basis to which one you select is that FireWire will capture the bottom field first, and an analogue signal with a break-out-box will capture the top field first.

Size

Size *is* everything, of course, but this will only be appropriate if you are transcoding for streaming media. If you want to keep a few more frames per second or you want a bit more quality in your image, then it's size that needs to be addressed for a stream. It's got to be as small as possible for transferring over data lines.

>3< If your film is shot in progressive scan mode, then there is no need to use fields. If you've shot in interlaced mode, then the fields setting will depend on how you imported the film from the camera.

>4< The pixel aspect ratio is a different ratio than that of frame size. It is the ratio of each pixel, the vertical divided by the horizontal. Whilst this may sound as though it is the same ratio as frame size, the variations in standard, widescreen, and anamorphic frame size dictate that it is the pixels that have to be understood at encoding.

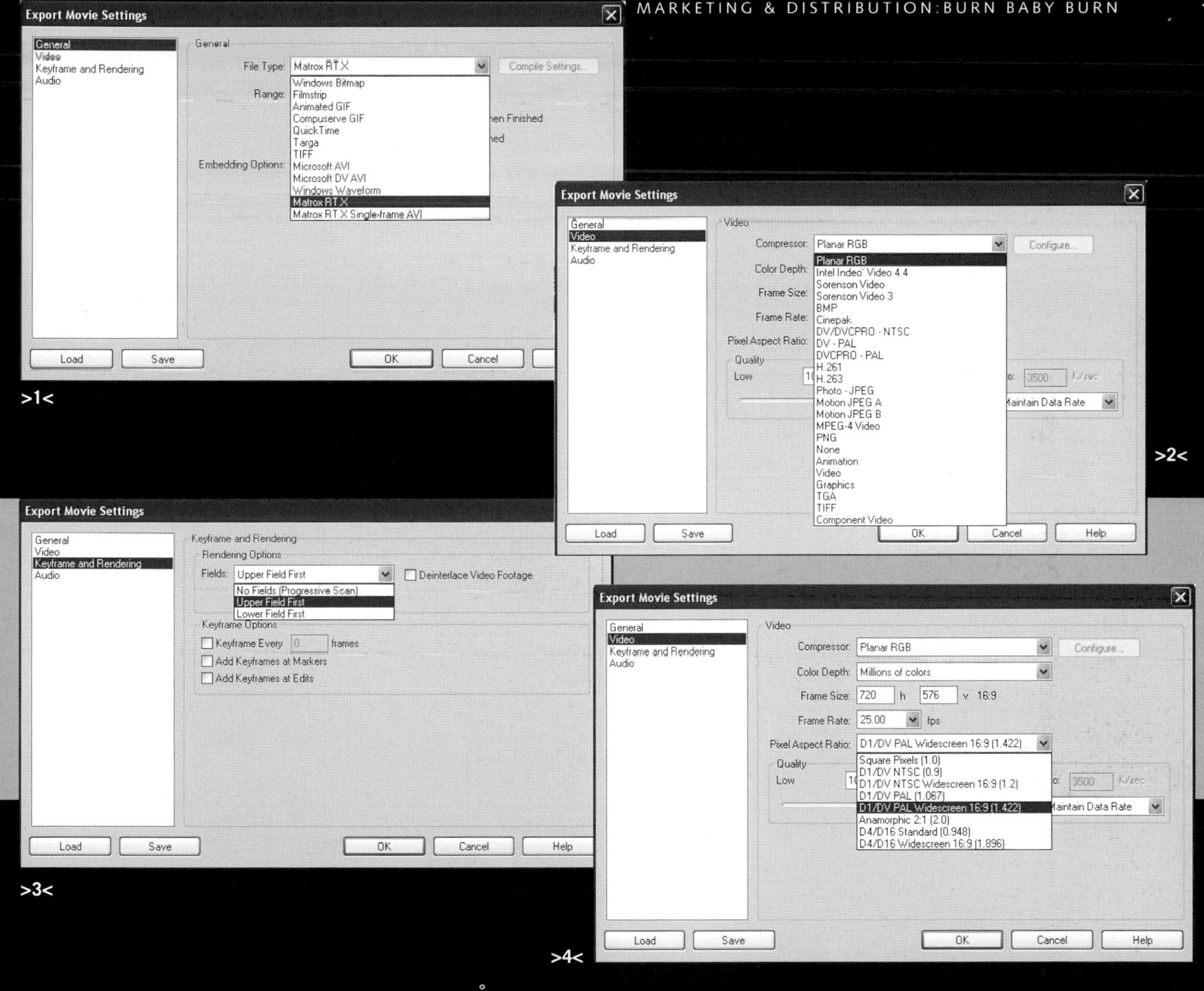

Getting your pixel aspect ratio wrong leads to loss of resolution and picture distortion. It shouldn't be necessary, given your software's intelligence, to option anything else. If you are faced with a list, here's what to use:

Pixel Aspect Ratio (PAR)	Original frame size	Encoded frame
D1/DV NTSC (0.9)	720 x 480 / 720 x 486	4:3
D1/DV NTSC WIDESCREEN (1.2)	720 x 480 / 720 x 486	16:9
D1/DV PAL (1.067)	720 x 576	4:3
D1/DV PAL WIDESCREEN (1.422)	720 x 576	16:9
D4/D16 STANDARD (0.948)	1440 x 1024 or 2880 x 2048	4:3
D4/D16 WIDESCREEN (1.896)	1440 x 1024 or 2880 x 2048	16:9
ANAMORPHIC 2:1 (2.0)	Use this for DV shot with an anamorphic lens	
NON-SQUARE PIXELS	Use this for pure graphics encoding	

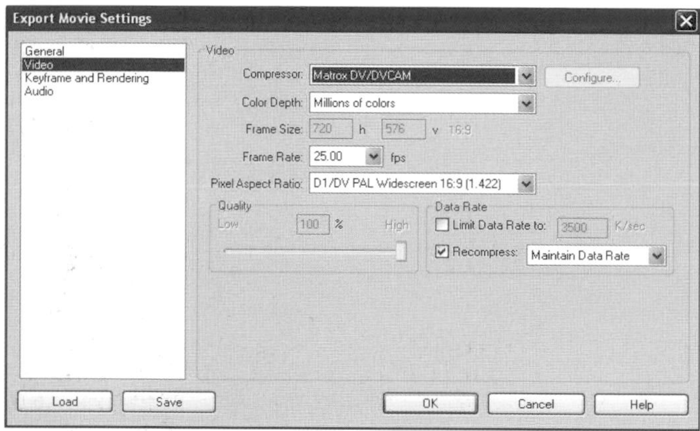

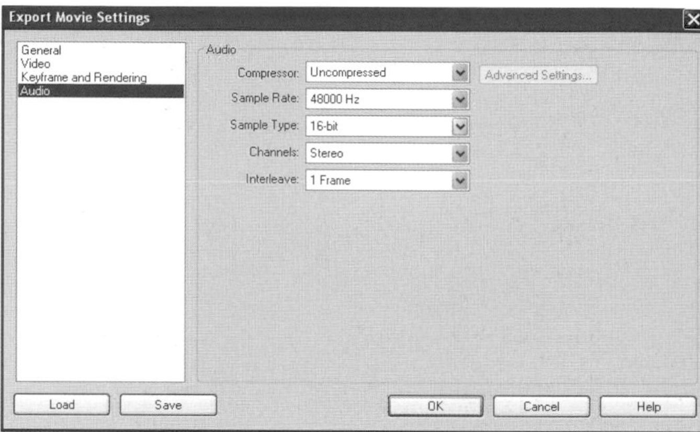

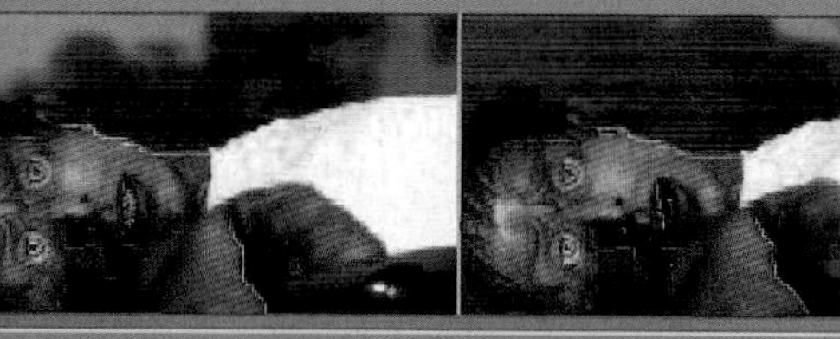

BURNING DOWN: **EXPORTING AND BURNING YOUR MUSIC VIDEO**

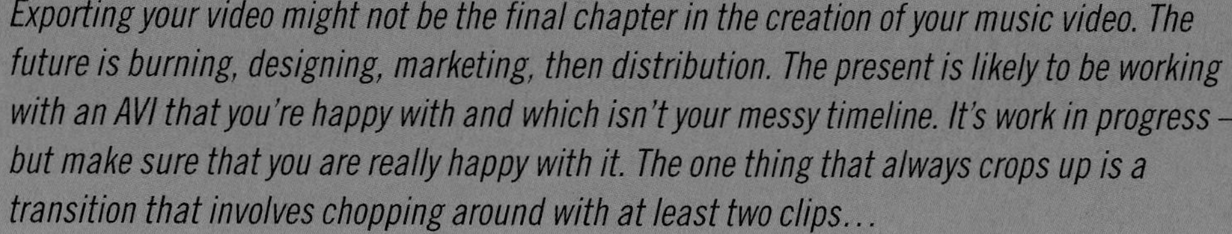

Exporting your video might not be the final chapter in the creation of your music video. The future is burning, designing, marketing, then distribution. The present is likely to be working with an AVI that you're happy with and which isn't your messy timeline. It's work in progress – but make sure that you are really happy with it. The one thing that always crops up is a transition that involves chopping around with at least two clips...

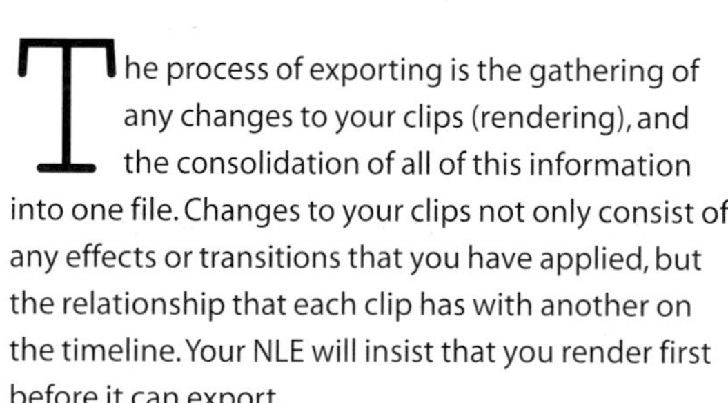

The process of exporting is the gathering of any changes to your clips (rendering), and the consolidation of all of this information into one file. Changes to your clips not only consist of any effects or transitions that you have applied, but the relationship that each clip has with another on the timeline. Your NLE will insist that you render first before it can export.

If this *is* a work in progress, it is essential that you maintain your settings as you have already done in the edit. The exceptions to the rule are when the clip itself is to be exported with an entirely different effect to the rest of your edit – such as a lower frame-rate to infer film effect.

LEFT: Your project settings are likely to stay the same, and your software application will hopefully use these by default. That is to say that frame-rate, aspect ratio, and audio settings will not change. Always check. Any changes to these three elements followed by import back into the project will not sit happily – if at all.

If you've been using a video card in association with your edit software, keep using it as your encoder.

BELOW: Unless you've been cutting to no audio or you intend to relay it, make sure that you maintain the same CD quality sound that you went in with.

LEFT & BELOW: Importing the exported file as a complete AVI back on to a new timeline is not only good housekeeping, it's a rewarding and reinvigorating experience. Time to start afresh...

Once your AVI is complete (i.e. master video and master audio, as well as trimmed top and bottom), it is ready for encoding. Cleaners encode as they clean; DVD authoring software encodes as it burns. Whether or not the new file is created in your computer or burnt straight to disc relies on this difference. If the new file, as well as the project created by the application demands a new lot of computer memory, now is the time to sort it out.

RIGHT: The process of DVD burning uses some form of content protection. This might be region coding, or it might be CSS (Content Scrambling System) – both offering encryption that protect the copying of your digital data. Whether or not this is what you want is up to your checkbox finger. The more audiences that you want to see your music video and to hear the music, the fewer obstacles you should put in their path. This, of course, works against you if there is money to be made from selling the product with an internationally controlled release.

BELOW: Burning to DVD takes time to transcode the AVI into an MPEG. Pre-mastering is the collection of data, the multiplexing of video and audio and some maths. Because the program is copying the AVI again to change the numbers – and incorporating the features of any menu, additional video, audio, and buttons – it needs a bit of room to manoeuvre. Make sure that your hard drive has space to cope with this.

BELOW CENTRE: Any other burning questions are likely to concern speed. If you're having problems with burning discs, look at the speed and make adjustments in your application to suit. If you get it wrong, the app is likely to stop with an error message – and if you're using DVD Writables, you might as well throw it away…

Either way, a mastered MPEG requires a codec (a decoder) that will play the DVD. Domestic DVD players offer more and more versatility to play domestically authored DVDs; computers aren't so willing. Computers – specifically PCs – would rather make even more money out of playback of a DVD that you've created inside it. The more encryption that you check, the more specific the codec needs to be. Alternatively, the process of ripping doesn't involve encryption, but simply transcodes MPEGs into something else that your hard drive can read. It's lossy and messy, and some rippers still require a program to extract this information on playback. The nature of the Internet, though, is that everybody wants something for nothing – and this includes ripping applications.

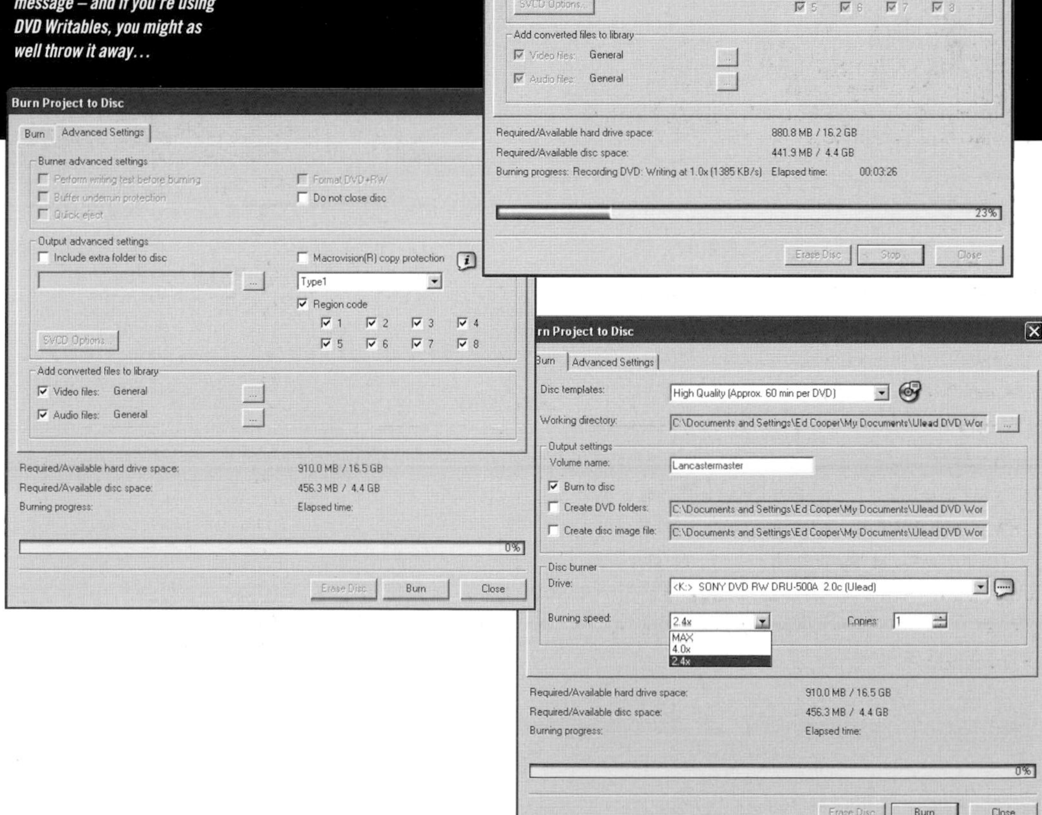

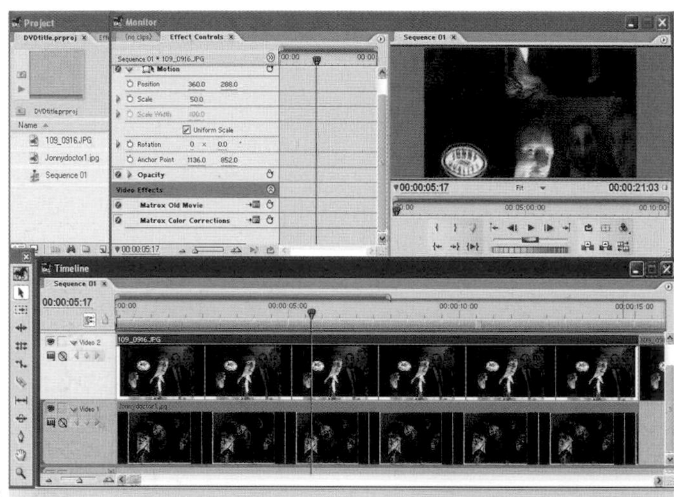

>2<

>3<

AUTHORING DVDS

>1<

DVD authoring software can be quite expensive. Shopping around and comparing utilities is the way to go. Beware of bargain Limited Editions (meaning 'limited' in capability), and address the software in the light of your product – i.e. if it's widescreen, make sure that the software can handle 16:9.

Look at a few of your own DVDs. What do they have that make the product look professional? This is like an effects question in an edit – although your authoring app may have the whizbangzooms, does it actually just make the disc look cheap?

The first stop is always to reach an agreement with the talent as to their marketing strategy. What is their logo? What is their font? This is all to do with incorporating the musicians' branding strategy into the video product.

>4<

>5<

Start
Capture
Edit
Menu
Finish
Borrowers.dws (249.1 MB)
Menu
Button
Text
Style
Attributes
Playlist
Frame
Shadow
Brightness (0:dark 99:bright):
50
Contrast (0:low 99:high):
50
Transparency (%):
13
Rotation (degrees):
7
Video - General
N03_PAL
R01_NTSC
R02_NTSC
R03_PAL
S01_NTSC
S02_NTSC
S03_NTSC
~Masterpr...
DVDtitle
Borrowersd...
Borrowersd...
DVDtitle2
JONNY QUALITY
MENU
Insert object or menu here
BLANK MENU

>6<

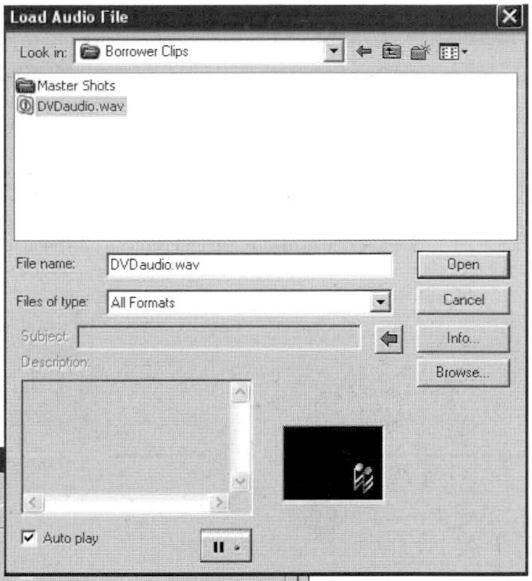
Load Audio File
Look in:
Borrower Clips
Master Shots
DVDaudio.wav
File name:
DVDaudio.wav
Files of type:
All Formats
Subject:
Description:
Open
Cancel
Info...
Browse...
Auto play

>7<

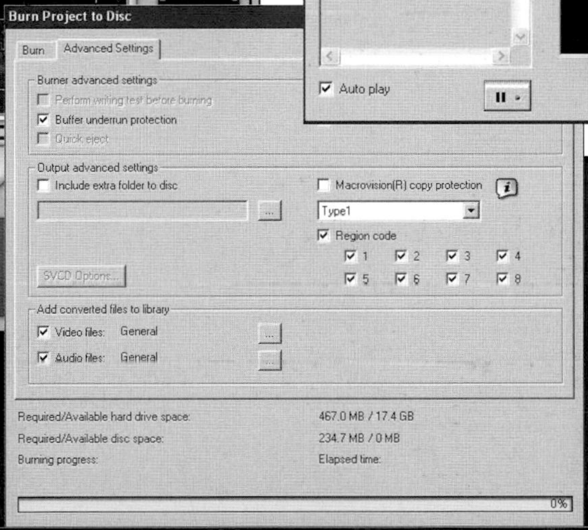
Burn Project to Disc
Burn
Advanced Settings
Burner advanced settings
Perform writing test before burning
Buffer underrun protection
Quick eject
Output advanced settings
Include extra folder to disc
Macrovision(R) copy protection
Type1
Region code
1
2
3
4
5
6
7
8
SVCD Options...
Add converted files to library
Video files:
General
Audio files:
General
Required/Available hard drive space:
467.0 MB / 17.4 GB
Required/Available disc space:
234.7 MB / 0 MB
Burning progress:
Elapsed time:
0%

>8<

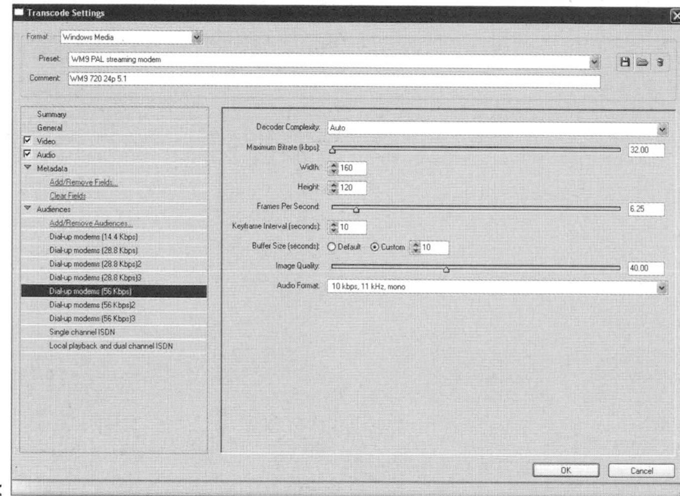

>1<

>1< Windows Media exports at only 6.25 frames per second (PAL) by default. Changing the fps for a smoother animation increases the file size (and thereby lengthens the download time). Taking the image quality slider down, or reducing the image size itself, balances the file size.

>2< The summary for QuickTime highlights the Packet Size Limit. This is the size of file that downloads to the receptor computer in a chunk before it begins to play. This doesn't change the file size of the entire video, but changes the way that the viewer perceives it. A smaller size limit means that the server delivers each 'packet' of video in small, frequent measures. A larger limit means that the viewer will wait longer at the start of downloading in order to receive an image, but will then experience the video for a longer duration while the next packet is being downloaded.

STREAMING DOWN: **MUSIC VIDEO ON THE INTERNET**

Cleaning picture and sound is both an essential and fatuous process when streaming (aka progressively downloading) your video over the Internet.

Even with broadband and a large bandwidth at your own side of the server, you still have to think of the intended audience. If it's a *general* Web audience (i.e. worldwide), then the lowest common denominator receptor computer will be a 56K modem, slow, and in dire need of a good clean-up and de-frag. This is precisely the source reason that your 1GB promo will need compressing.

Compressing a video to a screen size suitable for viewing, and file size suitable for downloading, involves the digital information being summarized.

PRIMARY DIGITAL INFORMATION

- **> Chrominance**
- **> Luminance**
- **> Video Sample Rate**
- **> Audio Frequency**

Your musician will be pleased to hear that the comparatively small size of the audio information leaves it pretty much negligible. By default, compression *does* change the kHz value (usually from 48kHz with DV), but for streaming or download media, 22kHz is adequate.

Chrominance and luminance levels are adjusted by algorithms. The algorithms are different calculations depending on the different streaming application used. Standard Windows PC choices are Streaming Windows Media, RealMedia, and Quicktime. The Apple Mac uses its proprietary Quicktime, and RealMedia.

The way that chrominance and luminance are affected is by limiting their permissible values. With chrominance, this means rounding off numbers to the nearest Web palette value, creating colours close to – but not true to – the original. Luminance similarly is given new and fewer greyscale values, and the original values are rounded to the nearest allowance.

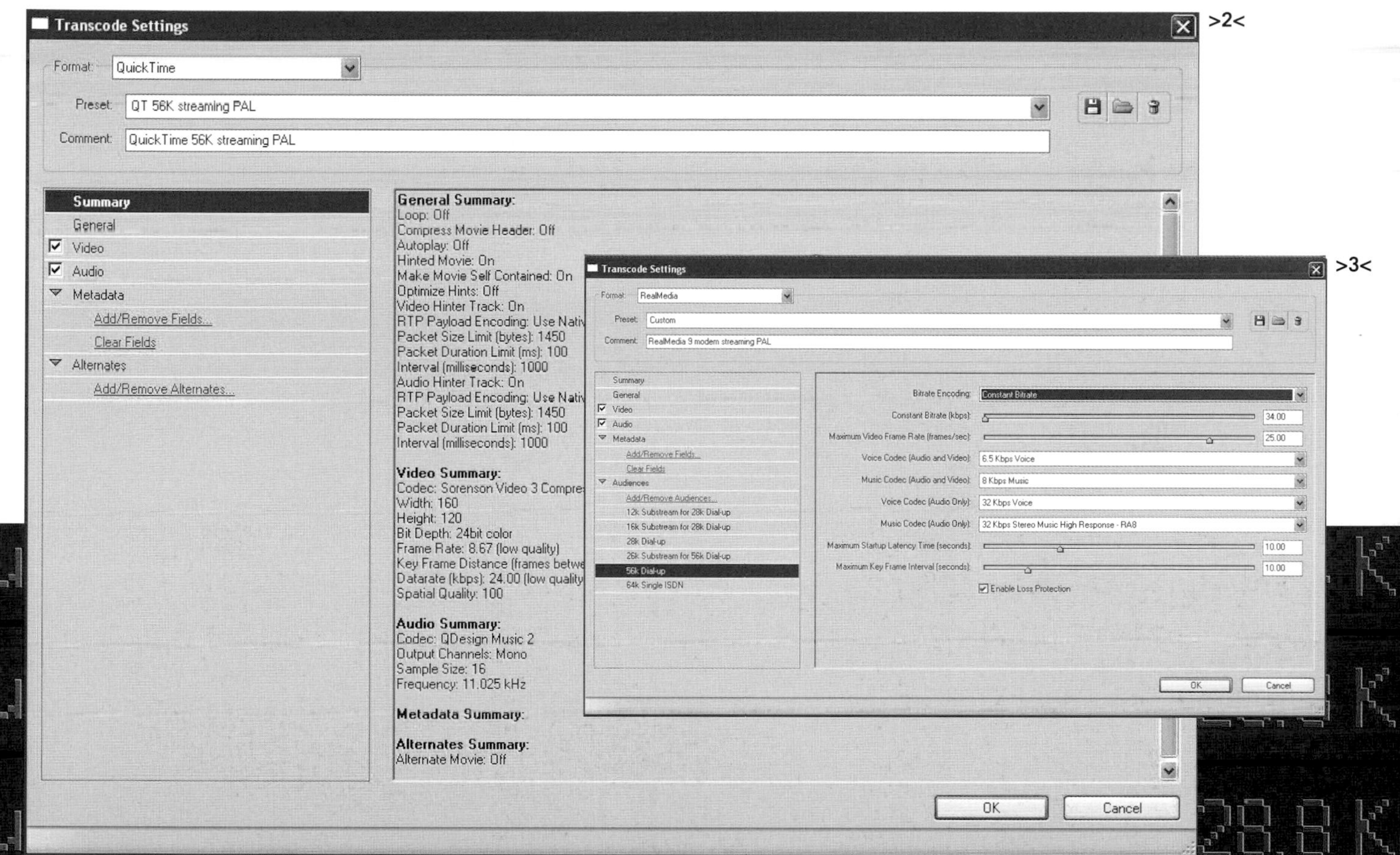

A change in sample rate is the most critical form of compression, where the war between bringing visuals to life, or stopping them dead in their tracks, begins. A low sample rate would be represented as a series of stills; a medium sample rate as an animated flick-book; and a high sample rate as the believable effect of motion in time that you've slaved to create. Of course, the former is information-lite, and the latter not so far off from the GB of promo that you originally mastered.

This promo is short and sweet. These are the variables as applied upon export under preset 56K streaming options. Of course, everything's negotiable, but always at a price.

The two different ways of delivering your music video to your audience are either through streaming or download. Each have their own boredom and frustration issues for a viewer. While the stop-start of streaming packets of information delivers viewing annoyance and incoherence, simple downloading takes time, but allows a user to do something else at the same time, and the privilege of saving the file to their hard drive for fluid playback.

Both methods rely on bitrates for their information to be received by the user. These can either be *constant* or *variable*. They work similarly to mortgage rates – a constant drips the same amount of data at a constant rate; a variable delivers information at different speeds depending on the complexity of each sample of video and audio coming through. If your video has intermittent simple visuals of low motion activity, a variable bitrate is a wiser move as the setting distributes the shorter time taken to stream such images along the course of the entire download.

>3< Instead of a packet, RealMedia's streaming is based on 'realtime' latency – that is, the time required by your computer to respond to the initial download. By default at 56K PAL streaming, this is set at 10 seconds: 10 seconds to gather information from the server before it begins replaying to the viewer. The *Maximum Keyframe Interval* applies to any keyframes that you've added for streaming. This allows exactly the same thing to happen throughout download at those specific frames, buffering and then releasing information.

ABOVE: Compression is always disappointing. While looking superb in Final Cut Pro, encoding and exporting this video to be played on a PC as a .mov made it very dark. It then had to be lightened back in FCP and the process repeated to get an acceptable luminance for the re-compressed video.

The key to getting the best possible visual and aural results while compressing is to shoot and edit the video for streaming purposes from the outset. Always bear in mind where the video is going to be played from way back in pre-production. The three factors that should influence the way that you shoot and the way that you edit to make streaming a quick, image-comprehensive, and altogether painless task are the control of motion, contrast, and detail with the picture.

Motion is perhaps the most important as it is held over a barrel by sample rate. Coupled with this, compression relies on any similarity in picture from one keyframe to the next to make calculations. If a background doesn't change, then the information doesn't have to be resampled with entirely different values, saving crucial download time. With fast motion, though, not only are the values from one image to the other different, but a higher sample rate is needed to register the fast motion.

The other ball in the juggling act is that of the server you choose. Delivering the goods to an audience can be done in different ways, depending on the flexibility of the server.

Unicast

A single data stream copied and sent to multiple viewers on demand.

Multicast

A single data stream accessible by multiple viewers on demand simultaneously.

Reflected Multicast

A (usually) Unicast or (occasionally) Multicast stream that makes a detour via another server to become Multicast.

LEFT: If your band have a tendency to move sharply – in this case, jumping with guitars is the order of the day – consider a higher frame rate so that the movement can be seen. This is far more appropriate for this video during compression at the expanse of colour saturation.

The choice is yours, but bear in mind that specialized media servers may also offer True Streaming, supporting realtime streaming (i.e. no cache file storage). All three, streaming architectures – Windows Media, RealMedia, and QuickTime – are catered for by the server, regulating the transmission rate to compensate for the available bandwidth.

The alternative to streaming is having your video placed on a server as a downloadable media file. This opens up encoding to allow not only for (non-streaming) AVI, MOV, and RM files, but for MPEG as well. Again, you're relying on your audience's boredom threshold. Instead of storing packets of information to your cache and playing them out in portions, a downloadable file simply downloads to a viewer's hard drive for them to play out when completed. The same compression laws apply, though, and the larger the file, the longer it will take the user to download.

What has to be considered is the desirability of the product, and any hype that you can put in place on the page to entice download. If there's interesting information placed on the same page in an entertaining and user-friendly design, then an audience is far more likely to stick with your site. If you're streaming and there are periods of buffering, bite-size chunks of information work well to distract briefly. If the video is available as a hard-drive download, try to keep a user's attention to stay within the pages of your site. Downloading is dull: always consider the audience.

ABOVE LEFT: Detail is one thing that streaming video is pretty terrible at if a lower resolution is chosen. Look at the video; find whatever it is that makes it work and try to preserve it during compression.

ABOVE CENTRE & ABOVE RIGHT: Crushed blacks and nasty whites are, again, an undesirable result of compression. If you've got high contrast in your video, consider the loss of detail as a result. Is it going to harm the video? Is it worth adjusting the gamma of the entire production before compression?

SELLING UP: **MARKETING STRATEGIES**

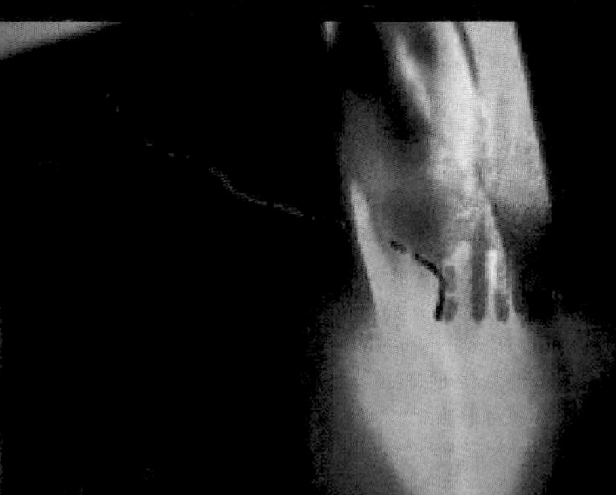

And so, at last, you've made your music video...what now? The answer is marketing, although this may not be your concern. It may be that your role ends at the point that you hand over the approved master to the client or the musicians.

TOP: The projected image of the musicians is a very useful tool for promotion. Work on this yourself, if you can, and come up with an iconic image to use for anything from DVD covers to forum posting idents.

Of course, it may absolutely be down to you – or at least down to you to incorporate some of your own ideas. This should have been planned from the start, based on your own contract or understanding of the ownership of the video with the musicians.

If the video is going online, let the world know. The musicians should have a website where the video is offered. From their home page, let any visitor know that there is a new video in town. Build it up, but not so that it can never live up to expectation or that it can be knocked down – a net-head can kill a download in a click...

Locate it aesthetically and significantly on a page, making it work with the text around it. Don't add anything that is just going to make download any more of a drag than it will be anyway – sometimes a small separate window that doesn't obscure the text of the page beneath it can work wonders. Make it easy on the viewers and easy on the eye.

Getting people to the site to see the video can take time. Search engines like Google take so long to register keywords that when the searches get results, the song's old hat. If this is workable, register keywords that make you stand out. If your track is burdened with an awesomely clichéd title, don't lose valuable keywords on it. The band should already have established their site to rank highly amongst search engines. If they haven't, start with their name, their hybrid genre, and make sure your *video* is attached.

Other ways to get noticed are by starting net rumors. Finding freeze-frame effects – the more surreal, the better – blurring them, creating fake histories, and assaulting news or sci-fi sighting sites broaden the demographic. Find one way of getting the video talked about and it will spread from there.

Post on sites that deal in music videos: *MVWire, Shooting People Music Video* – even some of the movie sites like them because they're short and sweet. At the same time, get the musicians to do the same with their own specific music sites. The music video is good for their news, too. It's ammunition against those without music videos. Get them posting as much as you are.

The Internet aside, your music video may well be a very sendable DVD. While the musicians' target list will be very different, there's no reason why you shouldn't exploit your directorial skills and send your own.

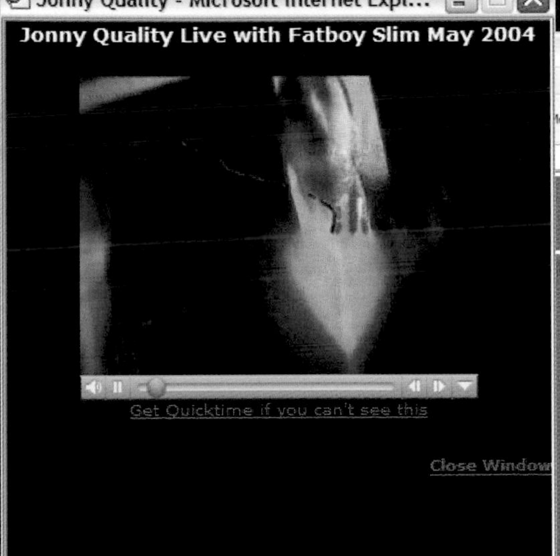

The Argus, Friday, May 14, 2004 — NEWS

DJ gives a lift to new band and promises they will b

by BRENDAN MONTAGUE

SUPERSTAR DJ Fatboy Slim is used to performing to hundreds of thousands of adoring fans.

But he gave his loyal Brighton following a chance to get up close and personal in an intimate performance to a capacity crowd at the King and Queen pub in Marlborough Place.

Hundreds of fans poured through the doors to watch the internationally-renowned DJ play his tunes from above a bar.

He was supporting band Jonny Quality's at their fourth gig in Brighton since they formed last year.

The DJ, who lives in Hove, will sample their music for his next album and has also promised to produce their debut once they are signed by a record label.

He said: "If the Beastie Boys had sex with a stray cat while the Jam were watching, Jonny Quality would be their love child. Watch out for a guest appearance on the next Fatboy CD for more."

His personal assistant and close friend Emma Coquet added: "I have never seen him look like that at a gig before – he was really blown away."

The DJ, aka Norman Cook, had agreed to warm up the crowd under an alias but word soon spread across the city.

Climax

Wearing his trademark blue jeans and short-sleeved shirt, the DJ launched himself into a buoyant, if relaxed, show after arriving half an hour late.

Then Jonny Quality's eclectic mix of scratch DJ samples, loud acoustic guitars and tongue-in-cheek rockabilly seemed to win them a new fan base.

Norman endorsed Jonny Quality after a chance meeting with member Sean Moody during a night out in Brighton.

The band bombarded their hero with CDs until Cook finally agreed to collaborate.

Sean, 29, from Kemp Town, Brighton, said he was delighted to be supported by the city's most famous star.

He said: "It was an amazing night and I had the time of my life up there on stage. This was the climax to a couple of years of hard work and we hope it will just get better.

"A huge thank you to Norman for giving us a jump – to see a producer up there

PERFORMANCE: Norman Cook, alias Fatboy Slim, get up close and personal with adoring fans during a spe

Fatboy's such great support

There are plenty of competitions (Web, national, and international) for music video directors. If you think you have demonstrated the right balance of creativity, interpretation, and directorial and technical skill, go for it. It is a highly competitive area of video-making.

If you're sending DVDs off, complete the package. Print out a jewel case sleeve and a disc label and tailor them to the theme of the video. If it's for your own purposes, differentiate it from those sent out by the musicians so as to promote yourself. Credit, after all, is what you are seeking to receive.

Above all, if you have found making a music video a pleasurable or rewarding experience, do it again. Find another band, do something different, broaden your skills, and possibly your scope, too.

Experience counts, and it makes you as valuable a commodity as the product you're selling. The bandwagon is becoming your chauffeured, fur-lined limousine – and it's rolling outta town

ABOVE: A website is an essential part of any band's marketing strategy today. It's not only somewhere that interested parties can go to find out more about the band, it's also somewhere you can show off the new video.

ABOVE RIGHT & RIGHT: With PR for your music video, hang it on the musicians. Find a story in your experience and get your video noticed. People will talk…

The Argus, Wednesday, May 12, 2004 — NEWS

PICTURE: TONY WOOD

Fatboy is our support act

by SIMON FLACKS

LESS than two months ago DJ Norman Cook was playing to thousands of revellers in sun-baked Rio.

Now he is swapping cocktails on the beach for pints in a Brighton local.

Norman will be performing at the King and Queen pub in Marlborough Place tonight supporting fledgling rockers Jonny Quality.

Band member Sean Moody, 29, from Kemp Town, met Norman after a gig at Po Na Na in West Street, Brighton.

He said: "We inundated him with CDs to begin with. Then he sent me an email and said he wanted to collaborate.

"He came to our show and fell in love with the music.

"To hear praise from someone like Norman is better than getting a million-dollar contract. It's amazing he's helping us out."

Jonny Quality have only played three gigs to date but hope tomorrow's event will provide a launch pad.

Sean, who describes the band's musical mix of hip hop beats and acoustic guitars as "rockabilly surf hop", said: "We are hoping there will be lots of music industry people at the concert.

"Norman wants us to get a record contract and then produce our album.

"There is a spirit and energy about him. He is so easy-going and welcoming.

"He said, 'I'll play with you but I'll try not to bore you'. We were star struck at first but his sense of humour erased that.

"As a band, you sometimes wonder if you are as good as you think you are, so recognition from someone like Norman really helps. But we are not too nervous about following him on stage."

Jonny Quality is made up of guitarist Sean, scratch DJ Nick Dunn, drummer Steve Joseph and bassist and lead vocalist Pete York.

Sean, who came to Brighton from San Francisco last year, writes, arranges and produces the music.

He sold almost all his possessions to launch the band in Brighton.

He said: "I came to Brighton because the music scene here is thriving. The people are more open to new styles of music. It's harder to break the scene in America.

"I'm hoping this will help save me from running out of money."

DJ Nick, aka Buck Wilde, joined the band after Sean heard about his scratching skills.

Nick said: "We are expecting a lot of people to come along. We are surprised at how fast this has moved."

Norman, who lives in Hove, said: "Jonny Quality will be guesting on a track on my new album and are my new playmates hence I recommend you check them out.

"I don't normally go to see live music but this lot are definitely alive."

Norman plans to warm up the crowd tomorrow with a set starting at 9pm. The band take to the stage at 10pm.

simon.flacks@theargus.co.uk

PUB GIG: Norman Cook

16:9 The widescreen ratio used by widescreen televisions, projectors, and some digital video cameras.

24p Digital video shot or shown at 24 frames per second, in progressive scan mode. This results in a more 'film-like' moving image.

4:3 The standard screen ratio of non-widescreen televisions and early Hollywood movies. Sometimes referred to as 1.33:1.

Aspect Ratio The horizontal versus vertical ratio of an image or screen, varying from standard TV ration (4:3) through 16:9 widescreen, to cinematic widescreen formats (usually 2.35:1).

Bars and Tone Default chrominance, luminance, and volume levels conveyed as colour bars and tone, and recorded onto a tape before shooting. These can then be used to set-up the editing system correctly for the footage.

Bluescreen/Greenscreen A blue or green screen used as a background during shooting, which will be keyed out in post-production and replaced by a new, simulated background.

Boom A long, adjustable bar used to position a microphone near actors but keeping the operator out of frame.

Capture The process of transferring video and audio data from a source, such as a digital video camera, to the hard disk on a computer.

GLOSSARY

ADC (Analogue to Digital Converter) A component within a digital video camera or other piece of digital video equipment, that converts analogue signals from a source (e.g. the camera's CCD) into digital data, ready for storage and processing.

Anamorphic The process of squeezing a widescreen image at capture, so that it fits onto a frame of film or a CCD, then stretching it out during playback so that it fits within a 16:9 ratio.

Artifacts A visual disturbance of an image – for instance, ugly blocks of colour – caused by flaws in the image-capture or storage systems.

Batch Capture Automated capture of a tape's images using a log of clips and the timecode embedded in the tape to transfer only the footage wanted from the camera to the computer without the user's manual input.

Bitrate The quantity of data in a stream of digital data, measured in terms of how many bits (digital 1s and 0s) go through the stream each second (bits or kilobits per second). As a rule in video, the higher the bitrate, the higher the quality of the audio or video, but the more demands placed on whatever carries, processes, or stores the data.

Cardioid The heart-shaped pattern of audio sensitivity around a microphone. This can also be super or hypercardioid, which narrows the shape and extends the range.

Chrominance The color values of a dot or pixel in an image, measured in RGB levels.

Close-Up A shot that shows a detail of a subject or object.

Condenser A microphone that uses a sensitive, electrically charged diaphragm to pick up sound.

Coverage The quantity of footage shot to ensure there is enough video to work with in the editing suite.

Cut An editing term that describes the finite end of one shot or scene, followed by the immediate beginning of the next without any transition in-between.

Cutaway An interposing shot – often a close-up – placed between two other shots to convey information, or to cover and blend a poor cut or awkward moment.

DAC (Digital-To-Analogue Converter) A device that converts a stream of digital data into an analogue signal. The DAC in a DVD player, for instance, converts the digital stream from the disc into an audio/video signal for output by a TV and surround sound system.

De-Interlace The isolation and combination of the interlaced fields that make up a frame of video to create a distinct still image or simulate the effect of progressive scan.

Depth of Field The range in front of the lens in which objects in the frame will appear in clear focus.

Digital8 A Sony digital video format, which uses the 8mm tape employed in the old Hi-8 analogue standard to store DV data. While inexpensive and backwards compatible, the quality isn't usually as good as MiniDV.

Dissolve An audio/video transition that mixes two shots through the lowering of opacity on the first with a simultaneous raising of opacity on the second.

Dolly A small vehicle running along tracks that supports the camera (and sometimes the operator) ensuring smooth camera movements that follow the action around the set.

Drop Frame The process by which NTSC rectifies 29.97 frames per second by dropping two frames every minute, with the exception of every tenth minute.

Dynamic Range The difference in audio signal level between the loudest and quietest parts of an audio track or program.

EDL (Edit Decision List) A list of timecodes, covering every In and Out point of every clip on the timeline.

Encoder A program that converts digital data from one format (e.g. DV) into the digital data required for another format (e.g. MPEG-2 for DVD).

EQ (Equaliser) A facility that allows for the amplification or softening of particular frequencies in an audio signal.

Establisher A shot, usually taken from some distance, used to establish the location of a sequence or scene.

Exposure The amount of light that is permitted to enter the camera via the lens, as dictated by the aperture.

Fade A decrease of opacity towards the end of the shot, usually fading to black.

Field Monitor A monitor that displays the action seen through the camera on location or set.

FireWire The Apple-coined term for the IEEE-1394 interface standard, as used by most DV cameras and capture cards.

Focal Length The distance between the CCD and the central (focal) point of the lens. A long focal length will magnify the image but narrow the angle of vision. A short focal length will not magnify the image, but widens the angle of vision.

Foley The recreation of sound effects for recording as part of the audio track.

Frequency The number of cycles per second of an audio waveform, measured in Hertz (Hz).

Gain An electronic circuit that amplifies a video or audio signal.

Gate A facility in an audio edit that continuously limits an audio signal to a designated level.

Grading In post-production, the adjustment of colour and tone in an image to maintain a consistent look across a movie or video, or to create a particular visual style.

HDTV (High Definition Television) A new standard for the recording and displaying of images, with close to double the resolution of standard TV.

Hot-Plugging Adding or removing hardware whilst the computer is fully operating, with the computer and the device communicating instantly and on-demand.

Hue The pure colour attributed to a pixel (e.g. red, blue) before saturation and brightness (or luminance) are brought into play.

IEEE-1394 A connection that allows data transfer of up to 800Mbps, and the standard interface between DV cameras and computers.

iLink Sony's term for IEEE-1394.

Interlacing The process whereby a conventional CRT television produces an image from two frames, one comprising the odd horizontal lines and one comprising the even horizontal lines, alternating between them at 60 frames per second to create the illusion of a single image updating at 30 frames per second.

Keyframe A concept borrowed from traditional animation, where a lead artist would draw the most important frames of a sequence and junior artists would then create the in-between frames. In digital video, keyframes are used to control an effect or animation. The user sets a keyframe, and altering the values of parameters or the position of an element, then sets another keyframe for the next change. The computer will then calculate the effects on the frames in between.

Keying A process where a video-editing or effects package selects an area of screen, based on either chrominance (Chromakey) or luminance (Lumakey), which the computer will replace with another image.

Lavalier A small lapel microphone, which may be wireless.

Lens Converter A ring that screws either onto the existing camera lens or onto the camera body to allow a different lens to be attached.

Li-ion (Lithium Ion) Now the most common battery type in DV cameras, Lithium Ion batteries are long-lasting and don't suffer from a memory effect, meaning they hold the same amount of charge during the whole of their lifetime.

Lock-Off A camera firmly mounted in place on a tripod for the duration of a static shot.

Long Shot A shot that frames the entirety of a subject in their surroundings.

Luminance The amount of light attributed to a pixel or image.

Master Shot One extended shot that covers the whole of a scene, sequence, or event, incorporating all aspects of the dialogue and action.

Matte A digital mask that defines an area of transparency for compositing or keying.

Medium Shot A shot that frames the subject from slightly above the waist to the top of the head.

MicroMV Sony's digital format that uses MPEG-2 compression to copy video to a tape smaller than MiniDV cassettes.

MiniDV Standard consumer digital video format, with DV format data recorded to a ¼-inch digital tape.

MPEG-2 File compression standard for digital video, principally for use by the DVD format, and set by the Motion Pictures Expert Group.

MPEG-4 File compression standard set by the Motion Pictures Expert Group, aimed at the distribution of streaming video across the Internet.

NLE (Non-linear Editor) A digital editing system, which allows a movie to be assembled in any order, so that shots can be shuffled or repositioned and effects or transitions added at will, without needing to work through the film sequentially. Non-linear editing is a more flexible and intuitive process than traditional movie editing or linear video editing.

NTSC (National Television Standards Committee) The TV standard used by the USA, Canada, and most countries in South America and the Pacific. NTSC uses a 525-line display made up of two interlaced fields scanning at 29.97 frames per second.

Opacity A percentage attribute given to a video clip in order to control its degree of transparency.

PAL (Phase Alternation Line) The TV standard used by the UK, Australia, and New Zealand, and most of Europe (except France, which uses a variant, PAL SECAM). PAL has a 625-line display made up of two interlaced fields scanning a 25 frames per second.

Pan A camera movement along the horizontal axis, or an audio movement from the left to right or right to left speaker.

Plug-in A small, separate program which 'plugs-in' to a larger application in order to extend or improve its features.

Post-Roll During a batch capture, the amount of time a tape continues to be captured after the Out point has been reached.

Practical An on-set light that is part of the set dressing and operates as an in-frame light.

Pre-Roll During a batch capture, the amount of time a tape pre-captures before the in point is reached.

Progressive Scan A way of refreshing a television screen or other display without interlacing. The image is displayed in one frame, running continually line after line, at 30 frames per second for a smoother, flicker-free display.

RGB (Red Green Blue) The three primary chrominance components of a colour video signal.

Safety Take A further take of a shot undertaken to ensure that there is something safe and in the can.

Sample Rate The amount of times per second an audio or video signal is sampled. The higher the sample rate, the closer the sample to the original signal, and so the higher the quality.

Saturation The strength of colour in a colour signal.

Scratch Disk Disk drive or disk space allocated for capturing and for previewing clips.

Setup The positioning and organization of everyone and everything needed for a single shot of a film or video including all the talent, the lighting, the set, and the camera.

Shoot Ratio The ratio describing the amount of footage shot on set to the amount actually used in the master edit.

Shooting Schedule A diary breakdown of all crew, talent, setups, and locations required to undertake a day's shoot.

Shutter Speed The number of frames per second that are sampled and captured by the camera's CCD.

Slowmo Running a clip at less than 100% speed in the edit in order to slow the clip down and give a slow-motion effect.

Sound Check A quick rehearsal prior to the shoot to gauge the levels of audio for correct recording.

Storyboard A narrative broken down into a series of images to present the angles, composition, and sequence of shots in a scene.

Sync Recorded sound that is created – or appears to be created – by a visual source on the screen.

Take A version of a shot running from 'action' to 'cut'.

Tight A close-in shot taken using a lens with a long focal length.

Tilt A basic camera movement where the camera pivots on the vertical axis.

Timecode A number given in hours, minutes, seconds, and frames for every frame of video, to enable it to be logged for batch capturer or editing purposes.

Timeline A single or multitrack line representing the length of video and audio clips during editing in chronological order. Clips can be dragged to the timeline, arranged in order, cut, and extended.

Tracking Shot A moving camera shot where the camera itself moves to follow a subject and keep them in frame. The name stems from the Hollywood practice of mounting the camera on tracks to keep such movement smooth.

Transition A change from one shot to another that uses an effect instead of a straight cut.

USB2 A computer interface standard allowing for high-speed data transfer between a PC and a peripheral device. Some DV cameras now come with USB2 connections, but FireWire remains a more popular standard, particularly as it allows for more connection options (camera to camera, camera to digital VCR, and so on).

Video Card An add-in card containing a graphics chip which turns data from a computer's CPU into a video signal that can be shown on a monitor or other display. Not to be confused with a video-capture or video-effects card, which allow video to be digitized from various sources or effects and transitions to be rendered in real-time.

White Balance Information sampled by or given to the camera to establish the median colour temperature of a shot.

Wide A shot covering more of the area around an object, shot with a shorter focal length than average.

Widescreen A screen ratio where the horizontal width is much larger than the vertical height. Widescreen ratios are standard in Hollywood movies. The term has also become used to describe the 16:9 ratio used in modern TV sets.

Wipe A transition that wipes a new clip over an old one.

YUV An alternative colour model to RGB, where colour is represented as signals of hue, light, and saturation.

Zoom The process of moving focal length from a loose, wide-angle shot to a tight, heavily magnified close-up.

INDEX & ACKNOWLEDGMENTS

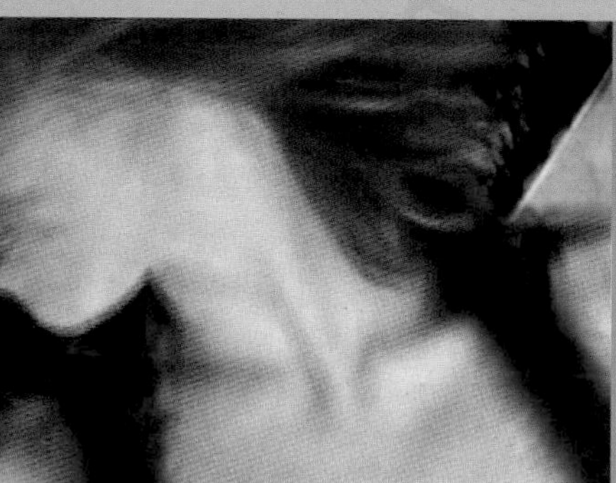

A
Abba 21, 50
absent musicians **16-17**
active pixels 66
actors 42
Adagio for Strings 31
Aguilera, Christina 99
American Pie 41
analogue medium 68, 137
anamorphic lens **66**
anamorphic widescreen 67
Ant, Adam 98
aperture 78-9
Apple 77
Armstrong, Louis 24
arrogance 25
art department 123
artefacts 83
as-lives **14-15**, 80, **163**
  and 8 bar **119**
  and props 102-3
Ashcroft, Richard 46
aspect ratio
  see pixel aspect ratio
attack 167
audience 14-15, 73, 111
audio 58
audio compression 166-7
audio editing **140-3**
audio intrusion 110
audio tracks **130-31**
authenticity 80
authoring DVDs **176-7**
auto controls 78
AVI 77, 172, **174**

B
B-Line **52**
backing up 168-9
balanced image 82
band 93, **96-7**
bandwidth 117
Barber, Samuel 31
Barbra 12
The Beastie Boys 38, 39
beat 52, 132
The Beatles 21
Beautiful 99
Bennett, Tony 21
Beyoncé 34
Bittersweet Symphony 46
Björk 46
Black and White 47
Black Box 12
The Blair Witch Project 69
block displacement 136-7
blue gel **82**
bluescreen **100**
Bohemian Rhapsody 8, 54
Bon Jovi, Jon 23
Boney M 12
Bono 10, 40
Boomtown Rats 40
bouncing ball 164
bouncing light 113
Bowie, David 21
Bragg, Billy 40
branding 8
break-beat 132
breathing 167
brightness **151**
Britney 39, 40
broadcast television 120
budget 47, 49, **60-61**, 70, 84, 91
  lights 77
  location 74
burning to DVD **174-5**
Bush, Kate 50

C
camera 58, 70, 76
camera angles **106-7**
camera lens **76,** 78-9
camera moves 34, 47, **108-9**, **117**
camera operator **71**
camera rigs **108-9**
captions 164-5
capturing 126, **127**
Carey, Mariah 80
Carlisle 50
CCD 66, 67, 82
CD-R 168
CDs 136, 168
Céline 12, 31
centre frame 105
charity record 40
charts 20
checklists
  production **84-5**
  setting up 88
chorus 50
chromakey 47, **82**, **100**, **146-9**
chrominance 68, 144, 178
cinema language 54
Clarke, Vince 96
Classic FM radio 30
classical music **30-31**
cleaners **174**
cleaning pictures **158-9**
clichés 89
Close to Me 46
close-ups 72, 104, **107**, **117**
clothes *see also* wardrobe
  and politics 40-41
  and sex 34-5
Cobain, Kurt 23
Coffee and TV 47
Coldplay 21
colour 113
colour correction **145**, **150-51**
Colour Pass effect **151**
comedy **38-9**
communication 49, 90
compatibility **77**
competitions 183
composing shots **104**, 105
compression 67, 83, 178, **172**
compression ratio 166
computer-generated
  graphics 28
computers 77
content protection **174**
Content Scrambling System
  (CSS) **174**
contingencies
  budget 60
  time 58
continuity 72, **101**
contracts 49, 60, 62-3
contrast 82-3, 113, **151**
copy and paste **127**
copyright 63
costs *see* budget
cranes and jibs 109
crash zoom 108
creativity 69
credits 165
crew **70-71,** 88-9, 123
CRT 160
cutaways 33, 72, 73, 96, **120-21**
  and close-ups 107
cutting 10, **129**
  to the beat **132**
C&W line dancing 28

D
D12 38
Da Funk 42
Daft Punk 42
dance **28-9**, 132
dark side 36-7

DAT 136
DAT recording 117
data compression
see compression
Davis, Miles 24
daylight 76
death **36-7**
decadence 25
decoder **175**
deconstructed set 103
deferred payment 62-3
defining parameters **129**
definition 66
defragmenting 168
degradation 144
depth of field **78-9**
Destiny's Child 24
dialogue 50
diffusers 113
Digital Diva 29
digital medium 68
digital stills camera **79**
directing 43
director 70, 90, 122
disc label 183
dissolve **138-9**
distance shots 97
distortion **160**
distressing pictures **156-7**
Dixie Chicks 40
dolly 109
downloading 179, 181, 182
dress-rehearsal 72, 101
The Drifters 24
drive 77
DV camera 66
DV tape 136
DVDs 77, 172, 182-3
DVEs 47
dynamic range 52, 116, **132**, 136, 166

E

editing 47
absent musicians 17
and sync 9
as-live 14, 15
film 68
HDTV 67
lipsync 13
settings and options **126-7**
editing software 77, 83
EDL (Edit Decision List) 168
effects **144-5**
8 bar **118-19**
Eminem 39
encoders and encoding **77**, 158, **172-3**
epilogue 50, 54
equipment 76-8
checklist 84
establishing shot **106**
Everybody Hurts 164
exporting 174-5
exposure 113, **112**
exposure setting 82
exteriors 75
external storage 168
extras 71
extreme close-up **107**

F

fastmo 109, 114
Fatboy Slim 17
fear 36
feedback 111
fetishizing 33, 107
fields 68, 172
50 Cents 53
file management 126, **127**, 168-9
film versus video 68-9
filters 79
financial considerations
see budget
Firestarter 74
FireWire connection 76, 77, 172
Fischinger, Otto 31
flare 111
Flint, Keith 99
fluorescent lights 76, 83
focus 78-9
formats **126**
formulation dancing 28
4/4 on-beat 132
frame rate 68, 137
framing 106
Friday the 13th 52
fun 38

G

gain 166
gamma values 82-3, **151**
Gaye, Marvin 24
gels 113
ghetto roots 24, 26
ghettoism 21
glam rock **23**
glides 34, 109
Golden Section 105
Gondry, Michel 31
Google 182
goth 36
grading 36
graphics **164-5**
grey areas 82
greenscreen **100**, **146**, **151**, **160**
greenscreen clipping **129**
Grohl, Dave 38
grunge 99

H

halogen lamps 76
Hamlet 36
hand-held shots 108, 156
hard-drive 168
headphones **53**, 80
High-Definition Television (HDTV) 67
The Hives 164
Holiday, Billie 24
hook 47, 118
horizontal axis 66
Horner, James 31

I

i-link 76
ideas and inspiration 46-7, 69
illegal grading 11
illustrating the lyrics 50
I'm Not in Love 52
image creation 98
image quality 83
in-camera moves 108
In Da Club 53
incidental music 42
instrumentals 30-31
instruments 53
interlaced scanning 67, 172
Internet 178
Ironic 46
irony 9, 50
isolating clips **129**

J

jacks 117
Jackson, Michael 40, 47
Jay-Z 24
jewel case sleeve 183
Jones, Howard 40
Jones, Tom 80
Jonze, Spike 42
Joplin, Janis 23
Julia 50

K

K-Tel 22
Keef 50
key changes 53
Kiedis, Anthony 38
King, Stephen 46
Koons, Jeff 9

L

Landis, John 42
language 26
The Last Broadcast 69
lateral thinking 9
lead singer **92-5**
legal issues 16, 17, 62, 83
Lennox, Annie 50
lenses *see* camera lens
light temperature 76, 83
lighting 58, 79, **76**, **82-3**, **112-13**
close-ups 72
equipment 76
mood 82
lighting crew **71**
linear edit 68
lipsync **12-13**, 80-81, 110, **114-15**
live feed 117
live gigs 54, 72, 81, **116-17**, **137**
live sets 88-9
location 46, 74-5
and props 102
and wardrobe 101
availability 91
lock-off **110-11**
locking tracks **131**
logical thinking 9
logos 164
London Underground 74
long shots and reality 15
Lowe, Chris 97
luminance 68, 144, 178
Lux (lumens) 82
lyrics 26, 38, 40, 42, 118
and developing ideas **50-51**

M

The Macarena 28, 80
Macs 77
Madonna 40, 41, 46
Main Offender 164
maintaining interest **129**
make-up 34, 58, 71, 88, **98-9**, 123
malcontents 36
Manson, Marilyn 40, 50, 99
Mariah 12

marketing 21, 48, 176, **182-3**
  pop music 20, 21
Martin 52
master-sheet **60-61**
master shot 90, 104, 106, 110, 117, 120, 136
meals 88, 89
medium shot **107**
meetings **48-9**
memorandum of particulars 58
Mercury, Freddie 98
metaphor 50
Michael, George 17, 39, 40, 41
microphones 80, **81**
Milli Vanilli 12
miming 12, **13**, 15, **114**, 115
Minelli, Liza 98
mise-en-scène 105
Mission Impossible 42
Missy Elliot 21
mistakes 160-63
mixer 117, 167
modem 178
mood 52-3
  and close-up 107
  and lighting 82, 112
Morisette, Alanis 40, 46
morphing 11, 47
movement and vibration 104, 111
movie soundtracks 31
movies 10-11, 13, 42, 106, 107, 120, 128
MPEG 77, 160
MPEG-2 67, **159**, 172
MTV 20, 46
Muller, Sophie 37
multi-camera set-up 70
multicast 180
music and developing ideas **52-3**
musical key 53
musicals 42
musicians 88-9, 90
  and acting 42, 96-7
  as personalities 47
  miming 15
  preparing for the shoot **48**
MVWire 182
My Band 38
My Heart Will Go On 31

N
narrative 42-3, 54, 102
natural light **113**
neutral density filters 79, 113, 166
night-time **74**
Non-Linear Editor (NLE) 67, 68, 72, 126, 174
Nothing Compares 2U 50
NTSC 66

O
Oasis 10
O'Connor, Sinead 40, 50
off-beats 132
Oh So Quiet 46
Only You 46
opinions 40
Orbit, William 31
OutKast 39
output medium 66
Outside 39, 41
outtakes **161**
over-runs 58, 91
overexposure 82, 97

P
P Diddy 39
pace **129**
PAL 66
Panasonic P2 system 168
paperwork 122
parody and pastiche **23**, 38, 164
payment 62
Pearl Jam 40
permission to use location 74
Pet Shop Boys 97
physical moves 108-9
pivot 108
pixel aspect ratio 66, 172, **173**
pixels 66-7, 144
plots *see* narrative
point-of-view (POV) shot 72, 73, 107
polarizing filters 79
politics **40-41**
popular music **20-21**, 132
Portishead 46
post-production 49, 60, 84
POV *see* point-of-view
PR 8, **183**
Praise You 17, 46
pre-production 60
  checklist 84-5
Presley, Elvis 21, 23
Prince 21, 80
The Prodigy 74
producer 70, 91, 122
production 60
production checklist **84-5**
production design 58
production designer 71
production issues 49
progressive scanning 67, 172
prologue 50, 54
props 58, 71, **102-3**, 123
pull-focus 109
pull-outs **109**
pumping 167
punk 25, 99
push 108

Q
QuickTime 181

R
R & B **24-5**
racking focus **78**
Radiohead 21
RAM 77
rap **26-7**, 40, 47, 104
Ray of Light 47
reality and lighting 112-13
RealMedia 181
receipts 122
recording live gigs 14
redhead 77, **82**
reducing costs 60
reflected light 113
reflected multicast 180
reggae 132
region coding **174**
rehearsing **72-3**, 89, **111**
release 167
release forms 63, 122
REM 164
renting equipment 123
resolution 68, **159**, 172
reverse shots 73, **115**, **153**, **155**, **163**
rhythm 52, **132-5**
rights 63
rock music **22-3**, 99
role-playing 94
Rolling Stones 21
rough cut 126
royalties 63
rule breaking 54
rule of thirds 105
rules of space and time 10, 128
runners 71

S
sample rate 140, 179, 180
saturation 160
Saturday Night 74
Saturday Night Fever 28
saving 169
scanning 172
Schenk, Rocky 37
Scott, Jake 164
scratch track **140-43**
screen ratio **66-7**
screen safety 165
scrims 113
script 89
search engines 182
servo intrusion **110**, 111
set-dressing 102
set-ups 54, 90, 101, 104-5, 120
sex
  and dance music 28
  and R&B 25
  and rock 23
sexiness **32-5**, 92, **93**
  and clothes 34
  and make-up 45, 98-9
sexual politics 41
shareware 60
shoot ratio 118
Shoot the Dog 17
shooting angles 58
Shooting People Music Video 182
shooting schedules **58-9**, 89, 91, 122
'show and tell' 50
sight gags 38
Simmons, Gene 23, 98
sin and evil 22
single-source lighting **83**
size 172
ska 132
slowmo 11, 33, 107, 114, 120
Smells Like Teen Spirit **52**
Smith, Robert 46, 99
Soft Cell 52
Soft Focus **145**
Sony megapixel cameras 76
Sony MPEG cards 168
sound recording 80-81
sound system 77
soundtracks 30, 43
speed, altering **152-5**
speeding clips **134**
split-screen 11
Standard Definition Television (SDTV) 66
star filters 79
static shots 104
Stay 37

Steadicam 109
stills photographer **71**, **73**
stopping down 79
story *see* narrative
storyboards **54-5**, 89, 123
streaming **178-81**
striking set 123
style 158
StyleWar 164
stylist 100
subwoofers **77**
Suede 74
symmetry 105
sync 117, **136-7**, **163**

T
tapes 122
technical run-through 72
telecine 68
telephoto lenses 79
television commercials 10
10CC 52
themes 50
thrash 132
3CCD cameras 76
three-point lighting 112
threshold 166
Thriller 42, 50
tilt-down 109
Timberlake, Justin 34
time 54
time-based media 54
Time Music 22
timesheets 122
Titanic 31
titles 164-5
transcoding 172
transitions **138-9**, **140**
trash-metal 36
tripods **104-5**, 108
True Streaming 180
tungsten lights 76, **82**, 83
Turner, Tina 23
TV Roll **145**
Tyler, Steve 38

U
underexposure 82
undersheet 60-61
unicast 180
unintentional humour 39
unlinking tracks **131**
urban areas **74**
Usher 24

V
Vanessa Mae 99
verbal humour 38
vertical axis 66
video and reality 69
video art 11
video card 77, 126, 174
Video Killed the Radio Star 8
Virtual Insanity 46
visual concept 46
visual intrusion 111
visual jokes 39
visual logic 120

W
wardrobe 58, 71, 88, 97, **100-101**, 123
Weapon of Choice 17, 47
website **183**
Where the Wild Roses Grow 37
wide-angle lenses 79, 104
wide shot **106**
widescreen 66
Williams, Robbie 80, 84
Windows 77
Windows Media 181
Wonder, Stevie 24
wrapping up 89, **122-3**
writer 70
Wuthering Heights 50

X
XLRs 117

Z
zoom 34, 47, 97, 108
Zoom Blur **145**
ZZ Top 50

Jonny Quality
Sean Moody
Lancaster County Prison
Shane McGowan
Kathryn Fleet
Clea Smith
Jane Lesley
Jonathan Rice
Chloe York
Charlie Finney
Louisa DuPrey
Barrie Dunn
Parveen Nabi
Kathryn Lamb, *KL Associates on behalf of Ulead Systems*
Dan Loshak, *Discreet*
Robin Charney, *Matrox*
All at www.MVWire.com

MUSIC VIDEOS AND IMAGES

Swamphouse: *"Caine"*
Ivisualise Films
Directors: Andrea Fellers/Blake West
Producers: Andrea Fellers/Blake West
Post: Ivisualise Films
www.ivisualeyes.com

Shahrzad Sepanlou: *"1001 Nights"*
Ivisualise Films
Directors: Andrea Fellers/Blake West
Producers: Andrea Fellers/Blake West
Post: Ivisualise Films
www.ivisualeyes.com

Daddy: *"Better Than You"*
Fink
Director: Ben Rollason
Producers: Charlie Mitchell/Ben Rollason
Post: Charlie Mitchell/Ben Rollason/Atacama
www.fink-base.com

Local B: *"American Football"; "Mountain Bike"; "High Tennis"; "Beach Golf"*
Local B Films
Director: Eduardo Brand
Producers: Gilson Val/Eduardo Brand
DP: Maurizio D'Atri
Post: Eduardo Brand/L Felipe Escosteguy
3D/CG: Raphael Braga
www.localbfilmes.com.br/english

Ziggy Ranking: *"Miserable Life"*
Aaron Mosher for Artical One
Producer: Aaron Mosher
Director/DP: Ethan Vogt
Editor: Ethan Vogt
www.aaronmosher.com

Jonny Quality: *"Borrowers"; "Smiling"; "Buses"; "Live with Norman"*
Fleshpuppets
www.fleshpuppets.com

Lancaster County Prison with Shane McGowan: *"Town I Love So Well"*
Fleshpuppets
www.fleshpuppets.com

images from *The Argus*

Ilex-press.com is the home of all things ILEX. Don't forget to visit our website for news on the latest ILEX books, tutorials, competitions, give-aways and online resources to get the best out of your ILEX books.

Get 20% off ILEX books
All purchases through the ILEX online bookstore will automatically save you 20% off the cover price.

Expert advice in the forum
Visit the online forum and share expertise with your peers, or ask ILEX authors and experts for advice on creative and technical issues.

Join our affiliate programme
If you run a website, newsgroup or online gallery, become an ILEX affiliate and earn 10% referral fees for books sold through links to our site.

www.ilex-press.com

www.web-linked.com

Join our email list
Sign up for the ILEX eNewsletter and get up-to-the-minute news on ILEX books, authors, promotions and speaker events.

Free online tutorials
Each month we'll be featuring free tutorials from the latest ILEX titles, so if you are looking for useful tips for improving your workflow or want to try your hand at creating impressive digital art, then check out our tutorials section.

Monthly giveaways
We will be giving away free copies of our latest books to registered members every month. Sign up today, and you could be one of the lucky few to receive a free ILEX book.

Web-linked.com is a unique online resource for every ILEX book that we publish. Make sure you visit the web-linked site for this book which you'll find at www.musvuk.web-linked.com to access useful links and download source files to get the most out of your purchase. You'll find directories of websites and organisations that will help you develop your knowledge and skills, and you can follow step-by-step tutorials in the books using the original artwork used by our authors.

ILEX